THINKING TOGETHER

RHETORIC AND DEMOCRATIC DELIBERATION
VOLUME 16

EDITED BY CHERYL GLENN AND STEPHEN BROWNE
THE PENNSYLVANIA STATE UNIVERSITY

Co-founding Editor: J. Michael Hogan

Editorial Board:

Robert Asen (University of Wisconsin–Madison)
Debra Hawhee (The Pennsylvania State University)
J. Michael Hogan (The Pennsylvania State University)
Peter Levine (Tufts University)
Steven J. Mailloux (University of California, Irvine)
Krista Ratcliffe (Marquette University)
Karen Tracy (University of Colorado, Boulder)
Kirt Wilson (The Pennsylvania State University)
David Zarefsky (Northwestern University)

Rhetoric and Democratic Deliberation focuses on the interplay of public discourse, politics, and democratic action. Engaging with diverse theoretical, cultural, and critical perspectives, books published in this series offer fresh perspectives on rhetoric as it relates to education, social movements, and governments throughout the world.

A complete list of books in this series is located at the back of this volume.

THINKING TOGETHER

LECTURING, LEARNING, AND DIFFERENCE
IN THE LONG NINETEENTH CENTURY

EDITED BY ANGELA G. RAY AND PAUL STOB

The Pennsylvania State University Press | University Park, Pennsylvania

Library of Congress Cataloging-in-Publication Data

Names: Ray, Angela G., editor. | Stob, Paul, editor.
Title: Thinking together : lecturing, learning, and
    difference in the long nineteenth century / edited
    by Angela G. Ray and Paul Stob.
Other titles: Rhetoric and democratic deliberation.
Description: University Park, Pennsylvania : The
    Pennsylvania State University Press, [2018] | Series:
    Rhetoric and democratic deliberation | Includes
    bibliographical references and index.
Summary: "Explores the myriad ways that people in
    the nineteenth century grappled with questions
    of learning, belonging, civic participation, and
    deliberation. Focuses on the dynamics of gender,
    race, region, and religion, and how individuals and
    groups often excluded from established institutions
    developed knowledge useful for public life"—
    Provided by publisher.
Identifiers: LCCN 2017053093 | ISBN
    9780271080871 (cloth : alk. paper)
Subjects: LCSH: Education—History—19th century.
    | Learning—History—19th century. | Lyceums—
    History—19th century. | Lectures and
    lecturing—History—19th century. | Deliberative
    democracy—History—19th century.
Classification: LCC LA126.T45 2018 | DDC
    370.9034—dc23
LC record available at https://lccn.loc.gov/2017053093

Copyright © 2018 The Pennsylvania State University
All rights reserved
Printed in the United States of America
Published by The Pennsylvania State University Press,
University Park, PA 16802-1003

The Pennsylvania State University Press is a member
of the Association of University Presses.

It is the policy of The Pennsylvania State University
Press to use acid-free paper. Publications on uncoated
stock satisfy the minimum requirements of American
National Standard for Information Sciences—
Permanence of Paper for Printed Library Material,
ANSI Z39.48–1992.

CONTENTS

Acknowledgments | *vii*

Introduction | 1
ANGELA G. RAY AND PAUL STOB

Part 1 **Disrupting Narratives**

1 The Portable Lyceum in the Civil War | 23
RONALD J. ZBORAY AND MARY SARACINO ZBORAY

2 Women's Entrepreneurial Lecturing in the Early National Period | 41
GRANVILLE GANTER

3 Mobilizing Irish America in the Antebellum Lecture Hall | 56
TOM F. WRIGHT

4 Authentic Imitation or Perverse Original? Learning About Race from America's Popular Platforms | 72
KIRT H. WILSON AND KAITLYN G. PATIA

Part 2 **Distinctive Voices**

5 A Lyceum Diaspora: Hilary Teage and a Liberian Civic Identity | 97
BJØRN F. STILLION SOUTHARD

6 Secret Knowledge, Public Stage: Joseph Smith's King Follett Discourse | 113
RICHARD BENJAMIN CROSBY

7 The "Perfect Delight" of Dramatic Reading: Gertrude Kellogg and the Post–Civil War Lyceum | 130
SARA E. LAMPERT

8 Talking Music: Amy Fay and the Origins of the Lecture Recital | *150*
   E. DOUGLAS BOMBERGER

9 Hinduism for the West: Swami Vivekananda's Pluralism at
   the World's Parliament of Religions | *169*
   SCOTT R. STROUD

   Conclusion: Placing Platform Culture in Nineteenth-Century
   American Life | *187*
   CAROLYN EASTMAN

Notes | *203*

List of Contributors | *237*

Index | *241*

ACKNOWLEDGMENTS

Scholarship is always collaborative, and an edited volume represents a concentrated form of collective endeavor. We are grateful to all those who have shaped this book, from its inception in conversation through its oral performance in an academic symposium to its print publication. We salute Bob Schurk and Jim Mackay, whose invitation to the Alexandria Lyceum brought us to Virginia in September 2015 to host an interdisciplinary academic conference titled "Popular Knowledge, Public Stage: Cultures of Lecturing and Learning in the Long Nineteenth Century." The event was jointly sponsored by the City of Alexandria, Northwestern University's Department of Communication Studies, and Vanderbilt University's College of Arts and Science. Contributors to this volume presented their work, along with the following scholars: Monika Alston-Miller, Trudy Bell, Yvonne Carignan, Virginia Garnett, Elisabeth Kinsley, Shirley Wilson Logan, Lisa McGunigal, Elizabeth McHenry, Johann Neem, Britt Rusert, and Carly Woods. Others joined as spectators and interlocutors: Christina Bevilacqua, Stephen Browne, Elizabeth Gardner, Johanna Hartelius, Jennifer Keohane, James Klumpp, Zachary Mills, Kevin Shupe, Sara VanderHaagen, and Courtney Wright. We appreciate all the participants' contributions.

Many have assisted us in bringing this project to published form. For their generosity and professional expertise, we thank Kendra Boileau and her colleagues at the Pennsylvania State University Press. We also extend gratitude for the encouragement and aid of co-founding series editor J. Michael Hogan and to current series editors Cheryl Glenn and Stephen Browne. Nicholas Taylor provided superb copyediting, and Robert Elliot Mills offered an insightful appraisal of the final manuscript.

Furthermore, Angela G. Ray acknowledges the indefatigable support of Harold Gulley, and she is grateful to Paul Stob for his camaraderie, his dazzling skill in juggling concepts and minutiae alike, and his kind and generous spirit.

Paul Stob thanks Sarah Stob and Elliott Stob for their unflagging encouragement. In addition, he thanks Angela G. Ray for her tireless work, amazing attention to detail, and vision for the Alexandria conference and this volume.

The discussions that began in Alexandria motivated this book and affected scholarship that appears elsewhere. We acknowledge all those who have "thought together" with us through the production of this volume, and we invite you, our reader, to consider yourself as part of this community, in which we seek to learn from the past and draw on that knowledge to influence the future.

INTRODUCTION

Angela G. Ray and Paul Stob

Scholars long have gathered at colleges and universities, have organized conferences and symposia, have discussed ideas in person or remotely through communication technologies from letters to video conferencing, and have read about the latest intellectual advancements in books, journals, and periodicals. Yet the future of thinking together—that is, of people assembling to pursue knowledge and to forge collective understanding—now seems uncertain. Changes over the past few decades have raised serious doubts about the viability of these norms, modes, and practices. Technological advancements, neoliberal economics, increased expenses, decreased governmental support, and a widening chasm between academic and public cultures—such changes have prompted questions about the pursuit of knowledge in the twenty-first century. Established models of higher education seem outmoded to many, inciting a chorus of commentators calling for change. William Deresiewicz, for one, chastises existing institutions for "exacerbating inequality, retarding social mobility, perpetuating privilege, and creating an elite that is as isolated from the society that it's supposed to lead—and even more smug about its right to its position—as the WASP aristocracy itself."[1] Richard and Daniel Susskind go even further by prophesying an end to collegiate education as we know it, particularly its system of certifying professional training: "In the long run, increasingly capable machines will transform the work of professionals, giving rise to new ways of sharing practical expertise in society" and decreasing the need for academically certified gatekeepers of knowledge.[2] Such criticisms imply that in the future people will be thinking together in very different ways than they do right now.

Yet scholars of intellectual history are demonstrating clearly that people in the past also thought together differently than they do now. In the United States, for example, collective inquiry did not always happen according to the professional models that the Susskinds and Deresiewicz now see coming to an end. Certainly in the nineteenth century, the norms, modes, and practices of thinking together were far from established. Experimentation, in fact, was the norm for people and groups who wanted to pursue knowledge together. Sometimes experimentation was born of necessity: through overt oppression or covert limitation, many people did not possess what Frederick Douglass called the "favourable circumstances and opportunities" of schools, colleges, and the wealth to enter them.[3] Whereas some people experimented with practices of learning because the doors of institutions were closed to them, the experimentation of others arose from a desire to extend or elaborate their formal learning. In consequence, nineteenth-century individuals sought insight in myriad ways and myriad places. Some participated in the creation of a distinctive literary or performance culture. Others envisioned associations for mutual learning as mechanisms for bringing intellectual or moral enlightenment to the world. Still others believed that a robust pursuit of knowledge could only happen through the creation of educational institutions designed for people long denied education. The histories of these and many other intellectual experiments suggest that the ways we think together are always changing, always in transition, always unsettled.

Today, as we face an uncertain intellectual future, we might find wisdom in the collective experiments of the past. This book takes part in that search, exploring some of the ways people in the nineteenth century, acting in community, tried to educate themselves, to deliberate about common problems, and to live intellectually rich lives. Perhaps the best-known instantiation of this search for knowledge was the lyceum, which involved a series of civic debating and lecturing associations created in communities across the country beginning in the late 1820s.[4] This volume investigates lyceums, but its scope is more sweeping, as contributors study lecturing and learning writ large—not only lyceum activities but the many ways people got together in different forums to speak, listen, and learn. What's more, the chapters that follow are especially interested in how people living on the margins of society managed to think together despite the many obstacles they faced.[5] Due to their gender, race, geographic location, socioeconomic status, or religious affiliation—or a combination thereof—they lacked access to institutions of higher learning and other traditional sites of intellectual power. Yet exclusion does not equal powerlessness; often people in challenging circumstances found ways to investigate the world together, on their own terms. They managed, to borrow John Dewey's conception of education, to find that which "enlarges and enlightens experience," that which "stimulates and enriches imagination," and that which "creates responsibility for accuracy and vividness of statement and thought."[6] They did this by getting together, sometimes in unexpected places, to deliberate about their world, to share concerns, and to investigate common problems. In that way, they engaged in the kind of deliberative encounter that Robert Asen sees as central for democratic society—that is, an encounter with one another that "may promote decision-making and collective problem-solving as well as helping us to discover a shared set of values."[7]

In pursuing the intersection of education and deliberation generally, this volume concentrates attention specifically on popular learning, a term that implies a contrast with the privileged learning that happened in established schools and colleges. Yet it is important to remember that the boundary between popular and institutional learning was permeable, and several of the individuals studied in this volume blended formal and popular teaching, formal and popular learning. Despite—or perhaps because of—their ambiguous relationships with established educational institutions, the people and groups who populate this volume created their own places, spaces, and discourses for sharing ideas, better understanding themselves and their world, and critiquing the society that surrounded them. For instance, letters that flew between the Civil War home front and battlefield reported news of books and lectures, linking distant kin in shared learning, while imprisoned Union and Confederate soldiers produced their own handwritten newspapers. Women teachers became educational entrepreneurs, entering the popular lecture hall to attract interest in their private schools. Immigrants gathered in great cities and small towns to ponder their relationships to the political and public cultures of the New World. African American women and men used music and theater to challenge the gaze of white eyes. In Liberia, settler-colonists created their own forums for deliberating about their new existence in Africa and their relationships to a U.S. homeland. On the American frontier, a group of Mormon believers who had been chased from the places they tried to settle came together for a message that blended inquiry, magic, and democracy. Back east, some white women learned to perform the words of others to entertain and edify diverse audiences while making careers for themselves. Others combined piano playing with popular lecturing, enthralling adults and schoolchildren alike. Near the end of the century, people gathered from across the world in the White City of Chicago's World's Fair to deliberate about religion, truth, and humanity, equipping themselves to navigate pluralism in a global context.

While it can be tempting to idealize these educational experiments, they were forged, to borrow Joseph F. Kett's characterization, "under difficulties."[8] That is to say, they typically emerged because of exclusion, because of opposition, because the mainstream institutions of learning were never as welcoming as they should have been. To be sure, thinking together because of exclusion and opposition can lead to problems of its own: insularity, dogmatism, resistance to the insights of others. But this volume focuses more on delineating the ways that people, places, and discourses structured intellectual communities than on assessing the quality of knowledge produced. When the chapters do evaluate quality, they demonstrate a prolific range, from the instantiation of white supremacy to a progressive politics of inclusion. This volume thus aims not to romanticize the past but to show the many ways marginalized groups creatively navigated their circumstances and still pursued knowledge in community.

The argument that links the subjects treated in this volume is that people and groups in the nineteenth century, many of whom had limited access to formal education, pursued learning and developed knowledge useful for public life, whether they would deploy such knowledge in local voluntary associations, in entertainment venues, in religious institutions, or in political forums. They participated in the production and circulation of knowledge for myriad purposes, from economic betterment to social change, from personal growth to public action. Together they considered the same questions that echoed through the nation's great halls of learning—questions about justice, equality, career opportunities, entertainment, war and peace, life and death, heaven and hell, the nature of the world, and the nature of education itself. Yet they considered these questions while facing difficulties, uncertainties, and opposition seldom encountered by those in power. Similarly, the practices of learning they adopted were consistent with their time but modified to respond to their own circumstances: they blended oral, scribal, and print production, as they debated, lectured, kept minutes of meetings, and wrote letters, diaries, essays, poems, stories, histories, town plans, and geographic texts. Their collective intellectual experiments reflect the profound value they placed on learning and offer salutary reminders of its many forms, functions, and results, reminders that may prove useful as we deliberate the future of education in our own time.

Before turning to the specifics of the collective intellectual experiments treated here, we need to explain three general dynamics of the forms of thinking together that pervade this volume—specifically, the dynamics of people, places, and purposes.

People

Historian David M. Henkin insists that "the heterogeneity of historical experience" is "the increasingly salient fact" about the past.[9] Heterogeneity certainly characterizes the people and groups studied in this volume who pursued knowledge together in the nineteenth century. Even as the chapters demonstrate the ubiquity of knowledge seeking and knowledge production, they also show wide variation among participants. At the same time, by enacting their own form of collective inquiry, they suggest the utility of a multidisciplinary approach to an exceptionally complex and multifaceted history. The scholars writing in this volume focus attention at different scales, investigating the ways nineteenth-century learning practices contributed to widespread assumptions about national belonging or transnational alliances while also examining the distinctive features of learning communities, which sometimes flouted ostensible consensus.

Put differently, while the volume showcases variety, it also seeks patterns and connections—and not just across the chapters but across the range of intellectual practices that defined the nineteenth century. Consider the following example, which illustrates the interplay of particularity and generalizability at the heart of this volume. In July 1832 William Lloyd Garrison's Boston-based abolitionist newspaper, the *Liberator*, reported a speech delivered by Sarah Mapps Douglass, one of the paper's contributing authors, at a meeting labeled a "mental feast." The daughter of Philadelphia abolitionists Robert Douglass Sr., a hairdresser, and Grace Bustill Douglass, a milliner, Sarah Douglass was a twenty-five-year-old schoolteacher and a member of Philadelphia's African American middle class. In 1831 she had helped to found the Female Literary Association of Philadelphia, in 1833 she would join her mother and other local women to organize the interracial Philadelphia Female Anti-Slavery Society, and in the early 1840s she would participate in the Gilbert Lyceum, the first mixed-sex literary association in Philadelphia's free black community.[10] At an organizational "feast" in 1832, Douglass companionably addressed her auditors as "my friends" and "my sisters" and marked the significance of their assemblage: "How important is the occasion for which we have assembled ourselves together this evening, to hold a feast, to feed our never-dying minds, to encite each other to deeds of mercy, words of peace: to stir up in the bosom of each, gratitude to God for his increasing goodness, and feeling of deep sympathy for our brethren and sisters, who are in this land of christian light and liberty held in bondage the most cruel and degrading—to make their cause our own!" She merged personal experience and public action, detailing her own convictions about the sin of slavery, her increasing cognizance of the rampant threats to all black lives posed by the slave power, her sense of responsibility "to elevate the character of my wronged and neglected race," and her faith in God's help. Finally, Douglass offered procedural recommendations, suggesting that future "mental feasts" begin with Bible reading and prayer, that study and conversation be "altogether directed to the subject of slavery," and that fare "for the body" be "simple," the better to promote an imaginative affinity with "those who have nothing to refresh body and mind."[11]

The *Liberator* and an anonymous participant in the Philadelphia women's group both credited the launch of the "mental feasts" to a suggestion of the white Connecticut minister, educator, and anti-colonizationist Simeon Smith Jocelyn, a recent visitor to Pennsylvania.[12] Yet the metaphor itself—of learning as a repast for the mind, a banquet for the intellect—was ubiquitous in the nineteenth century, used by educational reformers to explain the value of cooperative learning or by journalists to describe the experience of attending a popular public lecture.[13] It framed mutual study in social terms, emphasizing the pleasurable gathering together of individuals in friendship and kinship groups—friends, sisters, brothers—for nourishment and sustenance, and implicitly correlating the nutritional requirements of the body with the mental or spiritual requirements of the mind or soul. Cooperative sociability encouraged organizing among those whose circumstances were similar, and indeed, many antebellum educational associations were comparatively homogenous in membership—whether young white male clerks in urban centers, upwardly mobile white men in the Old Northwest, free black men in Northern or even Southern cities, white women workers in New England's textile mills, or, like the Philadelphia group, free black women with shared religious and political goals.[14] The "mental feast" was usually prepared for friends and family, but the metaphor also intimated a welcoming openness, since young and old, women and men, and all classes and conditions require food. It figured learning as consumption, to be sure, but ingestion for health and strength, intake that made knowledge part of one's own substance.

Douglass thus adopted rhetorical commonplaces of her time to conceptualize learning as social and sustaining, and she also adapted the religious tenets of Protestantism to claim a personal God who intervened directly in human affairs, offering nurture and empowerment. This was the same God who, according to contemporaneous reformers, granted people natural rights that surpassed the laws of the state, helped destitute families to overcome the evils of alcohol, and democratized religious knowledge.[15] Whereas such linguistic choices linked Douglass to millions of her contemporaries, regardless of sex, race, or condition, her call for intensive study of "the subject of slavery" was distinctive. The subject-specific focus marked the Philadelphia women's voluntary educational association as overtly antislavery and activist, with study and discussion identified as motivation and preparation for public action. Working within an arena that communication theorist Catherine R. Squires names an "enclave public sphere"—an "independent space" that allows participants the "freedom to innovate, draw upon their own traditions, and speak freely"—the Philadelphia women prepared to counter proslavery threats.[16] Indeed, the *Liberator* report itself represented a printed, public assertion of the group's presence and goals.

Communal learning proved efficacious. Historian Julie Winch notes that "some of the most able officers of the women's antislavery conventions, such as Sarah Mapps Douglass and Hetty Burr, served their apprenticeship in Philadelphia's female literary societies," and thus society activity became "an integral part of the antislavery crusade."[17] Rhetorical scholar Shirley Wilson Logan specifies the key features of that apprenticeship as speaking, writing, and generating argument, noting that the Philadelphia "women understood that finely tuned rhetorical skills could serve the abolitionist cause."[18] Further, literary scholar Elizabeth McHenry argues that African American literary societies, which fostered publicity through textual production, constituted "acts of resistance" to a "hostile racial climate," and historian Mary Kelley notes that they "stand as an indictment of [whites'] racism."[19] Across the disciplines, humanities scholars pinpoint the interplay of social learning and political action.

The notion of the literary society as an act of resistance raises an important point about lecturing and learning in the nineteenth century: namely, such activities always constituted a partisan, political act. Collective inquiry was partisan and political because it was carried out in service of social change, whatever its scope or valence. Whether they were African Americans in Philadelphia beset with legal threats and proslavery turmoil, Irish Americans generating a hyphenated identity in a new land, or incarcerated prisoners affirming their humanity, the nineteenth-century people and groups who thought together believed that the pursuit of knowledge could transform their world. Yet the same point about the partisan, political character of inquiry stands as well for those in power and those who aspired to power, whether Anglo-American frontier lawyers preparing for political careers or Liberian settler-colonists seizing the potential of self-governance.[20] Further, the forms of knowledge that circulated most widely—through oral, scribal, and print transmission—were (and remain) directly correlated to the distribution of authority. Thus, although this volume emphasizes the production and circulation of knowledge among people who often lacked cultural power—and sometimes had to live and learn in a clandestine fashion—it is important to acknowledge the larger contexts in which such learning occurred. This book is less a correction of scholarship emphasizing nationalism, imperialism, and Anglo-American and male supremacy than it is a shift of figure and ground—and a reminder that so-called mainstream culture is also partisan and particular, entailing continued rhetorical work to persist.[21] Commending innovation, creativity, and resilience should not discount the vexed interplay of the dynamics of power, from brute force to unacknowledged tolerance of status difference.

Places

The dynamics of power can be seen in spatial control and organization. The places that fostered nineteenth-century popular learning were as varied as the individuals and groups who promoted such learning. Whereas several contributors to this volume have participated in the internationalization of research foci, the book is Americanist in its geographic focus, demonstrating the heterogeneity of life and experience in U.S. territory or, in the case of Liberia, in a colony established by a U.S.-based organization.[22] At the same time, the volume challenges assumptions about the solidity of the nation-state, calling attention to mobility across space as a fundamental feature of nineteenth-century life—whether in the vagaries of soldiering; in the peripatetic careers of lecturers, readers, and musicians; in the relocation of immigrants proactively seeking a better life or driven from their homes by warfare or famine; in racially motivated diasporic settlement; in the migration of threatened religious minorities; or in the tours of international visitors. As people moved—across town, across the country, across the globe—their own experiences blended with knowledge gained through print and oral media to make meaning of their own moment and its relationship to the past and the future. This was true for Sarah Douglass, who published in the *Liberator* under a pen name that showed her esteem for Sophonisba, a Carthaginian noblewoman during the Punic Wars.[23] While writing in a culturally acceptable, "feminine" fashion under what McHenry labels "the veil of anonymity," Douglass configured herself as a confident and emphatic woman.[24]

Textual representation could enact the malleability of social place, even as physical spaces signaled the variable dynamics of power. It is likely that Douglass and her comrades met in a parlor, a space of complex political and cultural meaning for African American women that the visual communication scholar Jasmine Nichole Cobb has called "a place of reprieve and rehearsal."[25] Other groups of nineteenth-century learners also met in convenient surroundings, since mutual education societies required minimal resources, such as "shelter, heat, and light for meetings."[26] Whether in homes, churches, schools, or local halls, people came together in places under their control. For small groups meeting for the edification of their members, domestic or provisional quarters were often adequate, but individuals and groups that sought public audiences pursued larger venues. Itinerant lecturers rented commercially available space, and associations that promoted seasonal courses of lectures and other performances usually hired public halls; sometimes, if groups possessed sufficient wealth, they erected purpose-built edifices.[27] The design of such buildings often celebrated Western classical antiquity. For instance, the Salem Lyceum building in Massachusetts, opened in 1831 by local white Protestants, boasted fresco paintings of Demosthenes and Cicero. In Virginia, the Alexandria Lyceum's two-story Greek Revival structure, built in 1839, featured busts of Cicero and Seneca.[28] Such endorsements of classicism instantiated in architecture and decoration the cultural traditions that were also valorized as the basis of nineteenth-century learning. The emphases persisted throughout the century, as was evident on the main stage of the 1893 World's Parliament of Religions in Chicago, which displayed statues of Demosthenes and Cicero.

The names of the buildings in Salem and Alexandria disclose another terminological complexity in discussing the place of nineteenth-century popular learning: the word *lyceum*. A Latin term derived from Greek that appears in multiple chapters in this volume, lyceum was popularized in the United States in the late 1820s by reformers like the Yale-educated scientific lecturer Josiah Holbrook, an advocate for cooperative education. With promotional efforts yielding a bumper crop of civic associations called lyceums, the activities of these groups quickly transmuted the term into a rough equivalent of *literary society* or *debating society*. Such meanings were sustained across time, and yet, by the 1840s and 1850s, many lyceums were best known as sponsors of events that sought a fee-paying public: lectures, readings, and other performances, sometimes delivered by local people and sometimes by travelers on the expanding rail and water networks. Terms like *lyceum lecture system* and *lyceum circuit* arose, and then with the advent of commercial management

Figure I.1 The Alexandria Lyceum during the Civil War. This Greek Revival structure was built in 1839. Photograph by Andrew J. Russell. Courtesy of The Lyceum—Alexandria's History Museum.

bureaus in the 1860s and '70s such as the Redpath Lyceum Bureau of Boston and the Slayton Lyceum Bureau of Chicago, the term lyceum constellated a variety of public performance practices combining education and entertainment, including illustrated lectures, instrumental and vocal music, comedy, dramatic reading, and impersonation. As chautauqua circuits developed in the late nineteenth and early twentieth centuries, inspired by an 1874 Methodist retreat on Lake Chautauqua, New York, the phrase "lyceum and chautauqua platforms" became a ubiquitous rendering in publications promoting traveling talent of all sorts.[29] Whereas the term lyceum seems always to have connoted social respectability—in contrast to the theater—and, as Carl Bode remarked, always stood "grandly if a little vaguely, for learning," its denotative and connotative meanings varied markedly across space and time.[30]

Since lyceums were a protean site where popular education occurred in the nineteenth century, several chapters in this book examine the contours of lecturing and learning within such venues. Yet other chapters extend the volume's focus well beyond lyceums. As Ronald J. Zboray and Mary Saracino Zboray argue in the first chapter, the term lyceum can be taken as provocatively metaphorical, pointing less to a definite referent than to "a portable, mutable, transferrable identity" that people could adapt for circumstances as diverse as the wartime home front, the battlefield, the hospital, and the prison.[31] This form of learning could be practiced directly with friends and family, conveyed in letters to be experienced virtually and asynchronously, and shared through imaginative engagement with absent others. At once material and conceptual, the term lyceum in this volume—as in nineteenth-century history—is multiple and diverse, simultaneously a discrete setting where learning occurred and a symbol for envisioning learning itself. Yet because many chapters discuss phenomena that occurred in forums not named lyceums or imagined as such by participants, terms like *lecture culture* and *platform culture*—argot of present-day scholarship, not nineteenth-century usage—mark a broader range of public performance forms and signal the volume's thematic reach.

Sites of performance and the cultural meanings conveyed by such places also affected nineteenth-century interpretations of proffered presentations. It is possible, for example, that the purported earnestness of the lyceum and chautauqua platforms helped to solidify the impression for many white audiences in the late nineteenth and early twentieth centuries that white performers' imitations of "Negro music" or dialect readings provided an accurate rendering of black life and culture. At the same time and in similar venues, the versatility of African American performers like Anna Madah Hyers and Emma Louise Hyers presented the interpretive possibility that, as Kirt H. Wilson and Kaitlyn G. Patia put it, "perhaps there was no single identity for African Americans after all."[32] Illustrating the ways that lectures, musical performances, and dramatic readings—all configured as public entertainment—supplied educational content, overtly or subtly, this volume again confirms that education through entertainment media, widely recognized in our own time, was also an important historical phenomenon.[33] Networks of public entertainment showed how to identify one's place, but likewise could signal its contingency.

Purposes

The difficulties, uncertainties, and opposition that surrounded the people and places featured in this volume raise the larger question of purposes. Why was thinking together so important, even in the face of exclusion, and what did people hope to accomplish? Why, despite limited resources and, typically, few chances for social advancement, did groups assemble for collective inquiry? The answer to these questions is at once straightforward and nuanced.

On the one hand, people gathered for many reasons—social, political, personal, religious, instrumental, and more. Sarah Douglass, as we have seen, integrated learning and antislavery activism. Others hoped to advance their careers, as was the case with lecturer-teacher Eliza Harriot O'Connor, dramatic reader Gertrude Kellogg, and pianist Amy Fay, all studied in this volume. Some worked to forge a collective, civic identity, as was the case with Irish immigrants to the United States and members of the Liberia Lyceum. Still others sought religious enlightenment, as was the case with the followers of Joseph Smith and with those who assembled at the World's Parliament of Religions. Specific aims aside, practices of learning constituted a technology, a vehicle for self-development and self-assertion, that was applied by different people to varying ends. This was as true for those living on society's margins as it was for those in privileged positions.[34] In that way, lecture culture served as a nineteenth-century technology of learning much as the Internet serves users in the twenty-first century. From massive online courses and academic discussion forums to sites for professional development, self-promotion, and identity formation, online communication offers a space for collective inquiry with a similar diversity of purposes and a similar variation in quality of content as the spaces for lecturing and learning had in the nineteenth century.

On the other hand, there were also more subtle reasons—beyond self-improvement—that people in the nineteenth century gathered for collective inquiry, and these reasons offer an important counterpoint to many educational movements in the twenty-first century. For many nineteenth-century knowledge seekers, sociable learning was an end in itself. To be sure, inquiry was often instrumental in one way or another—as a means of extending professional influence or acquiring vocational knowledge, for instance.[35] Yet it would be a mistake to reduce the performances, debates, discussions, and lectures of the nineteenth century to instrumentality. Many people and groups, including many featured in this volume, thought together for the sheer joy and social sustenance of thinking together.[36] For instance, lecturing and learning during the Civil War was often necessarily removed from instrumental considerations, as the Zborays show. Sometimes lectures on the home front, or those shared in military encampments, avoided war topics so that people could forget the present crisis, however temporarily. Captured soldiers created their own educational forums behind prison walls not for professional advancement but as a way of retaining their humanity in horrifying circumstances. The Lyce-I-see-'em in Richmond's infamous Libby Prison energized prisoners' minds despite the deprivations of their bodies. Two decades beforehand and across the Atlantic, members of the Liberia Lyceum were often interested less in how thinking together could prepare them for work beyond the association—although preparation was part of it—than in stimulating their minds in the face of uncertainty in a new world. In many ways, then, lecturing and learning in the nineteenth century often resisted overt instrumentality in favor of sociability and the pleasure of inquiry.

This noninstrumental approach to education, in fact, was important to many intellectual collaboratives in the nineteenth century. Consider the case of the Breadwinner's College. Founded in 1898 by the arrogant, acerbic, but undeniably brilliant philosopher Thomas Davidson, the Breadwinner's College was a loose-knit group of working-class immigrants on the Lower East Side of Manhattan.[37] Despite what the name suggests, it was less a "college" in any formal sense than an intellectual collaborative for people who lived in oppressive, desperate circumstances. At the time, the Lower East Side was the most crowded neighborhood on the planet, rife with poverty, public health crises, and capitalist exploitation due to the seldom-regulated garment trade.[38] Participants in the Breadwinner's College were often first- or second-generation Americans who sometimes toiled twelve hours a day in sweatshops and stuffy tenement buildings.[39] After work, however, they got together at a neighborhood settlement house and pursued a rigorous curriculum in the liberal arts.

Davidson created reading lists, assignment prompts, discussion opportunities, and public-speaking scenarios for participants to pursue, but it was the neighborhood residents who made the group come alive. Their collective inquiry was divorced from typical settlement-house instruction, which usually comprised topics like grammar, civics, hygiene, bookkeeping, and nutrition. Instead they read Plato, Aristotle, Augustine, Aquinas, Descartes, Locke, Hume, Kant, Darwin, Spencer, and many other luminaries of the Western intellectual tradition. They discussed and debated world geography, comparative religions, ancient sociology, evolutionary theory, deontological ethics, and systems of governance.[40] Along the way they wrote and delivered papers on abstract topics that had little to do with their days in the exploitive garment trade. As Morris Cohen, a participant in the school, explained: the aim of the Breadwinner's College was "to afford young working people ... a systematic course of study which would provide the proper mental discipline and lay the foundations of liberal education. The course was primarily a culture course intended to make the pupils broadminded, willing and able to take an intelligent and active interest in the various important questions of life."[41] On New York's Lower East Side, immigrants, some of whom began with marginal English literacy skills, studied what it meant to be human—apart from any sense of career prospects or professional development—and they professed to love it. "The interchange of thought with that large, rich soul [Davidson] grew to be the keenest joy I had ever experienced," wrote Mary Ryshpan, a young dressmaker who lived and worked in the neighborhood. "Subsequently it caused my horizon to be somewhat broadened. He opened to me a world of literature, science, and art and philosophy that I had known only very vaguely before. He strengthened my desire to serve Humanity."[42] To be sure, the problems of the Lower East Side did not disappear with the formation of the Breadwinner's College, but many who participated in its courses and discussions satiated their intellectual hunger and gave their lives a newfound sense of purpose.

The culture of inquiry in the nineteenth century, especially in its noninstrumental manifestations, stands as a significant counterpoint to many of the educational trends in the twenty-first century, especially the rampant careerism that seems to pervade current debates. Contemporary commentators increasingly question the ROI (return on investment) of obtaining a four-year degree—and use managerial language like the initialism ROI—as they demand more institutional accountability for graduation rates and employment prospects.[43] In this environment, the intersection of lecturing, learning, and difference in the nineteenth century reminds us of the expansive possibilities of thinking together. Education, even higher education, need not hinge solely on questions of economic value. Those in the nineteenth century who thought together on the margins of society were excluded from formal institutions and had little chance of using collective intellectual spaces for social and economic advancement. Nevertheless, they understood the value of assembling wherever they could—from the parlors or lecture halls of the Northeast to the prairies of the American frontier and the sweltering tropical spaces of Liberia. They understood their need, as human beings, to ponder life's big questions with people in circumstances like their own. They used whatever resources they could to participate in the life of the mind. The scholarly studies that follow, then, underscore the value of a liberal arts education, even outside the walls of liberal arts institutions. Being human is motivation enough for thinking together.

Synopsis

In the following chapters, scholars from a variety of disciplines explore nineteenth-century popular learning and forms of difference. At the same time, the disciplinary diversity of this volume represents a collaborative thinking together in our own historical moment. Whereas each contribution investigates discrete archives and draws on discipline-specific concepts and approaches, jointly the chapters demonstrate that nineteenth-century popular learning pervaded diverse communities, occurred in a profusion of locations, and served various purposes.

The volume is organized in two parts: part I, titled "Disrupting Narratives," directly challenges common stories told by scholars about popular learning in the long nineteenth century, calling into question assumptions about where learning occurred and what functions it performed. Contributors ask what happened to the lyceum during the Civil War, when and why women began giving commercial lectures, whether the antebellum lecture hall was thoroughly an Anglo-Saxon, bourgeois phenomenon, and who was mimicking whom in performances saturated with racial—and racist—assumptions. In keeping with their emphasis on the generation of new historical and conceptual models, each of the chapters in part I surveys multiple individuals and groups. Following the four framing chapters of part I, the chapters in part II, titled "Distinctive Voices," offer in-depth studies of the work of individuals: writer and editor Hilary Teage, Mormon founder Joseph Smith, dramatic reader Gertrude Kellogg, concert pianist Amy Fay, and Hindu religious leader Swami Vivekananda. The chapters in the two parts function at different scales, and collectively they proffer additions and revisions to prior scholarship on nineteenth-century learning, emphasizing communities of learning that functioned through forms of difference, including racial, ethnic, gender, economic, geographic, and religious.

The first chapter in part I, by Ronald J. Zboray and Mary Saracino Zboray, profoundly disrupts the long-standing scholarly consensus that popular intellectual activities almost ceased during the Civil War. Drawing on an array of unpublished personal papers and their transcriptions of more than two million words about Civil War–era reading culture, the Zborays recover a multitude of educational and cultural activities among black and white women and men, North and South, on the home front, in battlefield camps, and in prisons. By exploring the varied people, places, and purposes of lecturing and learning during the Civil War, the Zborays articulate the central themes of *Thinking Together* while dramatically altering the way we understand the development of platform culture in the nineteenth century. Highlighting a wide variety of people, places, and conditions, the chapter sets the stage for the remaining chapters in part I to investigate comparatively defined groups—women entrepreneurs, Irish immigrants, and entertainers performing race. Further, the placement of the Zborays' chapter first in the volume—outside a chronological sequence—is a performative enactment of its disruption of narratives about wartime and the temporal progression of learning.

Chapter 2 thus moves back in time, as Granville Ganter turns to commercial popular lecturing and professional advancement in the early national period, long before Josiah Holbrook began his campaign for lyceum associations. Focusing primary attention on entrepreneurial white women such as Eliza Harriot O'Connor and Anne Laura Clarke, who used public lectures to attract clients for private schools, Ganter shows how these lecturers harmonized republican ideals for nationalist education with women's business practices in civic and social domains. Illuminating the little-studied phenomenon of early commercial lecturing by people often overlooked in studies of lecture culture, Ganter disrupts assumptions about gender and entrepreneurship on the early American public stage.

In chapter 3, Tom F. Wright expands the geographic dimensions of popular lecturing, exploring the role of Irish immigrants on antebellum U.S. platforms and their challenges to an "Anglo-American commons" that spanned the Atlantic. Focusing on such figures as Thomas Francis Meagher, John Mitchel, and John McElheran, Wright shows how such orators worked to reimagine and rearticulate a global Irish identity. Through spectacles of Irish nationalism and interrogations of "Celtic" and "Anglo-Saxon" racial theory, Irish immigrants carved a unique niche for themselves in transatlantic platform culture—a niche that Wright investigates to broaden our understanding of the people, topics, and goals that propelled popular education in the nineteenth century.

In chapter 4, Kirt H. Wilson and Kaitlyn G. Patia reveal the ways that nineteenth- and early twentieth-century American audiences gained impressions about racial difference by witnessing the platform entertainments of European and African Americans. To explicate the myriad roles that mimesis played on the public stage, Wilson and Patia range across time from minstrel shows to the performances of Polk Miller and His Old South Quartette, from the musical dramas of the Hyers Sisters to the plays of William Wells Brown. Along the way, they demonstrate how performative imitation challenged the assumptions of natural differences between whites and blacks and suggested, instead, that race was a matter of enculturation and imbricated in material opportunity. Wilson and Patia disrupt the often taken-for-granted racial lines that purportedly defined nineteenth-century lecture culture, detailing reifications of and challenges to conceptions of race on the public stage.

Following part I's disruption of conventional historical narratives, the five essays in part II locate distinctive voices that speak to lecturing, learning, and difference. In chapter 5, Bjørn F. Stillion Southard explores the deliberative practices of the Liberia Lyceum and the work of Hilary Teage, a speaker, writer, and editor in 1840s Monrovia who encouraged fellow settler-colonists to develop a black Liberian civic identity. Stillion Southard uses Teage's voice to show how print, performance, and deliberation in Liberia drew on the norms and ideals of lecture culture in the United States, while adapting and ultimately transforming those norms and ideals for the settler-colonists' geographic and political context. The Liberia Lyceum and the work of Hilary Teage show how people and places are as important as practices and purposes in understanding the life of the mind and its histories.

In chapter 6, Richard Benjamin Crosby turns to the marginalized community and distinctive voice of the early Mormon Church, analyzing how Joseph Smith's King Follett Discourse of 1844 helped adherents of this burgeoning religion to develop new practices of knowing on the American frontier. Crosby shows how the coalescence of lecture culture, folk magic, and radical democracy gave the much-maligned Mormons a distinctive yet quintessentially American voice. Smith's discourse, Crosby demonstrates, brought together markedly distinctive knowledge cultures and, at the same time, situated the church in a unique relationship to the forms of knowledge production that then defined mainstream inquiry.

In chapter 7, Sara E. Lampert moves into the post–Civil War era to investigate the work of Gertrude Kellogg, a successful performer of dramatic prose who modeled a way for middle-class white women to shape a national conversation about their public identity. Kellogg drew from, adapted, and recombined different platform practices to distinguish herself from scores of other dramatic readers. As Lampert shows, Kellogg managed not only to find professional success in a male-dominated field but also to use her own voice, through the words of others, to connect emotionally with audiences across the country. Kellogg's words may not have been her own, but the people, scenes, and roles she inhabited demonstrated that middle-class white women could extend the norms of Victorian womanhood into professional public culture.

In chapter 8, E. Douglas Bomberger draws further attention to the distinctive voices of women on the postwar public stage by explicating pianist Amy Fay's creation of the lecture recital, which combined musical performance with the oral presentation of information about the pieces performed. Not only did these recitals, which Fay called "piano conversations," help her to achieve professional success, but they also linked different audiences together in a larger public appreciation of music, discourse, and learning. Cultural elites in Boston, Midwesterners in Goshen, Indiana, and schoolchildren on Manhattan's Lower East Side—Fay's audiences saw education and entertainment merge into a provocative new form of thinking together, a form that would continue to morph along with the performative and technological innovations of the twentieth century.

In chapter 9, Scott R. Stroud homes in on the unique voice of Swami Vivekananda, a Hindu monk, largely unknown at the beginning of 1893, who challenged, inspired, and delighted audiences at the World's Parliament of Religions and, in the process, became a celebrated international representative of Hinduism. Amid some of the most important religious deliberations of the late nineteenth century, Vivekananda emerged as a pluralistic prophet who used his own religion to speak to the distinctiveness and unity of all religions. In that way, Vivekananda followed many other marginalized figures in the nineteenth century by combining different cultures, practices, and ideas into a provocative discourse that rose above the surrounding cacophony. By entering white Christian America at a time of rampant racism and xenophobia, a brown Hindu monk charted a way forward for an increasingly interconnected world.

Thinking Together concludes with Carolyn Eastman's deft assessment of the nine previous chapters, as she contextualizes nineteenth-century oral performance within broader historical trajectories that show the changing roles of Western audiences. "It is vital to recognize," she writes, "that the importance of audiences and public opinion had grown significantly by the era described here, and that these developments coincided with the gradual democratization of education, politics, print culture, and religion." These changing roles for audiences, Eastman argues, provided the substrate for innovations in genres of performance that expected audiences to reason logically and to respond sensorially, that prompted deliberative engagement, and that reinforced or challenged social norms. Interactions between speakers and audiences, between audience members, and across venues offer a crucial focus for present-day scholars who seek to understand what Eastman succinctly labels the "process-oriented aspect of the development of major American ideas."[44]

Today, in an environment in which educational commentators question the nature, value, and methods of learning, *Thinking Together* speaks to these issues by highlighting people, places, and purposes that disrupted conventional inquiry and diversified public discourse. The heterogeneity of the subjects presented here implicitly argues that all forms of difference are varied and variable, as the volume invites other scholars across the humanities to join in a burgeoning field of investigation. Itself an enactment of collaborative thinking, this book links scholars from multiple disciplinary traditions in conversation about nineteenth-century cultures of inquiry that tried to offer distinctive solutions to familiar problems of education, civic participation, and democratic deliberation. These histories, we believe, can offer new insights and more nuanced perspectives on how difference enhances the human project of thinking together.

PART I
DISRUPTING NARRATIVES

I

THE PORTABLE LYCEUM IN THE CIVIL WAR

Ronald J. Zboray and Mary Saracino Zboray

For most historians of the lyceum, the American Civil War marks the end of an era. Before the war, public lecturing fed the thirst for knowledge, educated the masses outside of formal schooling, helped to spread democracy, and fostered cosmopolitanism. After the war, lecturing became more highly organized, corporate, commercialized, reliant on a star system of speakers, and, according to some, devoted less to informing than to entertaining the citizenry.[1] Of what happened in between—that crucial time of transformation between 1861 and 1865—little is known. Very few works on the lyceum have addressed the war-era lecture system itself.[2]

One reason for this oversight is that the pioneering scholarly works on the lyceum, including Carl Bode's 1956 *American Lyceum* and David Mead's 1951 *Yankee Eloquence*, have discouraged the foray into the war years by claiming that the popular lecture either went into hibernation until better times, hobbled on with sparse audiences and lackluster speakers, or bellowed forth, every now and then, with crass patriotic propaganda. "Though lecturing itself continued as a form of activity within the American culture," Bode wrote, "its aim on both sides of the Mason-Dixon line shifted to helping win the war."[3] Another reason is that these influential works were shortsighted when it came to including women of all races, African American men, and others who were not the beneficiaries of Jacksonian-era democratization but who nonetheless attended lectures or struggled to gain access to the platform as speaker-reformers. Angela G. Ray reminds us in her *Lyceum and Public Culture* that the war "opened the lyceum lecture hall to explicitly political topics and discourse of social reform as well as to a greater variety of lecturers," granting greater visibility to white women such as Mary Livermore, African American women like Frances Ellen Watkins Harper, and African American men, including Frederick Douglass.[4] Still another reason for the paucity of wartime lyceum studies is that Civil War scholars have only recently begun to address cultural life on the home front and have, as yet, all but overlooked the popular lecture.[5] Finally, because so little primary-source research has been done to substantiate claims about the Civil War lecture system, researchers must go out into the field and reconstruct it for themselves, from the ground up.

That is what we did. Over the past fifteen years we have been transcribing extracts related to literary culture, such as reading and lecture-going, from ordinary Americans' wartime diaries, letters, memoirs, and account books to understand the transformations wrought by the war. We found relevant material in more than 5,500 documents written between 1860 and 1866 by more than a thousand Americans from all regions of the divided country. Our transcriptions, the largest body of data on Civil War–era reading culture to date, comprise more than two million words.[6] These include excerpts from personal papers authored by an equal number of male and female residents of both the Union and the Confederacy, and items written by both military personnel (mostly lower-ranking) and civilians. Of the total set of diarists or correspondents we consulted, 51 percent were working class. We actively sought out members of religious groups beyond mainstream Protestant denominations, including Jews and Catholics, as well as nonwhites and ethnic groups beyond British and Northern European ones.[7] Just over 7 percent of our material was authored by African Americans. Contained within all this material is information about specific lectures' settings, times, and speakers; auditors' transcriptions of lectures; the circumstances surrounding lecture-going; and responses to the content of lectures or the environments in which they were delivered. Several of our writers gave lectures themselves or debated, recited, or read aloud original handwritten newspapers, compositions, and printed materials before collectives. Much of what we present here, however, analyzes audience members' responses to lectures.[8]

The immense diversity of perspectives and the large extent of information represented in our material can hardly be filtered into an all-encompassing, let alone comprehensive, narrative of the lyceum's transformation. But we can say with some certainty that the lyceum was not consumed by the war effort on either side, nor was it severely disrupted or crippled, particularly in Northern cities and Western territories, which were not ripped apart by battles. Even for Southerners and Union army personnel in the embattled South, where cultural institutions were often literally destroyed, the lyceum never really died. For the lyceum during the war years was being spatially reconstituted as a portable, mutable, transferrable identity—a true "town meeting of the mind," to borrow Carl Bode's term—that, when called on to do so, could transcend the prior, conventional material conditions of its existence.[9] It could surmount brick-and-mortar boundaries and defy scheduled times for convening, and it required no established program of speakers. As such the lyceum could evade the material disruptions and dislocations engendered by war. Because of their long-standing involvement with the lecture and with lyceum-like activities such as reading aloud, creating literary newspapers, and debating, Americans had internalized a set of expectations associated with lyceum attendance that they were reluctant to discard with the first shots fired at Fort Sumter. Some of these internalized expectations included a hunger for new ideas circulated in social settings, group bonding, reaching beyond the mundane, self-improvement, escape from work or tedium—all experienced within a collective setting, and all transgressive of individualized, atomized, solitary, or silent pursuits.[10] In other words, Americans were so accustomed to "thinking together" that they struggled to maintain institutions that united individuals who craved intellectual stimulation. As we will see, the war also created new spaces of opportunity for innovating lyceum activities.

In this chapter we demonstrate some of the ways the popular lecture was imbricated in social, cultural, and political meaning-making among two major groups: those on the home front and those on the battlefield. These groups are somewhat contrived in that the intersections between the two, as we will show, are many. But we found this categorization the most expedient way to manage our data. We begin with the home front, homing in first on white women from the urban and rural North and West, who, along with children and non-enlisted men, enjoyed the greatest access to popular lectures during the war years and who probably filled the greatest number of seats. We focus here on women to compare their experiences with those we examined in our 2006 book *Everyday Ideas* and in our 2013 essay "Women Thinking: The International Popular Lecture and Its Audience in Antebellum New England." Because the lecture-going context had remained relatively stable over time for these white Northern women, they can provide a kind of baseline for locating any changes from the prewar era to the end of the war. After considering the changes in these women's lecture-going lives, we turn to the home front's free African American women and men as audiences for lectures and as members of literary societies. We highlight Emilie Davis, a Philadelphia seamstress immersed in the city's cultural offerings, and Christian A. Fleetwood, who helped to conduct the Galbreath Lyceum in Baltimore and who would win the Medal of Honor for his bravery during the 1864 battle at Chaffin's Farm in Virginia.[11] We follow him onto the battlefield—the topic of our next section, which explores the roles of soldiers, prisoners of war, and nurses in maintaining lyceum culture under the most extreme, disruptive conditions. Through their stories, perhaps more than anyone else's, we can witness the "town meeting of the mind" in its most expansive form.

Preserving the Lyceum on the Home Front

When abolitionist Sarah Browne of Salem, Massachusetts, sat down with her small pocket diary on 3 May 1862, she laughed at its jumbled blend of contents. "I am amused at the ridiculous manner in which I mix up home incidents with news of great public interest."[12] This avid lecture-goer summed up what most white women probably felt about their wartime existence: it oscillated between close-at-hand domestic concerns and momentous political events. The popular lecture was embedded in that divided existence. It could give women respite from housework and depressing thoughts of embattled loved ones, but it could also give them fodder for political discussion and war-related activism. Either way, the wartime lecture provided knowledge, sociability, and a sense of belonging to a collective outside of home and family.

Like their antebellum predecessors, war-era women moved within a gendered lyceum culture. They were still, especially in small towns, often accompanied to lectures by men, or they attended in mixed-sex groups. Embedded, as before, within a matrix of sociabilities that could include tea beforehand and dancing or going out for a snack afterward, the lyceum inspired discussions with company.[13] When that company was a beau, as it often was, the chatter could wax romantic. "This evening we all went to our Lyceum," Emily Hawley wrote in 1862 from Delaware County, Iowa. "James came home with me. We sat & talked awhile after the rest had all retired. Ah, those questions: 'do you love me, Emmie & will you be my bride?'" They soon married, as did many lecture-going couples.[14]

Women still marveled at the great crowds a popular lecturer commanded, but they also noted absences due to the war. While attending a Henry Ward Beecher lecture in Boston's vast Music Hall, of which "every niche and corner was occupied," Nellie Browne found that her mind wandered to her father stationed in Union-occupied Beaufort, South Carolina. "I thought of you and longed for you to be there," she wrote him on 20 January 1864.[15] In this way, women remolded the lyceum concept to include the absent who attended in spirit. Because their embattled husbands, sons, and brothers wanted to hear about what they were missing, women took mental notes about the lectures to write up in their letters to camp. When they mailed out these pieces of stationery filled with news from home, they were also mailing pieces of the lyceum.

Like women's wartime diaries, popular lectures themselves were sometimes a surprising compound of the mundane and the patriotic. It is often difficult to determine a lecture's topic by its title alone, but because we can call on diarists and letter writers to give lecture-going contexts, we get glimpses into content. We were able to identify in our material the content of 233 (out of 259) lectures that women from the North and West heard, and, of these, only 28 percent were obviously war-related—a stark contrast to women's reading choices, which showed a war obsession. Still, women frequently sought out war-themed lectures. One that a Brookline, Massachusetts, housewife audited called "Political Horoscope" lifted the spirits by predicting "a brilliant future for this country."[16] Lectures such as "The Rifle," "Munitions of War," and "Projectiles" may have helped women to understand what loved ones were up against.[17] While we can only guess at the specific topics covered in the declamations, recitations, and lectures given by young locals in Olney, Maryland, on 13 April 1865, the timing and the description of the small lyceum hall's windows, each decked with a *"beautiful pyramid of flowers, red, white, and blue,"* suggest that these presentations celebrated the war's ending.[18]

But most lecture-goers desired the occasional break from newspapers and war talk that a disinterested lecture provided. While some young women were at the cutting edge of a youth subculture that escaped war through solitary fiction reading, a broader spectrum of women preferred the sociable lyceum for diversion.[19] Some lectures, although not as many as in prewar decades, stimulated cosmopolitan women's global consciousness. These included talks such as "Whaling Voyage," "Maritime Cities of the Mediterranean," "Japan and Its People & Customs," "Garibaldi," "Florence," and "Palestine."[20] Catering to the scientifically minded were lectures like "Galvanism," "Circulation of Blood," "Physiology," and "Air."[21] Temperance lectures abounded. Out in Lockwood, California, they were one young woman's constant fare.[22] But airier subjects appealed as well. A talk on mental philosophy by Joseph Haven charmed one schoolteacher in Evanston, Illinois.[23] She wrote, "He led us into the ideal world,—into 'Cloud Land' as he called it . . . [and] cheered us by saying that we were by nature poets ourselves."[24]

If lectures like this were informed by war, then it was only by their blithe dismissal of it.

Auditors were often shocked when a seemingly nonpolitical lecture turned out to be a partisan plea. "Went last night to hear a lecture by Mr. O'Gorman," Maria Daly wrote from New York in 1863. "To our surprise, indignation, and disgust, the lecture was an infamous attempt to wrest the eloquence of [Edmund] Burke from its original meaning and make of it an ingenious appeal for the South."[25] Likewise, Sarah Fulton of Wilmington, Delaware, cringed when one of the phrenologist Fowler brothers, either Lorenzo Niles Fowler or Orson Squire Fowler, tried to recruit during the "public examinations" portion of his talk. After feeling the bumps on the head of a local doctor, Fowler announced to the audience that "he was a good surgeon, [and] ought to be in the army where his surgical talents would be brought into action."[26]

The Fowlers were but two of the better-known lecturers women heard. In urban areas, some speakers were already achieving a stardom that nudged some lesser lights out of the market and drew enormous crowds: Henry Ward Beecher, John B. Gough, George William Curtis, Wendell Phillips, Artemus Ward, Bayard Taylor, and Louis Agassiz. Women marveled at their appeal. "The thought came to me of the great power a man must have to hold the attention of such an audience," Nellie Browne exclaimed of Beecher.[27] Indeed, few women mentioned sparse attendance at any lecture—celebrity or otherwise—and even fewer attributed it to the war. Even in rural areas and small towns, lyceum life went on despite the upheaval. It is no surprise that in these areas women were more likely than those in urban centers to listen to local nobodies or people they knew personally. But rural women took a more active role in the lecture hall than their urban counterparts, mainly as poets, essayists, or editors of handwritten newspapers—paper sheets inscribed with news, verse, announcements, and other scribblings by locals, which were sometimes hand-copied in very limited numbers and distributed by being read aloud before groups. Women read these works on the platform more unapologetically than before.[28] In cities, the interstitial space accorded the amateur lecturer was likely shrinking as celebrity speaking loomed on the horizon.

The celebrity some women would achieve as professional speakers after the war is already evident in our transcriptions. Well on her way to national fame in 1865, Anna Dickinson stimulated discussion about her influence on neophyte speakers.[29] "A young woman here of eighteen is lecturing before large audiences upon reconstruction," Maria Daly in New York noted as the war closed. "I suppose she [is] fired by Miss Dickinson's success."[30] Although most of the women in our sample were still reluctant to praise the likes of Dickinson or Matilda Joslyn Gage, they moderated disapprobation with commendation or even backhanded compliments: Annie R. Stuart of Scipio, Ohio, for example, thought that Gage "was very interesting 'for a woman.'"[31] One "lady lecturer," probably a "Mrs. Bush" who remained composed under fire from the audience, won the admiration of Stuart even though she "did not like her." Stuart's neighbor and lyceum companion apparently incited the ruckus. "[Mr.?] Arndt and her had a spat and a good many acted very bad," Stuart wrote in her diary, adding that the speaker "did well and had any amount of brass."[32] White women in the North were more likely to hear and comment favorably on white and black abolitionist lecturers during the war than before—including Frederick Douglass, who was achieving celebrity by speaking regularly under the auspices of many white lecture-sponsoring associations.[33] In Wilmington, Delaware, Anne Ferris was awestruck upon hearing him in 1863: I "had no idea that his eloquence was of such a high order," she wrote. "I have never heard more than two or three orators that I think equal to him."[34] A diversifying set of speakers was framing white women's wartime lecture-going experience, opening their hearts to the rich amplification of voices previously muffled in the national arena.

That same year, in Philadelphia, Emilie Frances Davis, a free black seamstress and milliner, wrote in her diary, "Fred[erick] Douglass lectures."[35] On 17 March 1863, the Mother Bethel African Methodist Episcopal Church was packed when he delivered "The Crisis," also called "Men of Color, to Arms." Douglass's call for black enlistment included eliciting emotional pledges among male audience members and leading the crowd in singing "John Brown's Body." The next day the *Philadelphia Inquirer* wrote that "the church was shaken by outbursts of applause."[36] For Emilie, her escort Vincent, the black community, and white and black abolitionists in the audience, it was a transcendent moment.

Our sample of African American women diarists and letter writers is far too small for us to make confident generalizations about their collective lyceum experience, so we focus here on an individual, Davis, who left records for the years 1863 to 1865. During that period she attended at least seventeen lectures, and probably more. The small amount of space allotted to each day's entry in her ruled pocket diaries discouraged detailed writing, so she kept her comments brief. Her records, nonetheless, offer invaluable insights.[37]

Like the white women described above, Davis often mixed lecture attendance with other sociabilities. For example, on 19 February 1863 she wrote,

"In the evening, we went to the lecture. After witch [sic], we went over to Rachels, then up to Nellies. Jake had Nellie birthday presentats [sic]."[38] Vincent, a suitor, often accompanied her to the lyceum. One time he took her to a benefit lecture held for freedpeople and wounded soldiers. After hearing both William Darrah Kelley, an abolitionist congressman, speak on "The War and the Rights of Humanity," and Elizabeth Taylor Greenfield, the "Black Swan," sing, Emilie and Vincent chatted a while. "He is very affectionate," she wrote afterward.[39]

Although Kelley was white, most of the speakers Davis heard were black, something that marks her experience as different from those of the white women in our set. Davis came out for Frederick Douglass four times during the war: at the above-mentioned Bethel Church; at National Hall, where he spoke on "Affairs of the Nation" in 1863; and twice at Concert Hall, where he delivered his addresses "Our Work Is Not Done" and "Equality Before the Law" in 1863 and 1865, respectively.[40] Davis also attended Frances Ellen Watkins Harper's "The Cause and Effects of War" at Concert Hall and *Christian Recorder* editor Anthony L. Stanford's "The Fire of Malachi" (possibly Moloch?).[41] Several other black orators found their way into Davis's diaries: Institute for Colored Youth alumnus John H. Smith; the Reverend John Sella Martin; Davis's pastor, Jonathan Clarkson Gibbs; and Jacob C. White Sr., a Gilbert Lyceum founder and Sunday school superintendent of the First African Presbyterian Church.[42] Davis's consecutive round of Thursday night lectures held between January and March 1863 probably took her to the Banneker Institute, an African American literary society.[43] The only white lecturers other than Kelley whom she noted were abolitionists—Horace Greeley and Anna Dickinson, whom she did not get the chance to see.[44]

Davis's immersion in the local and national black lyceum community was one with her immersion in the ongoing war. Of the eight lectures Davis attended that can be identified, six were on war-related topics. It is likely that most other lectures she audited also addressed wartime concerns. The contours of Davis's lecture-going suggest resonances for other African Americans. Certainly, Charlotte Forten's antebellum diary brims with the names of white and black abolitionist speakers and as such shows a primary concern with issues that would later ignite the war.[45] During the first two years of wartime, however, she wrote much less often. One 1862 entry about Wendell Phillips might represent what remained unrecorded: "After Mr. P commenced speaking I forgot everything else. It was a grand, glorious speech, such as he alone can make. I wish the poor miserable President whom he so justly criticized c'ld have heard it."[46] After she moved to the South Carolina

Sea Islands to teach the freedpeople there, she carried with her a lyceum-like sensibility that helped her to advance literacy among them.

Both Forten's and Davis's records raise questions about the war's supposed dire effects on the lyceum. Certainly many of the lectures Davis heard were saturated with war. But they inspired her community, drummed up support for black regiments, and forwarded the cause of abolitionism. Yet Bode and others have seen the war lecture as a symptom, and even a cause of, the lyceum's supposed declension, without considering the varieties of war-related lectures—such as abolitionist ones—that fell outside the range from fire-eating to super-patriotic. Surely, lectures about wartime efforts to end slavery or to promote black enlistment that attracted African American audiences only served to advance the lyceum concept. Therefore, with Davis we are obliged to ask, About whom are we speaking when we speak of the lyceum? If we disembody the lyceum of its audiences—namely those that were racially and ethnically diverse—we risk abstracting it or, worse still, consigning it to an assumed citizenry of white voters.

The war-era diaries of Christian A. Fleetwood, a free black man in Civil War Baltimore, further complicate blanket notions of lyceum declension. Between 1860 and August 1863, the Galbreath Lyceum, an African American literary society, became a marked feature in his life that would shape his wartime experience. "Literary societies," Elizabeth McHenry has explained in *Forgotten Readers*, functioned as "vehicles of empowerment" that "became crucial to African Americans' assertions of their right to a place in the democracy." They carved out a "space where their membership might develop the ability and confidence to speak for themselves rather than be spoken for."[47] This was particularly true for Fleetwood.

After being raised as a child by his father's employer, John C. Brune, a white sugar merchant, Fleetwood traveled to Liberia and then studied at the Ashmun Institute in Oxford, Pennsylvania. Upon graduating in 1860, he found a position with G. W. S. Hall and Company, a Baltimore shipping firm trading with Liberia.[48] That year the nineteen-year-old joined the Galbreath Lyceum, founded in 1852 by James H. Hill and James H. Williams, students enrolled in Solomon Anderson's Howard Street school.[49] In 1862, Fleetwood began a pocket diary that faithfully recorded, in terse notation, the lyceum's Monday evening activities: debates, lectures, recitations, addresses, mock trials, and public readings of original essays. Members or locals usually held the platform. On 23 March 1863, for example, Fleetwood wrote, "Rec[ite]d [the] Raven; Speakers J.H.A.J. [Rev. James H. A. Johnson][;] Jno F. B. [John F. Brown][;] Butler [John Henry Butler] & Freeman" debate.[50] One debate, he noted, was "[u]proarious fun."⁵¹ Fleetwood lacked space to record lecture titles or debate questions, but some lecture details emerge. For example, we learn that the Baltimore doctor A. D. Dyer spoke on "Materia Medica."⁵² Another lecturer discussed "Languages."⁵³ At some point members heard "The Habits and Instincts of Insects."⁵⁴ Occasionally a famed outsider drew crowds. After the black abolitionist and educator William J. Watkins spoke, Fleetwood simply wrote that the house was "[p]acked."⁵⁵

In addition to participating in the Galbreath Lyceum, of which he was elected secretary in 1862,⁵⁶ Fleetwood went to the Baltimore Lyceum on Tuesday nights and to other offerings in town. He heard Liberian colonizationist Alexander Crummell deliver his "Progress of Civilization on the Western Coast of Africa" at Bethel Church on Saratoga Street.⁵⁷ Fleetwood pronounced Solomon G. Brown's lecture on "Geology" to be "excellent."⁵⁸ These presentations were imbricated in a larger world of print. Crummell asked Fleetwood to be his book agent in the United States,⁵⁹ and Brown, a naturalist at the Smithsonian, sent books and geological specimens for the lyceum's large library and cabinet.⁶⁰ Fleetwood encouraged women's literary societies,⁶¹ and occasionally he dropped in on sewing circles where men typically read aloud to seamstresses.⁶²

On 30 April 1863 the first number of the Galbreath Lyceum's newspaper, the *Lyceum Observer,* came out. It "sold like Hot Cakes," according to editor Fleetwood.⁶³ Agents in Philadelphia and New York extended its reach. Its nameplate motto, translated from an ancient Italian epigraph meaning to let well enough alone—"I Was Well, but Wishing to Be Better, I Am Here [in a grave]"—underscored the society's propensity for tongue-in-cheek humor.⁶⁴ The paper printed essays read before the lyceum, speeches, original poetry, local news, obituaries, and advertisements. In the *Observer*'s second issue, we see the war's influence in its reprint of J. E. Green's speech delivered on the first anniversary of emancipation in the District of Columbia, and a poem from the *Boston Recorder* titled "The Boy Who Has Gone to the War."⁶⁵ Fleetwood's editorship would be short-lived because on 11 August 1863, after being victimized by antidraft ruffians, he enlisted in the Fourth Regiment, United States Colored Troops, and was immediately appointed sergeant major. In September he bade his family goodbye and shipped off to Fort Monroe in Virginia.⁶⁶ "The close of the year finds me a soldier for the cause of my race," he wrote on 31 December. "May God bless this cause, and enable me in the coming year to forward it."⁶⁷ Even though he left the Galbreath Lyceum behind, he conveyed Baltimore's "meeting of the mind" to camp and battlefield, as we will see. Fleetwood, like other soldiers, kept the lyceum alive in his heart and mind.

We have shown that the lyceum persisted on the home front throughout the Civil War years as a vital forum for civilians "thinking together." It retained some of its prewar characteristics, such as a multivalence that allowed debates, newspaper production, and lectures to coexist as lyceum activities; a sociable sensibility that attracted groups out for an evening's entertainment, couples on dates, and homemakers escaping drudgery; and an openness to diverse lecture content that often encompassed cosmopolitan sensibilities. But the lyceum was changing, too. Audience members noted an emerging star system of speakers, more women and African Americans on stage and in the halls' seats, and equivocation in themselves over the degree to which war considerations had a place on the podium. For African American audience members, wartime content was often welcomed, especially when it related to abolitionism and black recruitment. But what if the podium was in a theater of war?

Transporting the Lyceum to the Battlefield

In July 1861, Amanda McDowell of rural Sparta, Tennessee, watched intently as her nineteen-year-old neighbor, Billy Stone, bid her father farewell before leaving for the front. "He took Father out, and told him that he would never forget the many good lectures he had heard from him [at Preacher's Hall], and that he would endeavor to profit by them." McDowell questioned whether the young farmer would be able to keep his promise under the duress of war. "[I] am afraid he will forget . . . all too soon, perhaps not though. I would not be hard on him, for I know he felt very deeply."[68] Had McDowell realized how much soldiers would cherish lectures throughout the war, she would have had no doubts about Billy. For when soldiers filled their knapsacks before heading out, they took pocket Bibles, blankets, socks, an extra pair of trousers, and perhaps a piece of pie, and at the same time they packed away indelible memories of the lyceum. These memories would nudge them to replicate lyceum culture under the worst of circumstances.

The most common way soldiers reproduced it was to experience it vicariously through civilian loved ones. The knowledge that life went on as usual back home allowed them to dream of peacetime. "Goodman wrote to me he gave you a standing invitation to go to the Lectures this winter," Lieutenant Colonel Marcus Spiegel, encamped near Memphis, Tennessee, wrote his wife, Caroline, in Ohio. "I want you to go . . . at least once a week, so that when I come home I [will] talk war and its incidents and you . . . , Lectures."[69] Letters about lectures made soldiers feel as though they were in the loop of normal affairs. In Pittsburgh, John Harper frequently wrote to his son Albert, a lieutenant in the 139th Pennsylvania, about lectures by Louis Agassiz, Bayard Taylor, and Parson William Gannaway Brownlow. "To night Wendell Phillips, the great Abolitionist, will lecture here, and I have got a ticket," Harper told his son. "He is perhaps the most eloquent man in America."[70] Even if a correspondent did not hear a particular lecturer, she could still fuel an epistolary conversation: "Last evening a young miss just sixteen years old lectured at the first baptist church . . . I would have liked to [have heard her]," Mary Emma Randolph wrote from Plainfield to her fiancé in the Eleventh New Jersey.[71] From a Baltimore hospital, Private Walter Dunn picked up the thread and replied to Randolph: "A few evenings since a Miss Anna Dickinson lectured in the Maryland Institute. Is she the same one that was in Plainfield?"[72] Dickinson was twenty-two when she spoke in Baltimore; the desire to communicate about lecture culture apparently overwrote fact-checking.

Instead of discussing lectures, civilians sometimes sent soldiers their manuscript lectures to read, but more commonly folks at home mailed printed material. A well-wisher from Baltimore sent both the *Lyceum Observer* and a letter to Sergeant Major Fleetwood just after he left home.[73] Fleetwood treasured the clipping as a symbol of the Galbreath Lyceum's sociabilities. Short of establishing his own lyceum in camp, he fashioned a collective literary environment, fostering what Shirley Wilson Logan calls "battlefield literacies" in her book *Liberating Language*.[74] From white officers he borrowed titles such as the *Atlantic Monthly*, *The Count of Monte Cristo*, and *Harper's Monthly*, along with unnamed newspapers.[75] Fleetwood sometimes read materials in comrades' tents. "Sat in Butler[']s all morning[.] read Les M.[iserables]," he wrote in 1864, probably about Private John Butler, a Baltimore friend in Company B.[76] With the former corresponding editor of the *Lyceum Observer*, Quartermaster Sergeant Alfred Ward Handy, he played dominoes and read Henry C. Deming's *Life of Ulysses S. Grant*.[77] On visits to the Reverend William H. Hunter, the U.S. Army's first black chaplain, Fleetwood read letters from Baltimore.[78] When the tables were turned, and one of Fleetwood's letters home was read before the Galbreath Lyceum, he felt "somewhat disgruntled."[79] Army personnel writing home habitually demanded that their correspondence remain private. "I don't like to have my letters read to every one," a chaplain complained to his wife. "It trammels me terribly in writing."[80]

Efforts to reconstitute the lyceum in camp were made by other officers who devised amateur lectures for their regiments or companies. In Tallahassee, Florida, Susan Eppes learned from one Confederate sergeant that officers gave lectures almost daily to members of the Georgia Twelfth Artillery Battalion. "These lectures are an education in themselves," she explained. "The boys are encouraged to ask questions and to debate on different points." The benefits were long-term. "Mr. Kellar, who is a mountain boy [from Rome, Georgia], says the Colonel [Henry D. Capers] taught him to read and write and now he is determined to get an education, when the war is over."[81] Chaplains, too, educated their men through talks. One Wisconsin minister "lectured on the use of tobacco and spiritous liquors," and another, from Minnesota, on the less didactic topic of "Geology."[82]

Sometimes lectures and debates were conducted through more organized literary associations, but many never got off the ground. Sergeant Major Fleetwood tried to establish one and encouraged Company H to form a debate club, but that, too, fizzled. Likewise, he once tried declaiming with a private.[83] The backing of a sympathetic commissioned officer went a long way in getting societies off the ground. "The major conceived [of] the brilliant idea of . . . felling the forest trees, sawing them into boards and timber, and building a large hall for . . . amusements," Captain Josiah Marshall Favill of the Fifty-Seventh New York wrote from winter quarters in Stevensburg, Virginia. "This palace of Mars," as he called it, "became the center of the social hospitality of the Second corps and lectures, concerts, dinners, and dances followed."[84] It was not exactly the lyceum, but it was the next best thing.

A more serious, elaborate, and well-sustained soldiers' lyceum was set up in Vicksburg, Mississippi, a few months after it fell in July 1863 to Union forces. A group called the Union Literary Society of Vicksburg, a joint effort among men mainly from the Sixth Division, Seventeenth Corps, Army of the Tennessee, was endorsed by the United States Christian Commission, an organization that supplied Union troops with supplies and religious literature. Tuesday evening meetings were held in the basement of the First Presbyterian Church, near the commission's reading room.[85] By December it had twenty members, but it invited outsiders to its "Soldiers Sociables," some of which lasted until 3:00 a.m.[86] The first was a rousing success, populated by officers, privates, and local women, who packed the church. After prayer, the Brass Band of the First Brigade, Third Division, Seventeenth Corps, struck up a tune, which was followed by lectures, essays, and readings from the society's magazine. The secretary, Thomas Christie of the Sixth Division's First Battery, Minnesota Light Artillery, boasted, "I have never seen a Harper['s Magazine] so interesting, and then it was all original matter. Poetry, Editorials, Stories . . . nobody expected to find such a high order of literary talent among the common soldiers," he continued, "it being generally thought that we are a rough set [but] . . . if they could hear the animated and profound discussions of abstruse subjects in our debates, they would alter their opinion."[87] In less than a year, the society had assembled more than two thousand volumes—a library larger than most at the time. Eventually, they called their meeting place "Lyceum Hall" and held public lectures there.[88]

Debate became a regular feature in the hall. One topic discussed was timely—"That it is policy for the government of the United States hereafter to keep a standing army of 100,000 men rather than to depend upon volunteers for national defense."[89] Another question was affirmed as "Love of country wields more influence over the masses than does Love of money."[90] Other, less well-delineated topics were pitched to auditors and judges to stimulate group participation. "There were several subjects given out and those that got one had to speak on that subject right off, without any Preparation what ever," William Christie, Thomas's brother, wrote. "I had 'War' for my theme, and Stephen Rollins had, our Lyceum for his subject."[91]

Establishing lyceums helped soldiers to pass hours of downtime in a profitable manner. But in frightfully unsanitary, disease-infested, and poorly provisioned prisoner-of-war camps, lyceum activity simply kept captives sane. Union officers at the infamous Libby Prison in Richmond maintained an astoundingly good sense of humor through the Libby Lyceum Association—pronounced, as they insisted, with reference to the insects afflicting them, "the Libby Lyce-I-see-'em."[92] Organized by a chaplain captured at Gettysburg,[93] the Lyce-I-see-'em offered lecture courses, debate sessions, and a handwritten newspaper called the *Libby Chronicle*, which was issued weekly, according to the editor, "from Prisoner & Co.'s steam press of thought" and delivered "postage free."[94] Copy that was written by "an extensive corps of able correspondents, local reporters, poets, punsters, and witty paragraphers" was collected and assembled once a week by the editor and read aloud in the prison's upper east room.[95]

The *Chronicle*, whose banner motto was "Devoted to Facts and Fun," posted upcoming debates and lectures. Some debates distracted the inmates from woe with their silliness: "Subject for discussion next week," the paper announced on 28 August 1863: "'Resolved, that men ought not to shave their faces.'"[96] More serious lectures resembled standard fare from home. "All will desire a good hearing of . . . 'Life and Manners in Cuba' by Lieut. Colonel Cavada, whose description of his native land from experience and observation will doubtless afford much solid information."[97] Another, less profound lyceum lecture course capitalized on a popular trend: "Major Henry's series of lectures on 'Mesmerism,' to be followed by experiments, will . . . form an era in Libby, especially if the Major can succeed in so mesmerizing any considerable number of us as to make us believe that we are amply fed and clothed and delivered from the 'pesky varmints' which are the *'bête noir'* of our existence here."[98] The course was apparently popular, and it was sardonically called by the editor one of the "three great lights . . . [in the] Augustan Age of Libby Prison."[99] In addition to these, the editor offered on "urgent demand" a course on phonography, a form of shorthand useful to prisoners encoding messages.[100] The transportable lyceum thus became a potential form of resistance.

Confederate prisoners in Union camps also fashioned handwritten newspapers out of practically nothing, but these tended to be more sober and genuinely instructive. The *Right Flanker*, a Confederate paper from Fort Lafayette in New York Harbor, was published "to relieve the monotony of prison life, by calling into action the taste and faculties of those who are capable of contributing to its columns [and] instructing and amusing those who cannot."[101] The *Rapidann*, a handwritten paper with a beautifully illustrated banner, published poetry such as "The Palmetto Tree" and editorials criticizing Robert E. Lee's policy on furloughs.[102] Created at Fort Delaware in 1865, the *Prison Times* featured a political and a miscellaneous column as well as ads for services that prisoners performed for barter, cash, or just to keep occupied. "Lt. W. S. White 33d N.C. is prepared to execute all kinds of engraving on metals with neatness and dispatch," one ad read. The *Prison Times*' carefully drawn banner with clock and book, and its neat penmanship, suggest that papers like it and the *Rapidann* were meant to be circulated from one small lyceum group that coalesced to admire the handiwork to another.[103] Discussion of intricate visuals no doubt anchored prisoners' wandering states of mind.

Newspapers were also published by army hospitals, especially Union-operated ones with long-term convalescents such as Armory Square in Washington, D.C. Its *Hospital Gazette*, a well-funded venture printed by patients and read to them by nurses,[104] reported on local events, including lectures such as Anna Dickinson's January 1864 speech at the Capitol.[105]

The relationship between hospitals and the popular lecture was an intimate one. Not only did lecturers come into the wards to speak, but soldiers well enough to get out and about and, in particular, nurses audited lectures in town. In this way, hospitals in or near cities existed in a kind of ever-shifting netherworld—a place between life and death, army and home front, the weakened morale and the resilient lyceum spirit.

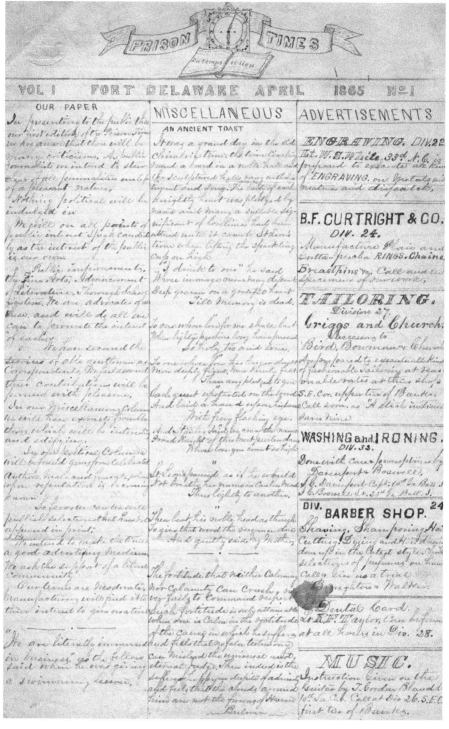

Figure 1.1 Prison Times, newspaper published by John W. Hibbs, April 1865. Image #ah00001, New-York Historical Society. Photography © New-York Historical Society.

Union army nurse Amanda Aikin Stearns provides a case in point. From December 1863 to February 1864, Stearns, with other staff from Armory Square hospital, got out to hear five lecturers, including celebrity John B. Gough on "Temperance"; historian John Lord, who spoke at the Smithsonian on "Civilization"; and Louis Agassiz, who lectured there on "Glaciers."[106] After hearing Anna Dickinson deliver "Words for the Hour" at the House of Representatives, Stearns recorded the following in her diary: "Her graphic pictures could not fail to bring unbidden tears to the eyes of many of her attentive listeners, and her final appeal to the patriotism of the young men was supremely eloquent." Stearns returned to the hospital "proud that such talent should have been given to a woman."[107] Although "completely tired out" one evening, Stearns would not miss George William Curtis's "Way of Peace." It "gave me a better knowledge of myself," she wrote.[108] Good conversation and liqueurs upon returning from lectures extended the life of these excursions away from pain and misery.[109] Often, however, escape eluded her. After one of her patients died, Stearns spent the evening writing to the man's family instead of relaxing with a lecture.[110] On another occasion a cancellation at the Smithsonian left Stearns and company disappointed. But because the lyceum's boundaries were mutable, they improvised at home that snowy evening by reading aloud to one another and entertaining their unexpected guest, Louis Agassiz.[111]

Lecturers transgressed conventional boundaries of lyceum spaces when they made the hospital ward their lecture hall. John Lord spoke several times in Armory Square's wards, and Curtis repeated the lecture Stearns heard in the hospital's chapel.[112] Clergymen and former prisoners of war, like Abel Delos Streight, gave lectures there, too.[113]

On 1 December 1864 Frederick Douglass made a visit to Alexandria's Soldiers' Rest, a hospice situated by the railroad for travelers and invalids.[114] Later that day he spoke briefly in a nearby hospital. The soldiers who assembled in the dining room listened with rapt attention and then sang "John Brown's Body" "with a will," according to onlooker Julia Wilbur, a white abolitionist relief worker.[115] That night Douglass spoke to a crowd at Alexandria's Liberty Hall, an exhibition space between Cameron and Royal Streets. Wilbur was there, too. She contemplated the moment and the past three years that had turned the city and, indeed, the entire nation, inside out. "To stand on the 'sacred soil' of Va. & talk against Slavery! It is truly wonderful. & 3 yrs. ago we would have hardly have thought it possible. I am glad he has been here. It has done him good & the people too."[116] So emblematic was the wartime public lecture that progress could be measured by its gauge.

Conclusion

As we have seen, rather than starving the population with insubstantial fare or, conversely, force-feeding it with shrill propaganda, popular lectures continued to nourish the divided country during the four agonizing years of civil war. In the North and West, popular lectures persisted, and many public halls remained crowded, especially when rising stars spoke in them. White women as audience members claimed an intellectual space there outside of home and family, and black women like Emilie Davis could find in the lecture hall a source of empowerment. Smaller, amateur lyceums also thrived, especially in rural areas where women were given a greater role to play. African American literary societies, like the Galbreath Lyceum, took on even deeper resonances as emancipation became a Union war aim in 1863, for they offered models for future educational uplift among freedpeople.

Between 1861 and 1865 countless lecture halls, particularly in the South, were converted into institutions that fed the war machine instead of the mind. The Alexandria Lyceum in Virginia, for example, had thrived for twenty years as a forum for learning before being refashioned as a Union hospital in the spring of 1861. Richmond's meeting places of the mind also became militarized. "The ladies are now engaged making sand-bags for the fortifications at Yorktown," Judith White Brockenbrough McGuire wrote in her diary in April 1862 during the siege. "[E]very lecture-room in town crowded with them, sewing busily, hopefully, prayerfully."[117] Yet everywhere, auditor and speaker alike kept lecturing alive by transforming the lyceum into a portable concept—a meeting place of the mind—that could be reconstituted at will with paper and pen, inside a parlor at home or under an army tent near the front. Civilians and soldiers held tenaciously to the lyceum concept in large part because they trusted that with the war's end, public lecture culture, as it had been, would simply resume. They assumed that the lyceum would pick up where it had left off, as if the war were just a nightmarish interlude. Of course, the public lecture, like the many people who survived the brutal conflict, would never again be quite the same.

Yet the Civil War hardly marked the death of an era. If we treasure the increased resonances of women's and African Americans' voices on the platform during those years, and cherish the ingenuity and sheer willpower expended by civilians and soldiers who believed that popular education could thrive under conditions of unbearable hardship, we might even say that the lyceum was more alive and well than ever before.

2

WOMEN'S ENTREPRENEURIAL LECTURING IN THE EARLY NATIONAL PERIOD

Granville Ganter

Although most accounts of commercial lecturing in the United States begin with the mid-1820s and the movement for adult education and entertainment known as the lyceum, the broad scope of early national lecturing is relatively unknown. Popular, entrepreneurial lecturing, typically linked to scientific demonstration, had been a growing practice in Europe since the early 1700s. In the American colonies, commercial lecturing began along the Atlantic seaboard in the 1740s, most notably with the electrical demonstrations of Ebenezer Kinnersley in the decades prior to the American Revolution.[1] By the late 1780s, lecturing recommenced with surprising force and variety, functioning as an important engine of knowledge production and circulation, as well as national and local socialization. The principal appeal was educational, but considerable entertainment spectacle was attached to entrepreneurial lecturing as well. In the new United States, audiences flocked to see electrical, chemical, and mechanical demonstrations in hotel ballrooms, private academies, taverns, and coffeehouses, as well as discussions of astronomy, history, agriculture, medicine, geography, and mnemonics assisted by apparatuses like astronomical orreries, microscopes, colorful charts, and large paintings. Americans also enjoyed listening to literary theory supplemented by examples taken from the theater and the history of Western oratory accompanied by stage histrionics.[2]

Women were important parts of this culture in at least two ways. First, they formed a significant portion of the audience, subsidizing lecturers with ticket sales as single women, spouses, or family chaperones. This participation was not merely passive consumption; as Ronald J. Zboray and Mary Saracino Zboray have shown, lecture attendance was part of a broad field of socialization, including courtship practices, entertainment, spirituality, and education.[3] Lecture culture was shared, exchanged, and lived, not just passively heard. Second, women also contributed to early national lecture culture as speakers themselves. Over the past two decades, scholars such as Lindal Buchanan, Mary Kelley, and Carolyn Eastman have drawn attention to the widespread practices of young women's declamation in schools, their exhibitions often advertised or published in newspapers, stewarded by schoolmistresses who were themselves well educated in public speaking. One explanation for such practices, according to Linda Kerber, was that oratorical training enabled women to become better republican mothers and teachers, to educate the nation's next generation of male leadership. The consequences of women's oratorical education could challenge the domestic norms that were simultaneously developing around middle-class women. In Eastman's view, however, women's education in belles lettres and oratory was also promoted as the sign of a universally enlightened age, when women's achievements would complement rather than rival men's professional status and political leadership.[4]

Extending the work of these scholars, this chapter demonstrates how women—particularly ambitious white women—used the educational warrant for public speaking to their advantage, a permission that also came with economic justifications. During the early national period, many lecturers were able to support themselves for short intervals, either giving lectures close to home or touring along the seaboard or waterways. Perhaps the best known is former Revolutionary War soldier Deborah Sampson Gannett, who toured the Northeast in 1802–3 giving a narrative account of her unusual life and then performing military drills on stage. Although Gannett's life has been the subject of several excellent studies, scholars have had difficulty identifying her as anything other than an aberration from social norms because so little has been documented about other entrepreneurial lecturers of the time.[5] In fact, other women in this period also took to the platform. Many were teachers augmenting their small school incomes; they often used the celebrity generated by their lectures to draw matriculating students to their private schools. While conducting a survey of more than twenty-five thousand digitized advertisements for "lectures" in American newspaper advertisements from 1740 to 1825, I have discovered that many prominent lecturers, particularly women, had some sort of affiliation with a school and frequently used lecturing to boost enrollments or their own social capital as educators.[6] Although it is sometimes argued that American lecture culture constituted a popular *alternative* to traditional education, it is perhaps more fruitful to think of the early American popular lecture as an epiphenomenon of the period's traditional educational practices—an *addition* to them rather than wholly distinct from them.[7] In the period from 1784 to 1828, entrepreneurial lecturing was less a means to financial independence (although it was for some lecturers) than a mode of advertising to build lecturers' social stature or to support their other economic ventures. Women's lecturing harmonized republican ideals for nationalist education with women's business practices in the civic and social domains.

To exemplify these dynamics, this chapter examines the careers of several women commercial lecturers of the post-revolutionary period who have previously not figured into accounts of American education, early national oratory, or feminist history. One of the most important is Eliza Harriot O'Connor (born Elizabeth Harriot Barons, 1749–1811), a schoolteacher who had the honor of lecturing to George Washington at the University of Pennsylvania in 1787, and who periodically gave public lectures for the next several years in Pennsylvania, Maryland, Virginia, and South Carolina, typically in cities where she planned to open a school. Another is Anne Laura Clarke (1787–1861), a Massachusetts schoolteacher, musician, and visual artist who toured the nation for a decade in the 1820s and 1830s, giving nationally acclaimed history lectures illustrated by magic lantern images and her own handcrafted chronological charts and geographic paintings. Clarke's use of the magic lantern, an early form of slide projector, and her astonishing infographic charts illustrate her fusion of the more spectacular features of the early national lecture with a deep knowledge of world history. In addition to discussing these prominent lecturers, this chapter considers the role of women as audience members. Although one might be tempted to consider early lecture-going audiences as passive consumers of theatrical and pseudo-scientific spectacle, lecturing also offered a genuine forum for women's education and social interaction. The lecture hall was a venue where respectable women—not jugglers, clairvoyants, or other kinds of traveling early national entertainers—could valorize themselves as both speakers and auditors of the public life of the mind.

Eliza Harriot O'Connor, Science, and Education

Immediately after the Revolution, commercial scientific lecturing, which had seen a vogue before the war, resumed in America with the sensational two-year speaking tour of Henry Moyes, a blind English scientist who spoke on "natural philosophy" (what we now call science). Landing in the United States in May 1784, Moyes spoke to audiences of up to a thousand people in many East Coast cities, in some cases raising large amounts of money for charitable humanitarian projects such as assisting the poor. Moyes's success inspired imitation. Counting more than two hundred people in Moyes's audience in Baltimore in 1785, young Noah Webster quickly realized the value of lecturing as an advertising tool. He transformed his own lobbying trip to secure state copyrights for his schoolbooks into a book promotion tour that lasted two years and took him to nearly fifty towns and cities along the Atlantic coast.[8]

Less than three months after Webster's promotional appearance in Philadelphia in 1787, an unusual advertisement appeared in the 2 April issue of Philadelphia's *Independent Gazetteer*:

<blockquote>
A LADY

proposes to read

A Course of LECTURES,

ON

Language, Eloquence, Poetry, Taste and Criticism,

BY SUBSCRIPTION.

IN the first lecture she designs to explain the origin, progress, perfection and beauties of the English language, illustrating every observation by selections from the most celebrated writers, ancient and modern, on this subject.

If it is universally agreed, that, example should unite with precept, in order to form a judicious and correct reader, she humbly hopes, that the liberal patrons of polite science, in the city of Philadelphia, will cherish a proposal subservient, in some degree, to the acquisition of an accomplishment, ornamental and interesting to the opulent classes of every community.[9]
</blockquote>

The price for attendance was one dollar per ticket for five lectures, typical for lectures of the period. The advertisement sought a subscription of fifty tickets to be sold before the date of the lectures was set. The following week, on 9 April, enough tickets had been sold for the lectures to take place, and repeat performances were advertised by 24 April. On 2 May, the Lady advertised a second course of lectures, charging one dollar for three lectures, which included readings of illustrative excerpts from William Shakespeare,

James Thomson, Alexander Pope, Edward Young, William Shenstone, and Sir William Jones. Later in the month, on 29 May, a reviewer for the *Gazetteer* noted that George Washington had been in the audience for the lecture on 18 May. His presence, the reviewer wrote, enhanced the Lady's "anxiety to express more copiously, emphatically, and distinctly, the sublimer parts of composition, which occurred in the course of the Lecture. This observation was evinced most clearly, by her pathetic recitation of the prayer, of Demosthenes, to the Immortal Gods, . . . *a prayer*, if reports are true, suitable enough at this period, to *every honest* orator in the State of Rhode Island." The Lady might have been surprised to find out that her lecture would be used as topical criticism of the antifederal Rhode Island delegates who had refused to attend the Constitutional Convention during the previous week, but no doubt she was pleased to see herself quoted as a friend of the United States.

Although no other excerpts from the Lady's speeches survive, the selection offered in the *Gazetteer* conveys a sense of the dramatic style of her presentation—calculated to move the passions and moderated by a tone of supplication and prayer. Read in the context of the other authors whom she advertised—such as Edward Young, whose lyric description of the stars in "Night Thoughts" was a commonly recognized example of the sublime in literature—the Lady seems to have chosen her reading selections for their emotional and romantic effect. In later lectures, she often highlighted excerpts from Sir William Jones, a popularizer of Persian and Arabian poetry, who forcefully argued that the "Asiatick languages" were second to none in their literary expressions of the higher passions.[10]

The Lady, whose name as a lecturer was never mentioned in her advertisements, was Eliza Harriot O'Connor, a thirty-eight-year-old woman with a worldly, upper-middle-class background, who likely would have had some exposure to transatlantic lecture culture. Raised between Portugal, London, and the British colonies, Eliza was a child of ocean trade, born into a family of successful importers of Madeira and fruit, living in the community known as the British Factory in Lisbon, where she was baptized in 1749 as Elizabeth Harriot Barons. Eliza's mother, Mary Margaret Hardy, was the sister of Sir Charles Hardy the Younger, a distinguished admiral of the Royal Navy. Eliza's father, Benjamin Barons, worked in a number of capacities, first as an importer of fruit between Portugal and London, then as Sir Hardy's secretary during his term as governor of New York (1755–57). Between 1759 and 1761, Barons was twice appointed collector of customs in Boston, but he was eventually removed for supporting Boston merchants over the interests of the Crown. Later, in 1764–66, he served as postmaster of the colonies south of

Virginia. Barons died in England in 1783, leaving a small annuity to his only child, Eliza, who had married John O'Connor in 1776. It is possible that the couple's inheritance enabled them to come to the United States, where Eliza had likely spent much of her childhood.[11]

When the O'Connors arrived in Philadelphia they immediately embarked on a formidable publicity campaign. Both husband and wife were of a literary turn of mind: John had just translated an edition of Pierre Nougaret's *Anecdotes of the Reign of Lewis* [sic] *the XVIth* in New York, and Eliza, who was fluent in French, had apparently worked as a teacher or governess there.[12] Just after Eliza's first lecture series, the couple began circulating a long advertisement speculating that her lectures "might be advantageously rendered the foundation of a permanent school for the Belles Lettres." The plan was ambitious: they would start a literary society for educating approximately twenty-six young men and women in French, and they would seek one hundred additional subscribers, each paying eight dollars a year, who would be able to attend public lectures given at the society's meeting hall every two weeks. At the same time, John sought to create his own language school: on 16 June he advertised an introductory public lecture on Latin classics, which would inaugurate a school that he hoped would enroll fifty students each paying six dollars per quarter.[13]

Although the O'Connors' literary endeavors seemed to promote humanities education, the couple explicitly advertised their work as part of Enlightenment science—the ongoing intellectual and creative work of demystifying the individual's relationship to the world. Writing to Sarah Franklin Bache, Benjamin Franklin's daughter, Eliza asked for patronage of her proposed school, arguing that she sought "to smooth the way to science." Indeed, the principal appeal for polite lecturing in this period was the diffusion of new and useful knowledge. At the same time, an important class and nationalist component to Eliza's letter to Bache also deserves note: because so many showmen and actors offered lectures, Eliza was attempting to make clear that she was no common puffer or entertainer. She positioned herself as one of the new nation's elite, engaged in a serious educational project with civic purpose.[14]

By July neither of the O'Connors' school plans had attracted enough interest to be viable, but Eliza began advertising another lecture series, this time on "The Human Mind," and she continued to promote her French Academy in the newspapers. While Eliza lectured, John sought subscriptions for two proposed books: the first a collection of his wife's Philadelphia lectures (never published) and the second a four-volume "geographical and topographical history of America." His expansive history advertised chapters on both South and North America, but it focused on the emergence of the United States, promising lengthy biographical entries of the nation's founders. This book, too, was never published, much to the dismay of the subscribers who complained when it did not come out.[15] By December the couple's school projects had received inadequate support, and they went south to Annapolis and Baltimore. There Eliza again gave lectures on eloquence, highlighting readings of Sir William Jones's exotic poem "Solima," a lush ode to the hospitality and benevolence of a fictional Arabian princess.[16]

In early 1788, the couple moved to Alexandria, Virginia, seeking George Washington's patronage for a girls' academy that Eliza ran briefly in the spring and summer. Washington was apparently not impressed by Eliza's lecture from the year before. Sensing a financial motive behind the performance, he wrote in his diary that he considered it "a charity affair" for a "lady in reduced circumstances," mistakenly identifying her as "Mrs. O'Connell." But upon the recommendation of his associate George Lux, who wrote to him that the wealthy and prominent Biddle family of Philadelphia vouched for the O'Connors' respectability, Washington invited John O'Connor to dinner at Mount Vernon in February 1788. Presumably Washington meant to learn more about John's proposed history of the Americas as well as the plans for Eliza's academy for girls in nearby Alexandria. When Eliza wrote to Washington in June, asking him to be a trustee of her school, he politely declined; but several months later he nonetheless invited her to stay overnight at Mount Vernon to discuss her school's prospects.[17] During this period, John kept his public profile high by getting literary notices published in the papers and giving a Fourth of July oration in Norfolk, Virginia.[18]

The O'Connors again used lecturing as a means of advertisement when they appeared in Charleston, South Carolina, in November 1790, promoting the Charleston Academy, later renamed the French and English Academy. Eliza gave more lectures on eloquence, explicitly advertising herself as "the LADY who proposes to open an academy for the younger part of her sex." Eliza's French and English Academy lasted a year and a half, and her students represented themselves well in two public examinations.[19] John, who seems to have been a boastful ne'er-do-well, worked at the school teaching grammar and literature and giving patriotic speeches about the girls' republican achievements. In 1791, he claimed to have published a geographic primer for student use, for which he hoped public subscribers would reimburse him, based on the plan of the late "Col. Ryan of Philadelphia." This text does not seem to have made it to print. He also tried to start a local lyceum, but he was obliged to retract his proposal and publicly apologize to a fellow Charleston schoolmaster, William Nixon, whose own plans to start a lyceum he had apparently threatened.[20] John's financial entanglements soon forced the O'Connors to auction off their property in nearby Dorchester. Their Charleston school closed by the summer of 1792, with John briefly visiting Ireland to engage in "selling American lands" and likely fleeing his creditors. Upon his return, the couple then moved to Columbia, South Carolina, where Eliza ran a school from 1793 to 1799, again employing her husband as a teacher. Eliza died in Columbia in 1811 with personal property amounting to about $290 worth of books and clothing. Her will, executed by a local friend, does not mention the existence of her husband.[21]

Speaking, Listening, and Maria Miller Stewart

Despite the hard times that seem to have fallen on Eliza O'Connor toward the end of her life, she and her husband illustrate the deliberate—and successful—use of the educational public lecture as part of a publicity program for professional advancement. Eliza was among the first in a long line of entrepreneurial lecturer-schoolteachers in the early national period who used commercial public speaking (i.e., charging admission for lectures) to recruit students to their schools or otherwise build their allied business endeavors through raising their social prestige. Using the same methods that O'Connor employed, dozens of such entrepreneurial lecturers advertised their appearances in early national newspapers. Representative examples include Thomas Adderley, a literary man who used a long lecture series to start a school in New York City in 1800; John Lathrop Jr., a Boston science lecturer and schoolteacher in the 1810s; Alexander Ramsey, an anatomist in Fryeburg, Maine, who recruited students to his school between 1806 and 1821; Nathaniel G. Senter, a schoolteacher in Hallowell, Maine, from 1814 into the 1820s; William Darby, a geography lecturer and schoolteacher from Philadelphia in the late 1810s and early 1820s; and David B. Slack, who opened his school in June 1822 in New Bedford, Massachusetts, but who first offered a series of public lectures on natural philosophy to advertise his educational expertise.[22]

Probably the most notable example of the relationship of public lecturing to school funding is Joseph Lancaster, who arrived in the United States from England in 1818 and lectured relentlessly through the 1820s to raise support for a school where he could draw the headmaster's salary. Lancaster was famous for the promise of his monitorial school system, where older students acted as teacher's assistants or monitors. Lancaster boasted that this method of schoolroom administration could enable one faculty member to teach a class of one thousand students. Lancaster's fusion of civic-minded oratory with commercial enterprise is typical of lecturing schoolteachers of this era and is well illustrated in Lancaster's industrial vision for educational progress.[23]

The reciprocal relationship between these practices of entrepreneurial lecturing and education had important consequences for women, both as students and as educators. As Michael Faraday, the noted theorist of electricity, would attest, it was his boyhood reading of Jane Marcet's 1806 *Conversations on Chemistry* that inspired him to become a scientist. Her book was itself a product of her attendance at Humphry Davy's lectures at London's Royal Institution from 1801 to 1803. As early as 1810, New York scientist and teacher John Griscom, who had just read Marcet's book, advertised his popular chemistry lectures with the announcement that his lecture rooms had "proper accommodations" for women.[24] By 1817 his annual lectures in New York included a series exclusively for young women, and his contributions to women's education in science would be favorably recorded in several stanzas of Fitz-Greene Halleck's 1819 poem "Fanny":

> [Fanny] was among the first and warmest patrons
> Of Griscom's *conversaziónes*, where
> In rainbow groups, our bright-eyed maids and matrons,
> On science bent, assemble; to prepare
> Themselves for acting well, in life, their part
> As wives and mothers. There she learn'd by heart
> Words, to the witches in Macbeth unknown.
> *Hydraulics, hydrostatics,* and *pneumatics*
> *Dioptrics, optics, katoptrics, carbon,*
> *Chlorine,* and *iodine,* and *aërostatics;*
> Also,—why frogs, for want of air, expire;
> And how to set the Tappan sea on fire![25]

Although Halleck assures readers that the young women are learning how to play a better part "as wives and mothers," it is hard to square those roles exactly with acquiring the technology to set the Hudson River's Tappan Zee on fire (setting water on fire was a common electrical trick accompanying lectures of the day) and developing a vocabulary that would challenge most twenty-first-century high school students. Indeed, Halleck's tribute underscores how far ideals of women's useful education had come in urban areas, even from the heady days of the 1790s when women's arithmetic and rhetoric were being championed as a radical improvement over the ornamental education of training in music, the visual arts, and dance. For example, in the early 1800s Susanna Rowson effectively promoted her girls' academy by publishing her students' speeches—implicitly demonstrating that young women could benefit from a rhetorical education as well as young men could.[26] Within a handful of years, women in New York, New Jersey, and Maryland had become chemistry students, largely sponsored by popular lecture culture.

Griscom was hardly the only science lecturer known for women's education in the 1810s. Baltimore science teacher and lecturer John D. Craig, active as a popular lecturer from 1802 to 1822, also advertised courses in experimental philosophy for women. The period's numerous botany lecturers, historically allied with medical knowledge, promoted botany as an appropriate domain of women's expertise. Most entrepreneurial American lecturers, even right after the American Revolution, sought mixed audiences of adult men and women no matter what their topic was, frequently offering discounts to pairs of men and women and families. As the Zborays have demonstrated, family-style ticketing, a system by which a man's ticket often gave women admission for free, was an important economic means by which women entered and sustained the American lecture system.[27]

The Zborays' recent scholarship on women's reception of popular lecturing is a crucial avenue for grasping the ways America's disenfranchised groups were influenced by early lecture culture. Although the Zborays examine the heyday of the antebellum lyceum, roughly 1830 to 1861, their work is suggestive for earlier periods as well. Their painstaking recovery of the journals, letters, diaries, and other papers of hundreds of New England women, mostly of the white lower-middle class but also including African American women and working-class white women, provides an index of women's internalization of the popular lecture as a social and educational event in their lives, in many cases leading their intellectual curiosity far afield of the traditional "bonds of womanhood." Although firsthand accounts of women's reactions to early national lecturing are rare, some do exist. In 1826, for instance, Elizabeth Palmer Peabody was impressed to hear that her friend Maria Chase went to a lecture every night when she was visiting in Philadelphia. Chase engaged topics as diverse as Milton, phrenology, lightning, King Solomon, Newton, Franklin, Isaiah, and belles lettres.[28]

Arguing that lecturing promoted many illustrations of "Women Thinking"—a gendered correlate of Ralph Waldo Emerson's "Man Thinking" of his 1837 "American Scholar" oration—the Zborays offer a provocative suggestion of the way lecture culture in Boston may have inspired women orators. One such orator was Maria Miller Stewart, a pioneer public speaker in American history. As Dorothy Porter and Elizabeth McHenry have argued, early African American literary culture was sponsored by social and religious groups whose meetings and sermons constituted an advanced educational arena for many participants. A number of African American self-help societies employed lecturers to address their members, and they also promoted public speaking among themselves. Boston's African Society, for example, booked lectures that were faithfully advertised by the mainstream Boston newspaper, the *Columbian Centinel*, from the 1790s through the 1820s.[29]

Raised by a Hartford minster, Miller received her early education through Sabbath schools. When she moved to Boston, she was married in the African Meeting House, a church where both she and her husband, John W. Stewart, were active. As best as scholars have been able to determine, her principal literary training was through these venues before she met the activist African American pamphleteer David Walker. Although Stewart's groundbreaking polemics about racial equality in the early 1830s were political, religious, and exhortatory rather than commercial and academic, her conduct shows how deeply she had internalized a culture of educational public speaking for women. Stewart was once critically hailed as the first adult American woman lecturer—black or white—to address mixed audiences of men and women, but she was part of a larger tradition of women educational lecturers who preceded her. It is little surprise that when Stewart left Boston for New York, she became an educator, moving from lecturer to teacher.[30]

Anne Laura Clarke, Teacher

Even before Stewart, women's engagement with educational lecture culture found expression as they became teachers and lecturing practitioners. For example, probably trying to augment her income and generate publicity for her school, a Providence, Rhode Island, schoolteacher named Miss Wheaton gave a thirty-five-lecture series on geography in 1821 with no controversy about the lecturer's sex or subject matter mentioned in the newspapers afterward.[31]

One of the most interesting figures in early national women's educational culture was Anne Laura Clarke, whose fame as a public speaker in the 1820s was eclipsed by the public furor over Frances Wright and the sisters Sarah and Angelina Grimké in the years after Clarke retired. Thirty-five years old in 1822 and desperate to build her private school in the competitive educational market of urban Philadelphia (like Eliza O'Connor before her), Clarke began offering public grammar lectures, then lectures on biblical history. She attempted to run a school using her lectures as advertisements, following the practices of her friend and adviser, the geographer William Darby. In 1825, after giving several successful courses of lectures in Philadelphia, Clarke decided to try to make her living exclusively as an itinerant history lecturer, buying a commercial slide projector and producing several charts and maps to illustrate her speeches on the history and styles of clothing throughout the world. A short fragment of her lecture on the toga still exists, as well as some thirty thousand words of her American history lectures. In addition to lecturing from the historical and anthropological slide collections that were sold commercially by Edward Carpenter, Clarke copyrighted a unique set of large historical charts that traced the cultural and political timelines of different societies side by side. Very well reviewed in the newspapers, she spoke over the next decade along the East Coast and as far west as Buffalo (and possibly in Ohio), staying a month in most cities and taking a short break only in 1832 before returning to her touring schedule. She was one of a handful of lecturers, male or female, who did not immediately fall back on teaching for an income after her lecture tours were over; instead, she invested her profits in real estate and Massachusetts bank stock. But she did open the Genesee Women's Seminary when she moved to the Buffalo area in the late 1830s to help rear her brother's children.[32]

The scope and intensity of Clarke's touring constituted a groundbreaking achievement for women public speakers, but her innovative techniques drew on a culture of science education that had been developing in the new nation for decades. Writing to her friend Amos Eaton—a botanist, lecturer, and cofounder of the Rensselaer School—Clarke in 1833 described her work as part of the "important cause of education," in which "science and literature are fast expanding themselves into every part of our land." Clarke had met Eaton in 1826 when she gave two courses of lectures in Troy and neighboring Albany. When the two discussed her prospects, he assured her that her educational endeavors would probably be more popular than any man's. The importance of their relationship is not in its novelty; rather, it is in the decades of science lecturing that preceded them—decades of "women

Figure 2.1 These copper plate sliders are part of a set purchased by Anne Laura Clarke to use as visual aids in her public lectures on world costumes. Courtesy of Historic Northampton, Northampton, Massachusetts.

thinking" alongside men—an epoch in American history that existed in contrast to the gendered prejudices of later periods.[33]

While speaking in Troy, Clarke also met Emma Willard, author of an 1822 student geography text and founder of the Troy Female Seminary. Willard came with her students to Clarke's introductory lecture, which was customarily given for free to entice paying clientele. Clarke and Willard were born only a year apart, and both had been educated in or near Hartford, Connecticut, internalizing their era's sense of the interrelation of geography, history, science, and literature. Formidable educators, both used schematic charts as mnemonic devices for teaching history. Yet the pedagogical practice of "mapping" had long been in the air. As Daniel Rosenberg and Anthony Grafton show, evidence of the creation and use of such infographics—even chronological charts of time—had appeared in American classrooms by the 1810s.[34]

As much common ground as Willard and Clarke shared, however, they did not get along personally, and Willard did not attend Clarke's later lectures. Clarke wrote home to her sister claiming that Willard was "vain," treating other women with neglect. In a later letter, written just before Thanksgiving of 1826, Clarke confessed that she was aware of the social prejudices she faced as a woman lecturer, and noted that she had no help from Willard: "Willard has gained nothing by her behavior toward me and is most deservedly censured by the community generally. There is a most violent prejudice existing against her in Albany and in Waterford, and her book is not used in the Academy *here* [Alonzo Crittenden's Albany Female Seminary]. I have been much *disappointed in Mrs. Willard*." Although Clarke confessed to great "distress" when it seemed that her lectures would be poorly attended, her friends in the area helped to ensure a sizable audience. Buoyed by strong newspaper reviews and testimonials, she even gave an encore course of lectures in Albany in 1827.[35]

Conclusion

Perhaps the paradigm that best captures entrepreneurial public speaking among white women in the early national period is the distinction proposed by historian Donald M. Scott. Explaining transformations in the profession of lecturing in a much later period—the 1850s to the 1880s—Scott characterizes public lecturing before 1850 as occupational rather than professional. He points out that the main economic problem faced by young middle-class men pushed off the family farm in the Jacksonian era was not whether they could become lawyers, doctors, or clergymen; it was whether they could *survive* in these positions. Many men, Scott explains, turned to entrepreneurial lecturing as a means of getting an edge on their competition and "finding a point of entry into a community that would enable them to secure a position or clientele sufficient to establish and maintain a career."[36]

Scott's insight has subtle consequences for understanding the trajectory of early commercial public speaking in the United States and the role of women within it. Previously, most narratives of nineteenth-century lecturing have sketched an arc of declension from ideals of popular education to commercial entertainment. The shortcomings of this nostalgic teleology of loss have been noted by Thomas Augst, Angela G. Ray, and others who argue that it oversimplifies the multidimensional aspects of lyceum participation, the roots of which show the interaction of various cultural forces. Studying women's lecturing as a manifestation of occupational work moves us away from an exclusive focus on their work promoting disinterested ideals of education (as either republican mothers or Enlightenment saints) and toward a more complex discussion of the simultaneous economic aspects of those practices. Women indeed exploited the educational justification of "shaping a sense of nationhood," in Ray's succinct words, and they did so with wide (although not unanimous) cultural approval that they should make a living at it.[37] Recent educational research chronicling how women became schoolteachers in the nineteenth century describes a slow and steady move into the mainstream, where only about 10 percent of primary and secondary schoolteachers were women in 1800, rising to 86 percent by 1920. But rarely have we spoken about public lecturing as a means for them to make this move in the first decades of the United States, or about how public speech might have functioned to compensate for their depressed salaries in their struggle with male teachers to enroll students.[38]

A second part of the story of women's public speaking in the early national period, however, focuses on widespread societal agreement over the importance of the propagation of science and useful knowledge. Although men outnumbered women as public lecturers, women lecturers made significant and novel contributions to this culture with surprising support and patronage from men. Furthermore, women's audience roles as intellectual participants, benefactors, and economic sponsors of the ongoing work of science, understood in its broadest sense, illustrate the depth of the intellectual resource that lecturing promised to middle-class America.

3

MOBILIZING IRISH AMERICA IN THE ANTEBELLUM LECTURE HALL

Tom F. Wright

The American speaking circuit occupies an indelible place in the history of what James Joyce called "our greater Ireland beyond the sea."[1] Given the presence of a large diaspora, a receptive political culture, and the prospect of support both moral and material, public appearances on the platforms of the United States have been a key arena of action for those seeking to shape visions of Ireland's future. The mid-nineteenth century represents an important chapter in this story. In the wake of the mass emigration of the famine period and the failed 1848 Young Ireland uprising against British rule, a great deal of cultural, political, and intellectual energy shifted west across the Atlantic, where the newly consolidated phenomenon of the American popular lecture system became a means by which the challenges and opportunities of global Irish identity could be articulated and reimagined. This chapter explores two distinct ways this was attempted during the antebellum period: through spectacles of Irish nationalism and through the words of orators eager to challenge dominant ideas about "Celtic" and "Anglo-Saxon" racial theory.

The list of nationalists who have made their case at American lecterns is a roll call of modern Irish political history: from Charles Parnell and John Redmond in the 1880s through Countess Constance Markievicz and Hanna Sheehy-Skeffington in the years surrounding the 1916 Easter Rising to Sinn Féin's Gerry Adams in the 1990s.[2] All have demonstrated a keenly instrumental understanding of what the lecture hall could mean in practical terms and what it could stand for as a symbol. In this chapter, I make the case that this political tradition effectively begins with the spectacular appearances of escaped fugitive nationalists Thomas Francis Meagher and John Mitchel in the early 1850s. Both used oratory as part of an array of flamboyant forms of publicity, with the aim of simultaneously mobilizing a radical diaspora and a counterpublic of Americans sympathetic to republican political ideals and reimagining the public lecture as political theater. However, as I show, during the same years the American platform also played host to other, more rarefied intellectual discussions of Irish and "Celtic" identity. Inspired by strands of popular polygenist racial theory, Irish lecturers such as John McElheran used pseudoscientific ethnology to push against the prevailing discourse of Anglo-Saxon superiority and to argue for the innate democratic potential of the Celt. In these ways, by thinking together in the lecture hall about the realities and illusions of apparent differences, and about the types of togetherness involved in political commitments, one of the most important generations of thinkers and agitators in Irish American history mounted a powerful challenge to an overarching "Anglo-American commons."

This last phrase is one that I use in my book *Lecturing the Atlantic*, where I argue that the lecture platform of the period was strongly patterned by its engagement with a quite different form of diasporic identity: that of an elaborate fascination with England and the Anglo-American connection.[3] Lectures about Oliver Cromwell or Shakespeare, lectures about travel in England and the "Anglo-Saxon race," or appearances by British writers such as William Makepeace Thackeray were among the most reliable crowd-pullers on any lecture program. The Anglo-obsession of lecture culture reached its apogee during the social turmoil of the 1840s, when it can be read as an assertive response to the pace of demographic change, especially in urban centers such as New York, where by the mid-1850s almost one-third of residents were Irish-born. Although the early lyceum promoter Josiah Holbrook had intended a diverse audience, the reality rarely lived up to this ideal. Thomas Wentworth Higginson observed of the period in 1868, "Foreign immigrants are apt to avoid [the lecture hall] or to taste of it, as they do of any other national dish, with courtesy, but not with relish."[4] As Andrew Chamberlin Rieser has noted, "The rise of nativism after the lyceum vogue is not entirely coincidental."[5] The ubiquity of lectures on British themes was one way the mainstream platform helped to enforce a normative ethnic identity.

My book argues that the lecture hall provided a galvanizing space where an "Anglo-American commons" might find its expression. I employ the term *commons* in two related senses. First, it refers to the sense of a shared ethnic lineage; second, and in a more abstract sense, it denotes the shared symbolic resources of culture, language, and history that were seen to unite Great Britain and the United States.[6] As I show, the American lecture hall was

Figure 3.1   Erin go bragh, circa 1879–85. This imaginary group portrait of patriotic Irishmen throughout history was published by New York's Fishel, Adler and Company. Its depictions include four Irish emigrants to the United States: Colonel Patrick Kelly, Thomas Meagher, John Mitchel, and Jeremiah O'Donovan Rossa. Courtesy of the American Antiquarian Society.

an arena in which ideas about an Anglo-American commons found some of their most prominent articulations. Yet as this chapter explores, it was also a space in which these ideas were challenged in powerful ways. In antebellum America, a range of performers questioned the relevance or importance of British inheritance, overturned historical myths, and revealed the material limits of a notionally shared culture. Native American lecturers, African American literary societies, and German-language lyceums, among others, all existed at the edge of this normative center, and as the present volume confirms, recent scholarship is continuing to uncover fascinating new evidence of the importance and scope of such groups. What follows is an attempt to begin something similar for the Irish American presence on the antebellum platform, an involvement that remains unexplored to date in most narratives of lecture culture, although historians of Irish nationalism and of Victorian scientific culture have touched on the experiences of some of the figures I discuss.[7] By drawing these contexts together, my aim is to offer a series of fresh, suggestive juxtapositions amid the tangled history of the Green Atlantic and to contribute to an understanding of lecturing as a rich and still overlooked element of a North Atlantic performance continuum that unites the worlds of theater, science, and political agitation.[8]

Meagher, Mitchel, and the Theater of Republicanism

Perhaps the most visible Irishman on the antebellum American platform was Thomas Meagher, the first of the leaders of the 1848 uprising to translate his experience for lecture hall audiences. Having dramatically escaped imprisonment in Van Diemen's Land (later Tasmania), he sought passage to New York by way of Brazil in mid-1852. In the words of Henry Ward Beecher, "When it was announced that Meagher had escaped from the convict-isle, the continent rang with congratulation."[9] The flamboyant, handsome Meagher was welcomed to North America as a global statesman, already famous for his oratory thanks to his widely reprinted 1846 "sword speech," in which he had memorably praised the "redeeming magic" of the American Revolution.[10] He soon bowed to the many invitations to speak on the public lecture circuit about his experiences, and his earliest U.S. appearances caused a sensation. The first engagement, at Manhattan's Metropolitan Hall, drew what one reporter thought "the largest audience ever assembled in this city to hear one man speak, where a charge was made for admission"; the event garnered "a larger sum than was ever produced by a lecture at New York."[11] Initially, Meagher spoke mainly about his prison experiences in the Australian penal colony, using such reflections to campaign for the "progress of republicanism in England and throughout the English colonies."[12] Soon he developed a wider repertoire, speaking to audiences across the country about "Great Irish Orators."[13] Having taken his reflections throughout New England, Ohio, Michigan, and Missouri, he also toured the South, and in 1853 he spoke before President-elect Franklin Pierce in Washington. He soon established himself as editor of the *Irish News* in New York, before finding lasting fame in his adopted country as a heroic Union general during the Civil War.

His fellow nationalist leader John Mitchel had read accounts of Meagher's exploits and transcripts of his lectures from his own imprisonment in Bermuda, where he was busy composing the *Jail Journal* (1854), which was to become a canonical text of Irish nationalism. Having resolved to follow

Meagher to the United States, Mitchel, too, secured escape and arrived in New York by way of California in November 1853. He was feted in much the same manner as Meagher and soon turned to the lecture platform himself, offering lectures that were even more militant and polemical than those of his compatriot. During 1854–55 he toured the Eastern seaboard and the Midwest with pieces including "The Position and Duties of European Refugees" and "The Ripening of Revolution in Ireland."[14] Mitchel's mixture of anti-imperialism and anti-industrialism was particularly attuned to the sensibility south of the Mason-Dixon Line. In 1855 Mitchel moved to Tennessee and later to Virginia, before becoming notorious in the North for his defense of slavery and staunch support for the Confederacy.

Just as the 1848 rebellion in Ireland had been more symbolic than militarily significant, so the U.S. lecture tours of the exiles were exercises above all in the political theater of global republicanism. Their arrival had come at a fortuitous time for such ideas. In the early 1850s, vocal interests in both North and South found common cause in venerating the heroes of recent European revolutions, either as part of the developing sectional dispute or through the internationalist solidarity, captured in Pierce's 1853 inaugural address, toward "the oppressed throughout the world . . . [who] have turned their eyes hitherward."[15] Crucially, Meagher and Mitchel also came hot on the heels of the visit of another hero of those European struggles. In 1851, Lajos Kossuth, the leader of the short-lived Hungarian Revolution of 1848–49, had arrived in the United States on a mission to raise funds for his nation's independence. The intense positive reception he received became a crystallizing event for the Young America movement and had a wider role in promoting fascination with European radicals.[16] It also suggested a route for the rebels of Ireland's own 1848 uprising. From jail in Bermuda, Mitchel had written of reading, "with a sense of returning life, the glorious Governor's impassioned harangues" as "the world once more hung enraptured on the fire-tipped tongue of a true orator."[17] Those seeking Irish independence could do worse than to emulate the illustrious Hungarian's exercises in mythmaking through oratory and public display. Lecturing offered not only an effective fund-raising exercise for the cause and for their own personal support but also a propaganda tool by which to cultivate an Irish American counterpublic and a broader network of liberal republican sympathy.

When their own turn came, this "theater" was stage-managed for maximum impact. Crowds camped out to await the arrival of Meagher's and Mitchel's ships; the men were paraded around Manhattan and Brooklyn at functions, receptions, and civic galas, and during 1852 the "T. F. Meagher

Polka" was performed nightly at Niblo's Theater.[18] From the outset, Meagher and Mitchel made speeches that were widely transcribed in the press, and although some took place at dinners and other events, their public lectures were to prove the most lasting. When they lectured, they brought a sense of spectacle with them. Their stages were shared with noted veterans of previous Irish uprisings: "nearly three thousand" cheered Meagher on stage in Philadelphia alongside "John Binns, one of the patriots of 1798," providing what one reporter called "a singular link" between the generations. In New York a band played Irish airs mingled with "Yankee Doodle."[19] When Mitchel spoke at the Broadway Tabernacle, "behind the platform was suspended the flag of the Irish Republic," and a feverish ovation heralded his arrival.[20] Lecturing in Brooklyn in 1853, Meagher was presented with "a magnificent sword," and his speech was followed by numerous celebratory tributes.[21] The previous year, the Convention of Civic Societies agreed to place Meagher at the head of a parade, with a stagecoach "handsomely decorated, to be drawn by six grey horses, banners, mottoes, &c."[22] The two men sometimes shared the stage as twin exiles, doubling the frenzied atmosphere.

Reports and accounts reveal Mitchel as the superior writer but Meagher as the more powerful orator. Some sources describe both in conventional fashion as "fiery" and "manly."[23] Their fervor and "frantic enthusiasm" were valued and read as moral authenticity: watching Meagher speak made a *New York Tribune* reporter's "breast swell with patriotism . . . he appeared to *feel* all that he said, and his audience felt with him."[24] Such histrionics were almost demanded by audiences, as when the press in St. Louis anticipated Mitchel's 1856 appearance by hoping that it would be "in the style of the pike and vitriol school of popular insurrectionists."[25] However, other observers appeared appalled by the overblown artifice of Meagher's style in particular. The New York correspondent for *Frederick Douglass' Paper* offered a skeptical account of seeing Meagher, describing him as "a man of some brains and more pretensions, [who] possesses all the wildness and ferocity of his class, tempered only by education and refinement."[26] This writer also captured something of the mobile nature of the Irishman's platform style:

> Irish hatred is now to be called up. Watch him. Observe every lineament of his face, every gesture, every expression. Now, he is the sly, cunning cat, sitting at the mouse hole, now—now to pounce upon his tiny victim . . . now he is the savage butcher, with sleeves tucked up, ready to strike his *victim*, the big, burly, *English bull*. . . . So wrapt [the onlookers'] feelings, so complete his acting, so perfect and intense his

performance. A low, savage growl, and then a wild shout, and a fearful rush, and then the cry is "the English, the English, the hated English; up—up boys, and at 'em!"[27]

Yet curiously, others found Meagher and Mitchel not the firebrands they expected and instead described a controlled mode of public delivery. One reporter reviewing Meagher's performance in Philadelphia thought that he had "less fire and energy than we supposed; more brilliancy and more grace ... seldom does he leave the calm and regular strain of speech and rise with kindling warmth. But when he does so, all the orator shines in him."[28]

Mitchel was explicit about his intended audience, claiming that it was his aim to "address the Irish-born citizens of America upon the one great topic of this age."[29] At times, when speaking before Hibernian Societies or other exclusively Irish organizations, this was certainly the case. We have little sense of the social makeup of such groupings, but the account of Meagher's lecture in *Frederick Douglass' Paper* demeaned one crowd as a Celtic rabble, frothing and animalistic:

> Were you ever in a *menagerie*? . . . Passing Broadway, when just opposite the Tabernacle, the name Meagher caught my eye. After a moment's hesitation, I entered. What a sight! Here were thousands of wild Irish vociferating and gesticulating with a fury; the wildest imagination could not portray, and I shall not attempt a description. With their long scraggly hair over low brows, and narrow faces, with huge projecting teeth and dull sluggish eyes, they presented to the beholder a collection, overmatching in apparent ferocity, any wild animals hitherto gathered in this country, or I venture to believe, in the combined Zoological gardens of Europe.[30]

Such descriptions seemed to owe more to the racialized anti-Irish nativism of Know Nothing bombast than to the emancipatory ideals of one of the nation's premier reformist papers. Yet they remind us of the wedge that Irish newcomers drove between reform movements, from abolitionists to Whig educationalists. To some observers such lectures provided simply "a fair exhibit of the wild Irish in America."[31] For most of Meagher's and Mitchel's public lectures, accounts confirm that there was often a majority Irish base of support—and not just in the Eastern cities. In Cincinnati, for instance, a June 1860 lecture by Mitchel was described as filled "mostly by countrymen of the lecturer."[32] Yet in other locations the audience seems to have been more mixed. Meagher's first biographer, for example, recalled the "fervid enthusiasm" of an Albany lecture that crossed "distinction of race, creed or class ... equal portions of native and naturalized citizens."[33] As one might expect, Meagher's and Mitchel's lectures and movements were heavily debated and covered in the Irish American press, including the *Nation* in New York and the *Pilot* in Boston. Later both men established their own publications to help sustain and energize the nationalist community. Further, as the lecturers knew, transcripts of their words were also presented in the most prominent newspapers in each city as mainstream cultural events with mass appeal to readers beyond an ethnic audience. For instance, Mitchel's appearances in Boston were described in the first column of the *New York Herald* in 1853, and the *New York Times* carried full transcriptions of Meagher's lectures.[34]

In this way, their performances had a dual rhetorical thrust. On one level, they functioned to shore up Irish diasporic identity, continuing the transatlantic political discourse prevalent since Daniel O'Connell's ascendancy a generation earlier. As Kerby Miller has argued, the East Coast Irish diaspora was "particularly receptive to nationalist interpretations of their experiences," and the predicament of exile and emigration was fertile ground for Young Ireland mythmakers to exploit.[35] But rather than just mobilizing the Irish population of the Eastern cities, these lecturers were simultaneously speaking to a wider constituency of American liberalism. Both used emotive accounts of Irish struggle and misery to elicit sympathy, with Mitchel sketching the Ireland he left as settled into "a deeper and darker pall than ever.... Her children lay dying by myriads round her coasts, mourned only by the hoarse Atlantic."[36] Both also deliberately inhabited the language of the American Revolution, with Mitchel opening a talk in Boston by praising "that famous spot of ground which your fathers held so nobly against the beleaguered battalions of England."[37] He customarily peppered his speech with denunciations of the "malefactors ... who now govern Europe, and more especially the Queen of Great Britain and Ireland," sentiments that elicited "immense cheering."[38] Their lectures, however, appealed to subtly distinct kinds of understandings of what a diasporic community or identity might entail.

Meagher was particularly keen to make his audiences identify not only with what he called "the inalienable inheritance of my poor country" but also with a broader culture of republicanism.[39] He offered the vision of a global liberal commons and invited audiences to place the American republic within it. "The example of America," he told crowd after crowd, had taught

Ireland "lessons of citizenship . . . those lessons of national spirit, industry and ambition, of religious toleration."[40] And such a global commons was not only transatlantic but also transpacific. "To you, the citizens of America," he told audiences with reference to the future status of the Australia in which he had been imprisoned, "it must be pleasing indeed to behold a new republic, rising up to share with you the labours and the glories of a future before which the conceits of the old world shall be humbled."[41] The energies that such a new republic might let loose, he maintained, would secure Irish freedom itself: "The seed will multiply, and borne back to the ancient land, will make the wilderness rejoice."[42] He asked American audiences to place their nation within a revised teleology of global freedom, by doing so himself.

Similarly, Mitchel's lectures aimed to construct a new language of nationalism and a commons based on sensibility and shared opposition to monarchical oppression. He particularly appealed to "those whose taste or whose destiny had led them to interest themselves in the great public transactions of mankind. . . . Men might pretend to look on this old world drama with indifference," he conceded, "they might say the Eastern world was in its dotage, but in vain could they shut their ears to the echoes of the mighty revolution there going on."[43] Having conscripted audiences into this global humanitarian consciousness through images of shared connection, he offered an opposite image to caution listeners of Britain's attempts to make the United States a pariah: "Think of it, to be shut off—God help us—from the diplomatic circle—to be held for Arabs and Gypsies—drawn off from civilized society, with whom it is impossible to be classified—to be stigmatized as a people bound by no compacts, respecting no law, dreaming of no justice, by whom? . . . It seems America is out of the pale of society according to the [London] *Times*."[44] In his own person on the platform, Mitchel offered a living rebuke to such attempts at untying. "Though not long present in the body," Mitchel claimed on more than one occasion, "I have been many a year an American in spirit."[45]

The lectures of Meagher and Mitchel were therefore performances that resonated on multiple levels. First and most obvious was the outlet they provided for patriotic celebration from the Irish community. Also present was an element of cross-cultural curiosity on the part of a wider American public for such sentiments. A similar desire was well captured in a Dublin reporter's response to witnessing Kossuth lecture in England: "It is a grand thing to look upon such a very wonderful and admirable man—the man whom a noble and gallant people regard with intense and passionate veneration, as their leader, and humanly speaking, the star of their hope."[46] In the United

States, fascination with the broader history of 1848 was in evidence throughout 1850s culture, including various lectures on "The French Exiles."[47] But what could be a more enticing prospect than the sight of an actual world-historical fugitive? Third, the speeches were appealing directly to the antimonarchical, Anglophobic spirit of the age; as one *New York Herald* report confirms, Mitchel consistently "wound up amid frantic enthusiasm with a stirring appeal to the hereditary hatred of England."[48] This was a sentiment, of course, that cut across the sectional divide. Meagher's and Mitchel's performances were rare examples of "acts" whose appeal genuinely straddled South and North, and they spoke widely in both. Finally, as famous escapees and exiles, both Meagher and Mitchel used the lecture hall as an extrajudicial extension of their trials, appealing to an imagined court of global public opinion and carrying over an earlier sense of testimony and defense. Yet as their tours continued, some of this initial import seemed to drain from the events: although Meagher was promoted on the East Coast in terms of the "fame of the orator and the cause," by the time he arrived in California his lectures were advertised simply as "an intellectual luxury."[49]

The tours of Meagher and Mitchel were in fact far from uncontroversial or universally celebrated. Ralph Waldo Emerson was among many who saw their reception as simple celebrity worship: "Some foreign celebrity passes by . . . Kossuth, or Dickens, Lord Morpeth or Meagher . . . the shout of welcome is echoed and caught from city to city . . . an oriental superlative of adulation."[50] The Catholic press, partly incensed by Meagher's praise for anticlericals like Kossuth and the Italian revolutionary Giuseppe Mazzini, held a similar view. The *Boston Pilot* complained that "we cannot but smile at the adulation which a certain clique in that paradise of cliques, New York, continually throw at his face. . . . These insufferable toadies, who live on some passing excitement, continually assure him that he *is* the leader of our race in America."[51] A glimpse from Meagher's New York lecture on Australia testifies to the controversies between the church and the nationalists: he railed against how "the Roman Catholic clergymen . . . did dishearten and restrain them. [Cheers and hisses. A voice—'They will never do so again.' Loud cheers.] Ah! in that voice, continued Mr. Meagher, do I recognise the future freedom of down-trodden Ireland. [Vehement cheering.]"[52] Others simply bridled at Meagher's and Mitchel's overly shrill Anglophobia, with audiences and booking committees in New Orleans and in Sacramento, California, taking offense at Meagher's "direct insult to the British nation."[53] Moreover, their theatricality was not to everyone's taste. The *New York Herald* thought that their speeches were merely rhetorical display: "Amid the flowers of language that fell in great profusion from the speaker's lips, a single principle of practical application or immediate usefulness will be sought in vain."[54]

Celts, Refugees, and Racial Theory

While crowds were being roused into republican fervor by these exiles, the fate of Irish identity was being discussed in a quite different register elsewhere. The second way that speakers from Ireland thought together about the meanings of the diaspora was by posing as educators of their mixed audiences on questions of identity and culture. During the 1850s, a range of performers spoke on such themes and articulated versions of Irishness more nuanced than the shrill identity politics that surrounded Meagher's appearances. In the hands of some lecturers, this took the form of the simple celebration of culture. One illustrative example was the Wexford-born dissenting Unitarian minister Henry Giles, who became a successful speaker during the 1840s, championing Celtic culture with lectures on such topics as "The Spirit of Irish History" and "Irish Character, Mental and Moral."[55] He later informed his audiences that he had been "heard with generous interest . . . in city halls and in village lyceums" since the early 1840s, but by the end of that decade and the deepening of the famine and emigration crises, the story of Ireland had become "no longer novel. It is now not a story, but a drama; a black and fearful drama."[56] Confronted with the mass immigration resulting from that "drama" and the demonization of the new Irish population, Giles aimed to forge common ground with non-Irish Americans through shared affection.[57] At least one New York reviewer found the attempt convincing, arguing that "the pathos of his presentations of the sorrows of his favorite, Ireland, never fails to touch effectively all who listen to his story."[58] Giles's project was shared by other performers such as William E. Robinson, whose 1852 talk "The Celtic and Anglo-Saxon Races" offered to redress "the American ignorance of Ireland," arguing that "in every department of art, literature, and science, the Celtic genius commands the world, and I must be pardoned if I decline to join in the general depreciation of this great race."[59]

As the title of Robinson's lecture reveals, such themes were often expressed using the problematic language of popular racial theory. The 1850s was a high point for pseudo-ethnographic typologies, thanks in part to the work of Scottish anatomist and popular lecturer Robert Knox.[60] Ideas of Anglo-Saxon racial distinction and supremacy were common currency in high and low culture of the period. Traces stretch from the pages of the penny press to those of the *London Times* or New York's *Christian Intelligencer*, and from the incendiary speeches of urban controversialists such as Ned Buntline and anti-Catholic firebrands such as Charles Levin to the supposedly more rarefied addresses of Transcendentalists such as Theodore Parker and Ralph Waldo Emerson, both of whom devoted lectures to the topic during the early 1850s.[61]

However, whereas Knox had argued for the superiority of the Anglo-Saxon, key Irish American cultural figures transformed his polygenist theories into an opportunity to counter negative stereotypes of savagery and superstition by celebrating the achievements and qualities of an imagined Celt. One of the most influential was Thomas D'Arcy McGee, another Young Ireland émigré and editor of Dublin's key nationalist journal, the *Nation*. In 1848, sought by British authorities for attempting to incite rebellion, McGee escaped for the United States, where he became a leading ethnic spokesman.[62] In the years before his emigration he had promoted a messianic theory of Celtic destiny, claiming that "Irish Catholic Celts were on a providential mission to transmit the One True Faith to the New World."[63] In the pages of his journal the *American Celt*, he encouraged Irish Catholics to respond to nativist hostility with a politicized ethnic pride, promoting a magnificent Celtic past and the promise of patriotic Irish Americans as guarantors of democracy. When he took these ideas to the lecture platform in the mid-1850s, he was one of a number of speakers making a similar case. As lecturer Peter McLaughlin argued in his talk "Characteristics of the Irish Celt: Moral, Social and Religious," delivered in Brooklyn in 1854, the migrant crisis of the previous decade meant that his topic was not marginal to a broader American public but a fundamental "subject . . . that concerns us all."[64]

The most intriguing lecturer on this subject was John McElheran, a Belfast surgeon whose subversive ethnological theories had already earned him notoriety on the other side of the Atlantic. He had come to prominence after attacking what he called "the Saxon lie" in a series of articles and public talks in Dublin during 1850–51, turning Knox's hierarchy of Saxon and Celt on its head. When McElheran's ideas were denounced in the *Times* of London, he defended them forcefully in a much-reprinted letter.[65] Politically he, too, had become involved not only with Young Ireland but also with the Celtic Union, labor rights, and the universal franchise, and he spoke at the prominent 1854 "national banquet" in Dublin to celebrate the safe arrival of John Mitchel in New York. By the end of that year he had come to the United States and begun advertising himself as a "lecturer on the races of men" whose notoriety preceded him.[66] To the Irish American press, McElheran's apparent triumph over the anti-Celtic antipathies of the London press had made him both a true patriot and a figure of curiosity to a wider audience interested in the controversies of pseudoscience. His 1854 lecture at New York's Academy of Medicine, on the "comparative anatomy of the human cranium," was reprinted in the *New York Journal of Medicine* and the *Boston Pilot*. The piece aimed to provide a maverick physiognomic basis for the Pan-Celtic resistance to the American nativism of McGee and others. McElheran's point of departure was still that of correcting misleading views of British history: "I appeal to history, but more to existing facts," he told audiences, "against the theory that England is Anglo-Saxon."[67] In the United States he fleshed out this theme considerably, claiming that Celts, not Saxons, were the universal proponents of civic republican ideals and, further, that Celts were bulwarks against the "Saxon" erosion of liberty in the republic. Moreover, he reassured his audiences that due to "superior religiosity . . . by the Celts alone would Christianity be perpetuated here, and if American civilization and progress were to partake of the Christian character, it would be controlled and directed by the Celtic element."[68]

These lectures are also important because, rather than offering mere dry rehearsals of contemporary scientific arguments, McElheran played racial distinctions for laughs. Reports suggest that he was as much entertainer as professor, interspersing the science "with a variety of Irish jokes, original versifications and occasional flights of Irish oratory."[69] The highlight of his performances was a sequence in which he used illustrations to compare the cranial shape of notable Celts with those of the U.S. Founding Fathers. A reporter for Meagher's *Irish News* captured the scene of an 1856 lecture by McElheran at the Broadway Tabernacle:

> Upwards of one hundred large cartoons of the human head and face were cleverly used . . . in support of his position that the strongly marked Yankee physiognomy is absolutely and purely Celtic. Great interest and laughter was excited. A sketch of a Paddy with a short pipe and battered hat was unmistakable. The Doctor removed his pipe, clapped on him a goatee, and presto he was a Frenchman. Away with the beard and his military cap and there stood revealed the noble features and brow of Washington . . . the lecture gave great satisfaction.[70]

This was popular science at its most accessible and deceptively frivolous. But its resonance was immense. By unveiling the portrait in this way, and revealing the presence of Transcendental Celt in unexpected places, McElheran not only made the Irish white, in Noel Ignatiev's phrase, but he transformed the very conception of the republic into a Celtic achievement. The stripping away of layers offered a fascinating lesson in civics and the ironies of hyphenated identity, allowing the immigrants among audiences a dramatic metaphor for their own routes to assimilation and acceptance.[71]

The quest to understand the possibilities of global Irishness also became the key theme of Mitchel's work as editor and lecturer in the early years of his American exile. Speaking under such probing titles as "The Duties of the Immigrant," he demonstrated a willingness to move beyond shaping the myth of '48 into promoting a nuanced identity politics. In Boston, a city beset with a major migrant crisis, he addressed local concerns in a dual way. In a December 1853 speech at the city's Revere House, he addressed members of the Irish diaspora and asked that they remember the duties they owed to the American republic in return for its protection: "I cordially join you in your just and hearty appreciation of the broad-based freedom and the all embracing generosity of this great republic. Let us remember what we owe to America; and, by faithfully and loyally discharging the duties of citizenship, let us endeavor to show both our gratitude to her, and our fitness for Democratic freedom and powers."[72] For a broader audience at the Music Hall on the same day, he met head-on critiques of the foreign sympathies of his countrymen, arguing, according to one reporter, that "it would be simply treason toward the commonwealth if he should pay more regard to the national claims or necessities . . . than to those of the new country whose nationality he has voluntarily chosen to take upon him [immense applause]."[73] To native-born Bostonians he underlined the point that all Americans were seeking asylum of some kind: "We are all equally Refugees; to us all alike the great free Republic of America opens her hospitable door and offers the sanctuary of an inviolable home." And he predicted that the republic might well find Irishmen the most eager and useful of recent immigrants at a future time of military strife: "War may come, and if it do, I know the land will have no more devoted defenders than her Irish citizens [tremendous applause]."[74]

Yet when that conflict came, the most prominent Irish Americans studied in this chapter found themselves on opposing sides of the Civil War: Meagher for the Union, Mitchel and McElheran for the Confederacy. This fact is unsurprising given that the issue of slavery served as a problematic absence in much of the lecture hall commentary I have discussed. The causes of Irish nationalism and abolition had long been in conflict—a result, in part, of the widespread fear among Irish nationalists that the antislavery movement would undermine American support for Irish political independence. The reframing of republicanism in Meagher's lectures had proved popular in the South, where many sympathized with his characterization of himself as trapped in a "fatal quarrel with a formidable government."[75] But other speakers discussed above went further. McElheran was not alone in insinuating in his lectures that abolition was a Saxon plan with London interests behind it. Mitchel also offered his audiences a skeptical view of the ineffective "transatlantic philanthropy" of Daniel O'Connell's abolition, and he began to argue for the expansion of slavery, offering a vision of an Irish American commons based on racial subordination.[76]

Mitchel's support for slavery was a rejection of one strand of Anglo-American commonality. "The Irish appear to think no other people on earth deserving sympathy or liberty but themselves," wrote one observer.[77] As a reporter from the *National Anti-Slavery Standard* put it, "It is plain from the opinion now expressed by Mr. Mitchel that he wages his warfare with England without any real principle of liberty at the bottom."[78] Despite the iconic role played by the Irish lecture tours of Olaudah Equiano in the 1790s, Charles Remond in 1841, or Frederick Douglass in 1845, the overlaps between the antebellum Green and Black Atlantics were deeply fraught, at least in the lecture hall.[79] Thinking together about the differences between Celt and Saxon often happened at the expense of African American sympathy.

Conclusion

Irish themes and speakers maintained their presence on the lecture stage into the postbellum period, and within the first fifty years after the Civil War the circuit would play host not only to nationalists such as Charles Parnell and Michael Davitt but also to those embodying Irish culture such as Oscar Wilde and W. B. Yeats. It was in the antebellum years, however, amid the turmoil of the Irish immigrant crisis, the low ebb for political opposition to British rule, and the divided loyalties of émigrés caught between North and South, that lecturing played its most important role in reimagining Irish America. As more is discovered by ongoing research, particularly into the social makeup and development of independent Irish lecture societies, this germinal moment will be fleshed out in far fuller fashion. Yet even in skeletal form, the Irish case study suggests a number of key truths about the nineteenth-century platform.

The examples discussed here demonstrate that the lecture hall was not simply a place for the flattening out of social identities or conformity, but for the expression of complex ethnic affiliations. For many, lyceum attendance was intrinsic not just to the formation of bourgeois class identity but also, at a moment when ethnic hierarchies were coming into being, to the creation of a distinctively "white" public. Engagement with institutions perceived as civic, such as the lecture, was a marker on the road to social respectability, legitimacy, and prestige. The Irish case reminds us that we need to see the lecture as part of a continuum with other, more flamboyant, carnivalesque forms of nationalist expression, such as parades. Lecturing might have been a subtler, more muted space where nationalism overlapped with education and performance, but it was by no means separate from the larger animating forces it both reflected and helped to direct.

Equally, this chapter underlines the extent to which, for some groups, particularly marginalized or contentious subcultures, the lecture hall has been, above all, a space of politics. For Irish American performers and audiences, with particular conceptions of an oratory of resistance, the idea of the lecture was interchangeable with that of political agitation. Their history brings the role of lecturing as secular preaching into relief. The nationalism present on the podium and the Catholicism of the pulpit were engaged in a bitter struggle for the soul of Irish America, and both were frequently at odds with the ideology of individualism that lecture culture more broadly sought to promote.

During this crucial antebellum period, in which the East Coast, urban political class was struggling to know what to do with the energies of Irish nationalism, the lecture hall played a vital role in constructing new global Celtic identities. For Meagher and Mitchel, and for those sympathetic to their cause, the lecture hall became a voice of the exile community. It provided the perfect platform from which to cement the myth of '48 and to catalyze the next generation of Irish activists and thinkers, at home or throughout the diaspora, through the constant flow of newsprint coverage of their words at American lecterns. At the same time, the platform also became as powerful a medium as any other for those trying to define, challenge, or forge anew public understandings of Irish American identity. Multiple commentators responded to the supranational threat of Anglo-Saxonist ideology with a supranational response, constructing a Celtic international community joined by blood, customs, and history.

4

AUTHENTIC IMITATION OR PERVERSE ORIGINAL? LEARNING ABOUT RACE FROM AMERICA'S POPULAR PLATFORMS

Kirt H. Wilson and Kaitlyn G. Patia

The nineteenth century was a remarkable period of public education when the practices of print and oral cultures intersected.[1] Between 1741 and 1861, U.S. magazines evolved from a dubious business venture into a robust mechanism for distributing religious ideas and general entertainment.[2] In the century's second half, America's periodicals expanded to include magazines about civic and political interests. Across the century, first at lyceum halls and, later, on the chautauqua circuit, noted authors, scientists, social reformers, and journalists delivered speeches on a wide array of subjects.[3] Sometimes print and oral cultures were so intertwined that they produced a single work, such as William James's *The Varieties of Religious Experience*, or a celebrity, such as Ralph Waldo Emerson.[4] At other times the intercourse between print and oral cultures was subtle, because the forms of expression both within and between the two cultures were diverse. We contend that knowledge about racial differences and similarities was one important subject that crossed between the print and oral cultures of the nineteenth and early twentieth centuries.

In 1884 the *Atlantic Monthly* published an essay by Harvard professor Nathaniel S. Shaler titled "The Negro Problem." That a geologist would write about U.S. race relations for a commercial magazine was not unusual. Shaler's mentor, Louis Agassiz, had been a biologist, a geologist, and an ethnologist.[5] Agassiz had stood at the intersection of print and oral cultures to advance polygenism, the theory that different races were different species. His arguments were attractive to antebellum proponents of slavery who claimed that the institution was an economic necessity and a public good.

Shaler agreed.[6] Furthermore, he shared Agassiz's conviction that science should educate the public about the human traits that made the races distinct.[7] To our knowledge, Shaler never followed Agassiz's example to become a popular lecturer, but he did advance public knowledge by writing for nineteenth- and early twentieth-century periodicals.[8]

"The Negro Problem" would become one of Shaler's most influential essays, because it provided a label for a widespread social anxiety that had grown after the Civil War. This anxiety was evident in conversations about blood quantum laws, justifications for lynching, and debates over public education, but a single question encompassed much of what was meant by the phrase "the Negro Problem": What place should African Americans occupy in society?[9] Shaler answered this question by considering a second question: Were African Americans the same as or different from European Americans? He wrote that white people without much interaction with black populations were "charmed by [the black man's] admirable and appealing qualities, and so make haste to assume that he is in all respects like themselves." But "if they have the patience and the opportunity to search closely into the nature of this race they will perceive that the *inner man* is really as singular, as different in motives from themselves, as his outward aspect indicates."[10] This unaccountable, hidden inner difference led Shaler to resolve the "problem" of the "Negro" by suggesting distinct roles for each race. He said that when whites treated blacks as if they were no different from themselves, mistakes in race relations and public policy ensued. Under such conditions, people of African descent would become a threat to the nation's well-being. However, if European Americans respected racial difference and acted accordingly, if they allowed each race to occupy its separate place in society, then the races could live harmoniously. Segregation, in other words, was the solution Shaler preferred.

Throughout his writing, Shaler was concerned about the capacity of African Americans to hide or obscure their authentic selves. In an 1890 periodical he wrote, "The negro is a very imitative creature; in no other feature does he so well show the strong, sympathetic quality of his nature."[11] According to Shaler, imitation was the means by which blacks hid their difference. In a book-length study of human relations titled *The Neighbor*, he explained further:

> It is, indeed, evident that so far as their remarkable imitative faculty has carried them they have come nearer molding themselves on the mastering race than has been the case with any other subjugated

people known to us. So complete is the likeness which has been thus brought about, that, led by their categoric motive . . . men very generally suppose that the Negro is in his essential qualities what our own kind would be if their skins were black. This appears to me to be a most erroneous conclusion; one that has already led to grave injustice to the black people and certain if it stay[s] uncorrected to lead to yet greater evils.[12]

These ideas were not unique to Shaler. Similar claims had been expressed in print and from lecterns since at least the 1840s. For just as long, African American abolitionists and intellectuals had struggled with these ideas and argued against their use as a justification for white superiority.

In this chapter, we examine Shaler's concern and ask: What forms of racial imitation existed in the nineteenth and early twentieth centuries, and how did imitation create public knowledge about racial similarity and difference? Certainly essays and lectures by Shaler and Agassiz, as well as the rhetoric of Frederick Douglass and W. E. B. Du Bois, shaped how Americans understood race, but the impersonation of race on public platforms was also a mechanism through which ordinary people gained knowledge about their own identity and the identities of others. We contend that the nineteenth-century stage became a special scene of imitation. Consequently, it was also a space where the potential subjectivities of African and European Americans were made and remade in public culture and consciousness. Through that process, the commonsense assumptions and refined knowledge that characterized black Americans were put under tremendous strain. For some black performers, this instability offered an opportunity to resist racism and to obtain some personal autonomy. For many white performers and audience members, this instability was disruptive, producing dissonance about what, precisely, differentiated the races. Race on the public platform became a complex matter of both reason and performance. It was a taught "truth" of material difference that was affirmed with certainty even as its contingency and instability were demonstrated over and over again.

Our analysis proceeds from three assumptions. First, we approach nineteenth- and early twentieth-century racial instruction as an activity that involved multiple and divergent kinds of public expression—lyceum and chautauqua lectures, scientific demonstrations, dramatic readings, musical recitals, educational sermons, and even minstrelsy. For the sake of space, we focus here on oral performances that were forms of entertainment, but we agree with both Angela G. Ray and Sara E. Lampert that although America's oral culture evolved across the nineteenth century, instruction and entertainment were intertwined with each other from the beginning.[13] Second, we focus not on a single historical context but on a general rhetorical strategy—racial *mimesis*—which we define as the imitation of allegedly distinct racial attributes.[14] We show that the mimetic performance of race persisted and evolved along with the public platform from the 1830s through the 1910s. Third, because mimesis is constituted in multiple forms of expression, our chapter is organized topically rather than chronologically. We identify and analyze racial mimesis as distinct types of performance that might differ according to the audience, location, performative expectation, and performer but that are all united in a constitutive attempt to define the appropriate places and social roles of African and European Americans.

We begin by examining how European Americans imitated African Americans, from the well-known practice of minstrelsy in the 1830s and '40s to subtler forms that included demonstrations of black dialect and the performance of black music, which became popular in the 1880s and continued beyond 1910. We then analyze forms of imitation evident in two African American performances, the first produced by Anna Madah Hyers and Emma Louise Hyers, known as the Hyers Sisters, during the post-Reconstruction era, and the second by William Wells Brown during the antebellum period. Finally, we conclude by reflecting on how practices of imitation, and the issues of sameness, difference, and "authenticity" that they raised, affirmed the contingency of race even as the rhetoric of difference became a matter of public policy called Jim Crow.

Authentic Imitations? European American Forms of Imitation and Entertainment

When European Americans wrote or spoke about the political and moral implications of racial mimesis, they focused on how people of color imitated whites. They rarely turned their attention to their own mimetic behavior, because the white commentators who analyzed race treated whiteness as a non-raced norm from which blackness deviated.[15] In practice, however, European American performers frequently imitated the traits and behavior they identified with African Americans. At one level, this practice was an attempt to describe and perform what black difference looked like, but at a second level, the impersonation of African Americans by European Americans was as much about establishing a white identity as it was about defining blackness. The best-known example of such racial mimesis is blackface minstrelsy, which involved the performance of alleged blackness by Irish immigrants and, later, by other European Americans.

In 1830, Thomas Dartmouth Rice, a white ship carver's apprentice from New York, hit on the idea of blacking his face with burned cork to mimic the skin color of a fictitious character named Jim Crow. W. T. Lhamon Jr. writes, "When he began, what T. D. Rice did was unusual. Then it mushroomed into a pop craze. Then it settled into convention."[16] Minstrelsy, a form of theater in which white performers imitated people of color, was deeply intertwined in the tensions of race and class that emerged in the first half of the century. Social fragmentation due to disparate wealth conditions, recent immigration, poor labor conditions, and ethnic rivalry spilled onto the public stage. Lhamon argues that "poor and disaffected whites, like Rice . . . latched onto" the unruly and disruptive blackness "to mark their own dispersal and disruption."[17] Thus, many of the performers who "blackened" their faces with burned cork and the audiences who laughed at characters like Jim Crow, Sambo, and Doctor Quash were from the North's urban working class. "Minstrel entertainers fashioned a theater in which the rough, the respectable and the rebellious among craft workers could together find solace and even joy," writes David Roediger.[18]

Yet the social function of Negro minstrelsy was not simply a release from the hardship of daily labor, nor was it only a catalyst for class solidarity. Often performed before mixed-race audiences, the minstrel show conveyed a kind of "truth" that defined people of color and the working-class whites who impersonated them. The public performances envisioned by T. D. Rice and Josiah Holbrook, the founder of the lyceum movement in the United States, seem to be miles apart. The former seemed intent on undermining high culture with a theater that violated just about every norm of decorum that one might imagine in 1830. The latter envisioned a space of early industrial education where individuals would obtain "useful knowledge" away from the "grogshops" and vice that plagued the urban North.[19] Nevertheless, the lyceum and the minstrel show were responses to similar social conditions—the arrival of immigrants into the United States and a perceived need to educate foreigners for the purposes of assimilation. The lyceum could teach those lessons that were essential to one's civic duty, while the minstrel show instructed audiences in the subtle, and not so subtle, hierarchies that defined citizenship as distinctively white. Further, the lyceum and the minstrel show managed the social shifts that Jacksonian democracy created in a diverse population. Increases in the political and economic power of the working class challenged the authority of upper-class Anglo-Americans, but the lyceum and the minstrel show worked from opposite ends of the public platform to ensure the continuity of white supremacy and a belief in American exceptionalism. Josiah Holbrook emphasized the lyceum's educational mission, but from the beginning he "had unabashedly joined 'instruction and entertainment' as part and parcel of the same venture."[20] T. D. Rice sought commercial success by entertaining his working-class peers, but instruction about racial differences and similarities emerged as a by-product.

The minstrel show created a new blackness, and in the process, a new whiteness also was born. One of the recurring themes of minstrel songs and jokes involved the impersonation of African American characters who "put on airs" in an effort to be white. That is, white minstrel performers often created black characters who, within the context of the comedic sketch, imitated whites. One of the most famous examples of this was George Washington Dixon, a white actor who performed the song "Zip Coon" and embodied the blackface character who gave the song its title.[21] In songs such as this one, the act of imitation was doubled; performers identified imitation as a distinctive trait of black Americans, but they illustrated this point through an act of imitation in which they performed a "black" imitation of "whiteness." In the process, white minstrel performers lampooned "the pretensions of [white] high culture and the society of manners" without explicitly making the critique in their own person.[22] It was a black fictional character, often a buffoonish fop, who revealed the faults of elite society in the skits of minstrelsy. The imitation made possible a new white culture of the laboring class, many of whom had not been viewed as white because of the distorted racial logic of white supremacy, which in the nineteenth century defined immigrants from certain European countries as racial Others.[23] But while the minstrel performer used satire and mimicry to make fun of the divisions between immigrants and natives, the rich and the poor, the performance conveyed a second message: African Americans were pretentious and, as a race, did not know their proper place. The education offered by minstrelsy was that African Americans tried to imitate ideals and manners that they could not comprehend or hope to attain. Through this dual rhetorical strategy, white working-class performers critiqued the upper class from which they were estranged and affirmed their superiority over black Americans who could never quite measure up despite their repeated efforts to do so.

But racial mimesis is a tricky business, and even the imitation of exaggerated stereotypes complicates the subjectivity of performer and audience alike. For example, on 26 January 1854 an essay titled "Negro Minstrelsy" appeared in the New York–based *Christian Advocate and Journal*. In the essay Augusta Browne condemned minstrelsy. One passage of her essay spoke directly to the threat she felt it posed for white Americans:

> To the present prevalence of negro songs, none can deny, is attributable much of the slang and low breeding found even among circles where better might be hoped. Said a gentleman of fine taste to the writer, speaking of a lady who had frequented one of the Ethiopian exhibitions during a fortnight of consecutive evenings, "Why, Miss —— has gone so often that she is nearly *black*." A significant and just criticism. There exists in every one enough of the faculty of imitation to enable him to adopt any manner, style, or habit which may chance to impress his fancy . . . and, as in this present fallen state of being, our nature is by far more ready to copy evil than good, we are, consequently, especially susceptible of bad influences. The negro-minstrelsy, acting on this foible, is therefore exercising a more extensive and injurious influence upon society at large than many would imagine, not only as regards the progress of musical science, but also of morals and religion.[24]

Here Browne declared that upstanding *white* citizens—including women and children—were corrupted by the imitative performances of minstrel players.

In many ways Browne's admonishment reflects a concern that the Greek philosopher Plato expressed several millennia before. Plato, too, was concerned about mimesis. Mimetic impersonations could be a threat to a republic, Plato argued, because the ability to impersonate others convincingly made it difficult to distinguish the helpful rhetoric of a true citizen from the harmful rhetoric of an alien. In the *Republic*, Plato recommends sending away the skilled impersonators from foreign cities and avoiding mimetic performances altogether, because the impersonator would confuse citizens. He states that Athenians, "for our souls' good, should continue to employ the more austere and less delightful poet and taleteller, who would imitate the diction of the good man and would tell his tale in the patterns which we prescribed in the beginning."[25] Augusta Browne would likely concur. The ease with which white minstrels put on and pulled off a black face was entertaining, but the stain of such performances always remained. We become the things we imitate, but we also become the imitations that we watch and enjoy, Browne warned.

After the Civil War, subtler forms of imitating black behavior began to appear on the public stage. Sparked, in part, by a desire to recapture a romanticized notion of antebellum life and by the concern to diagnose and resolve "the Negro Problem," white audiences flocked to performances that promised to demonstrate what Southern black life and culture were really like. Lyceum and chautauqua bureaus were happy to oblige. From the 1880s through the second decade of the twentieth century, one of the most popular forms of platform education and entertainment involved "Negro music" and stories of the old plantation. The widespread interest in black culture offered an opportunity for African American ensembles such as the Fisk Jubilee Singers and the Tuskegee Band and Glee Club, but it also provided a more respectable space for European Americans to imitate African Americans. In fact, many white audiences learned about spirituals, slave songs, and humorous folk melodies from white Southerners who claimed a special knowledge of the former slaves.

For example, Estelle and Harriet Turner performed as a duet and promoted themselves as "Georgia girls of culture and refinement" who specialized in "quaint negro melodies."[26] According to a *Washington Times* interview with Harriet Turner in 1922, the sisters moved from Georgia to New York, likely during the 1890s, "pretty, penniless and alone . . . a-seeking wealth and fame." They received a letter of introduction from William Randolph Hearst, and as Harriet proclaimed, "The rest was easy."[27] The sisters played "their banjos and mandolins while they sang the folk-songs of the cotton field and the cane break [sic], their sweet voices, faintly tinged with the soft, delicious drawl of the South."[28] They toured the United States and Europe, catering especially to "royalty, nobility, or [other audiences of] distinction," since, Harriet said, they "paid best."[29] In 1902 First Lady Edith Roosevelt invited the women to perform at the White House.[30] The Turner sisters built their careers on their claim to "wide knowledge of the sweet appealing songs of the South," melodies authored and sung by enslaved laborers before the Civil War, and one publication claimed that the sisters' performance was authentic because their family had held slaves.[31]

Although often rhetorically associated with Southernness, their mimicry resulted in a calculated, "special study of negro stories and dialect," according to *Music News*.[32] Reflecting on this process later, Harriet observed the challenges of accessing the oral tradition of prewar African American songs and spirituals: "We searched all over the South for genuine, old-fashioned negro melodies. No longer did mam[m]y croon a sleep-song to the grandchild on her knee, while the hoe cake baked on the hearth for daddy. No longer did

Figure 4.1 Estelle and Harriet Turner, with a Miss Estes, performing as the Southern Trio. Detail of "Southern Trio and Mart King," 1900/1909, Redpath Chautauqua Collection, Special Collections, University of Iowa Libraries.

young people dance and sing to the dear old banjo. . . . We learned Creole love songs that no white woman had ever sung, and we found quaint lullabies that only negro mammies had sung before."[33] In 1925 Harriet Turner would compile and publish these songs.[34] Her words suggest how the sisters offered their performances: audiences were invited to enjoy them from within the affective experience of nostalgic memory. In the late nineteenth century, as the country moved swiftly toward regional reconciliation, recollection took a romantic turn, and tales of the South often were coupled with depictions of the faithful, happy slave. For white platform performers, the imitation of black folk stories and songs claimed to be an authentic recollection of a romantic past.

Distinct from both the minstrel show and the musical revue, imitations of black dialect became yet another important stage performance at the turn of the century that provided both instruction and entertainment. This was particularly evident in the press that surrounded the popular "monodramist" Josephine Able Chilton. Described as "a typical southern woman, beautiful in person, attractive in manners and with a voice whose cadences are like music," Chilton experienced commercial success on the lyceum and chautauqua circuits through her ability to imitate African American dialect and laughter.[35] Her advertising circular claimed that her parents "were among the pioneer settlers of Oxford, Miss.," and her Southern roots were used to legitimize her portrayals.[36] The *Chattanooga News* declared, "Being of southern blood, she thoroughly understands and appreciates the negro, and her impersonations were perfect when introducing the negro dialect in the fascinating stories by southern writers."[37] Audiences were encouraged to compare her performance to the actual lives and behaviors of her subjects. The *Lyceum Magazine* praised Chilton for her "inimitable" work portraying "dialect stories of the southern negro" and declared, as an addendum, "Of course you must have first-hand knowledge of the negro of the South to appreciate her art."[38]

Chilton's repertoire included dramatic readings of popular stories by Thomas Nelson Page, Ruth McEnery Stuart, and Joel Chandler Harris that relied on racial caricatures. An 1897 *New York Tribune* report of one such performance noted, "Mrs. William Calvin Chilton . . . is considered a great success in her portrayal of the Southern darky. Mrs. Chilton was a delegate to the recent convention of elocutionists, and made a decided hit in a reading from Ruth McEnery Stuart."[39] Chilton's reviewers frequently acknowledged that they had received an education about who and what African Americans were along with an evening of amusement. The rhetoric of white performers like Chilton asserted a knowledge of the South and, especially, a particular vision of Southern blackness that they offered to the rest of the nation. This was particularly true of Polk Miller.

In 1895 the *New York Observer and Chronicle* reported that the summer season at Chautauqua, New York, was remarkable for the "draught on the Southern states for some of their best talent." According to the review, "Gen. John B. Gordon, United States senator from Georgia, thrilled the great audience in his very sensible and eloquent lecture on 'The Last Days of the Confederacy.' Rev. Dr. A. W. Lamar, of Galveston, Tex., was enthusiastically received in his lectures on the Old New South. Mr. Polk Miller, of Virginia, though young on the lecture platform, won a lasting reputation in his vivid representations of old times down South."⁴⁰ Miller was a Confederate army veteran, the owner of a pharmaceutical business in Richmond, and a rising star of late nineteenth-century lyceum and chautauqua stages.

Miller grew up in Prince Edward County, Virginia, and "spent a great deal of time with his father's slaves."⁴¹ He claimed to have been fascinated with black dialect, culture, and music. He learned to play the banjo from one of the slaves on the plantation, but as he approached adulthood he put the instrument aside because, he said, the banjo "was looked upon as a 'nigger insterment' and beneath the notice of the cultivated."⁴² Miller attended his first local Chautauqua Society in October 1889, but according to Jacques Vest, he found very little there to "excite his imagination." Then in 1892 he accepted an invitation to perform at the society's closing ceremony. Vest writes that Miller performed "the banjo tunes and dialect recitals that he had so long hidden from his respectable neighbors." He was so well received that he began performing on a semiregular basis, and within two years he had made appearances in Richmond, Washington, Atlanta, and Chicago. Vest writes that at first "Miller developed a solo act best characterized as a 'lecture' or 'address.'"⁴³ During his act he would tell stories of the Old South, sometimes speaking in the first person and sometimes in black character.

Like other white performers of his era, Miller characterized the antebellum South in romantic terms. He called it a "Garden of Eden for white man and black man alike." He claimed, "The best, the dearest and the truest friends that [white men of the South] ever had were the colored boys with whom they played on the farm."⁴⁴ Not everyone agreed with his characterization. While white audiences found his performance comical and endearing, African American audience members did not. A delegation who attended the New York Chautauqua in 1895 sent a letter to the organizers objecting to his performance. They wrote that Miller's "picture was not that of the aspiring negro of the South, thousands of whom fill the schools supported by the churches and philanthropists of the North. We feel that a great injustice has been done those negroes and those who are members of the Chautauqua in having only that grotesque and illiterate side of the negro presented, and by one who is not his friend."⁴⁵ Reactions like this did not discourage Miller from his new career; he expanded the act, adding a black quartet. The small troupe performed as Polk Miller and His Old South Quartette for the next thirteen years. In 1909, the group recorded songs on audio cylinders for the Edison Company.⁴⁶

The addition of a black quartet highlighted the questions of authority and authenticity that were at the heart of racial mimesis. Richard Mook writes that Miller was able "to harness the diverse and powerfully nostalgic quartet repertory from black-face minstrelsy including sentimental ballads, spirituals (and parodies of spirituals), and other dialect songs."[47] Sharing the stage with black singers legitimized his performance. Miller went so far as to claim that his biracial troupe offered a superior representation of black music and culture when compared to the then popular ensembles comprising only African Americans. Barbara L. Webb notes that after Polk Miller added the quartet, his advertisements contrasted their performances with those of "the students from 'Colored Universities,' who dress in pigeon-tailed coats, patent leather shoes, white shirt fronts, and who are advertised to sing Plantation Melodies but do not." Miller's broadside declared that unlike such groups as the Fisk Jubilee Singers, the black musicians in his ensemble "do not try to let you see how nearly a Negro can act the White Man while parading in a dark skin." The members of Miller's quartet were described as "uncultivated" and "natural," allegedly proving that they, and Miller by association, were the real reflections of Southern blackness.[48] According to this logic, people of color who dressed in tuxedos and sang in a manner that revealed their classical training were only imitating white characteristics to hide their natural difference. This logic established a strange dichotomy between the behavior of white and black performers. When European Americans imitated African Americans, they purportedly revealed the authentic nature of blackness, but when African Americans imitated European Americans, the dominant presumption seemed to be that they were perverse originals. Nathaniel Shaler's logic would lead to the conclusion that blacks used their remarkable mimetic abilities to obscure their true selves in a false image of whiteness.

Perverse Originals? African American Forms of Imitation and Entertainment

Attempts to distinguish Miller's ensemble from African American performers who also performed the sorrow songs reveal just how significant and complicated imitation was at the turn of the twentieth century. The imitation of race and culture had become an expression of social knowledge concerning inherent racial ontologies that allegedly separated African and European Americans. It was central to Shaler's claim that black and white Americans were very different despite what a casual assessment might conclude. African American stage performers may have contributed to Shaler's concern that inattentive observers might presume the races were similar. Whereas white imitations of supposed black culture and behavior sought to demonstrate how different the races were, black imitations of culture marked as white questioned whether those distinctions existed at all. A good example of the disruptive potential of racial mimesis is evident in the post–Civil War musical careers of two African American sisters.

In 1867, at the ages of ten and twelve, Anna Madah Hyers and Emma Louise Hyers enthralled an audience in San Francisco with their operatic recital. The *San Francisco Chronicle* declared that "those who heard them last evening were unanimous in their praises, saying that their rare natural gifts would insure for them a leading position among the prima donnas of the age. Miss Madah has a pure, sweet soprano voice, very true, even, and flexible, of remarkable compass and smoothness. . . . Miss Louise is a natural wonder, being a fine alto-singer, and also the possessor of a pure tenor-voice."[49] From 1871 to 1876, the sisters toured New England to similar acclaim. Their success drew the attention of James Redpath, and in 1875 the Redpath Lyceum Bureau of Boston took over their professional management and transformed the Hyers Sisters Concert Company into a dramatic troupe with a black supporting cast. Redpath announced in August 1875, "The Sisters are the most wonderful vocalists that the colored race in this country has so far produced. The Company will try and bring out an original Operetta for next season, illustrative of the progress of the colored race."[50]

The Hyers Sisters' performances exemplify a type of imitation that philosopher Elizabeth Belfiore calls "versatile mimesis." As discussed above, Plato was ambivalent about imitation, acknowledging its beneficial role in education but maintaining a reservation about its potential to corrupt citizens. Belfiore argues that Plato's real concern was not with obvious, mundane acts of imitation, but with a type or practice of versatile mimesis. In this type, a person imitates the actions or virtues of someone else so perfectly that the audience no longer views the performance as an impersonation. The imitation becomes real. For example, a person imitating birdcalls so perfectly that an audience believes it hears a bird is one example of versatile mimesis. Convincing bird impersonations are an innocuous example, but Plato believed that versatile mimesis could undermine social cohesion by presenting a false representation so convincingly that audiences accepted the perverse version as an accurate reflection of reality.[51] It is possible to read the Hyers Sisters' performances as precisely this type of versatile mimesis.

The Hyers Sisters Concert Company developed musical dramas with the Redpath Bureau on themes such as Southern plantation life and the progress of African Americans after the Civil War. At the same time, Anna Madah and Emma Louise also performed cultural forms traditionally dominated by European Americans, such as opera, *within* the black cultural scenes of their plays. In an era when racial difference was thought to exclude normatively white expressions from African American performers and black situations, the Hyers Sisters Concert Company played with the truth about black character by mixing allegedly distinct racial forms. Theater historian Jocelyn Buckner writes that the sisters were popular among white and black audience members precisely because they moved back and forth across the color line with such ease.[52]

Their act of versatile mimesis was not a form of passing. The Hyers Sisters were proud of their African heritage, but their performances illustrated that popular knowledge about black culture did not define them or their ability. They sang the most popular European operettas of their day, but they also sang slave-era spirituals. They performed in the finest concert halls, but they sometimes traveled with lowbrow black minstrel shows. They performed plays that featured African scenes and costumes but sang music that reflected European aesthetics. As actors, they imitated the habits of various characters, not just moving back and forth between racial identities but also across the lines of gender. Emma Louise's alto voice fit well with male roles, and together the sisters performed duets and romantic sketches as lovers. They imitated different musical styles so successfully that their performance was no longer viewed as an imitation and their racial identity no longer seemed to matter to audiences. Buckner writes, "The Hyers Sisters' manipulations of their vocal sound and their audiences' aural reception of it, in combination with their corporeal identities, created an opaque performance event onto and into which audiences and critics could read a myriad of possibilities for the performers' artistic capacities and socially constructed identities."[53]

The two women were so adept at moving back and forth across the color line that their performances prompted audiences to consider that there was no single identity for African Americans after all. Perhaps people of African descent were "the same" as whites because they shared similar capacities of intelligence and accomplishment. Consider this review, which appeared on 19 December 1871, after the sisters' debut in Cleveland:

> [The Hyers Sisters] had been announced as singers of more than ordinary accomplishments, and withal were colored girls from the "Pacific Slope," which is noted for its production of wonders. . . . They were

called to break down the barrier which had so long interposed itself between Society and Art. But as real Art has no prejudice, the task was not so difficult as might be supposed. They were received wherever they made their appearance with respect and after being seen and heard, their merits were acknowledged; and we find the highest compliments extended from sources where least expected.[54]

The Hyers Sisters became a fixture in many towns and cities along the East Coast, and newspapers like the *Bangor Daily Whig and Courier* gleefully announced each return visit. It is interesting to note that by 1875, Anna and Emma's race was rarely mentioned in these accounts. In the entertainment ecology of the nineteenth century, black performers typically were marked as black. The fact that the Hyers Sisters could be referenced apart from a racial designation indicates both their celebrity status and the subtle way they had shifted their identities from the stereotypes that haunted people of color both on and off the stage.

The importance of this versatile mimesis from within the context of a respectable public stage should not be underestimated. Strategic acts of black imitation that resisted racism were already taking place in vaudeville acts, but refining that behavior into a form that could exist on a lyceum circuit was an important innovation. In some respects, the Hyers Sisters and Redpath were taking advantage of a unique situation. As the post-Reconstruction lyceum blended its educational mission with more commercial endeavors, the Hyers Sisters moved into new theatrical territory. With the support of Redpath, the small troupe developed two popular examples of musical theater—*Out of Bondage* (1876) and *Peculiar Sam; or, The Underground Railroad* (1879). Redpath's advertising circular described the play *Out of Bondage* as "novel and ingenious." With the inclusion of Sam Lucas, a popular black minstrel performer of the era, the troupe engaged in "the most beautiful music, comprising plantation, jubilee and slave songs." Nevertheless, insisted the circular, "this company must not be confounded with a 'minstrel show.' It is entirely novel in its character and is a high-class dramatic and musical entertainment, appealing to the most cultivated portion of the community as well the general amusement seeker."[55]

The sisters did reflect aspects of traditional minstrel comedy, but they simultaneously incorporated the recital styles that many presumed to be the exclusive domain of Europeans and European Americans. A clever business decision, this choice also opened the door of black performance to white audiences and exposed audiences to new networks of meaning. The

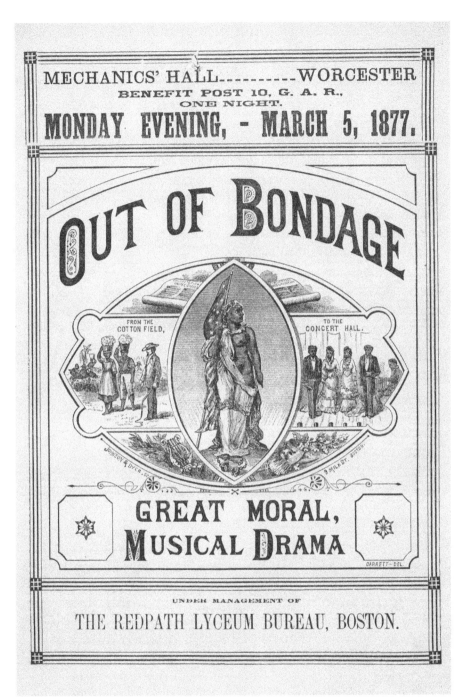

Figure 4.2 Playbill for a March 1877 benefit performance of the Hyers Sisters' *Out of Bondage*, Worcester, Massachusetts. Courtesy of the American Antiquarian Society.

Hyers Sisters performed their strategic act of versatile mimesis in the same spaces where, on other nights, ethnologists, phrenologists, and white Southern storytellers argued that the racial differences between white and black Americans were real, inherent, and inescapable. Thus, in many respects, the Hyers Sisters represented the opportunity and promise of equality that many African Americans hoped for after the Civil War. Certainly James Redpath viewed *Out of Bondage* and *Peculiar Sam* as progressive statements about the evils of slavery and the possibilities of freedom. It does not seem coincidental that the Hyers Sisters' career began during Reconstruction and ended at some point between 1891 and 1893.[56] This was a period of great contingency in the United States when many African Americans insisted on equal rights while many European Americans resisted that effort.[57] This tension was at the heart of the social anxiety Shaler called "the Negro Problem," and acts of versatile mimesis such as those performed by the Hyers Sisters seem to be precisely what Shaler worried about most.

The versatile mimesis of the Hyers Sisters had an important precedent from an earlier period of social conflict, the late antebellum era. In 1857, the African American abolitionist and novelist William Wells Brown introduced audiences to his play titled *The Escape; or, A Leap for Freedom*. It featured multiple dramatis personae. Brown presented all the characters himself, giving recitations at lyceum halls in the Northeast and Midwest.[58] He charged patrons ten cents apiece. In an 1858 review, Henry C. Wright declared, "Nobody could write such a drama but one who, himself, had been a slave, and had been born and trained in the mysteries of that 'sum of all villainies,' American slavery. The Drama is written with much power, and Mr. Brown reads it with a most happy dramatic effect. The audience listened to his reading—or, rather, reciting—with deepest interest, and the only regret seemed to be, that it was too short, though the delivery of it occupied an hour and a quarter."[59] Brown's recitals were so successful that the *Liberator* reported that he quit his position with the American Anti-Slavery Society to earn a living from his lyceum performances.[60]

Northern abolitionist audiences received Brown's performance in much the same way that they read *Uncle Tom's Cabin*: though fictional, the play's events, people, and situations seemed to many an accurate reflection of life under slavery. The play contained a comedic, though cutting, account of slaveholders. It contrasted the horrors of sexual exploitation under slavery against a romantic love affair between two slaves who expressed their affection in the sentimental style of nineteenth-century fiction. It even depicted a house slave, Cato, who exhibited all the negative behaviors associated with the stereotypes of minstrelsy. Cato's broken dialect, his exaggerated affectations, his frequent use of the term *nigger*, his willingness to blame others to avoid responsibility for his own misdeeds, and even descriptions of his appearance convey the presumption that at least some African Americans were perverse originals quite different from the white majority.

But why would Brown and his abolitionist audiences find any pleasure in such a character? There are at least three potential answers to this question. First, white abolitionists were not free from the prejudice that made portrayals like Cato funny to the general population. Second, even as they laughed, audiences could take comfort in the idea that Cato represented the perverting influence of slavery, not the immutable character of an entire race. Abolitionists often argued that bondage destroyed people's character. It made the white master mean, lazy, indolent, and irreligious; it made the slave servile, ignorant, and imitative. In many respects, Cato offers a cautionary lesson about what slavery could do to the mind and morals of a human being. Third, from the perspective of the author and performer William Wells Brown, Cato provides an illustration of how imitation could be a form of resistance and a mode of self-transformation.

Consider the first scene in which Cato appears, helping his master Dr. Gaines with his medical practice:

> DR. G: Well, Cato, have you made the batch of ointment that I ordered?
> CATO: Yes, massa; I dun made de intment, an' now I is making the bread pills. De tater pills is up on the top shelf.
> DR. G: I am going out to see some patients. If any gentlemen call, tell them I shall be in this afternoon. If any servants come, you attend to them. . . . Feel their pulse, look at their tongues, bleed them, and give them each a dose of calomel. Tell them to drink no cold water, and to take nothing but water gruel.
> CATO: Yes, massa; I'll tend to 'em.
> [*Exit Dr. Gaines, L.*]
> CATO: I allers knowed I was a doctor, an' now de ole boss has put me at it, I muss change my coat. Ef any niggers comes in, I wants to look suspectable. Dis jacket don't suit a doctor; I'll change it. [*Exit Cato—immediately returning in a long coat.*] Ah! Now I looks like a doctor. Now I can bleed, pull teef, or cut off a leg. Oh! Well, well, ef I aint put de pill stuff an' de intment stuff togedder. By golly, dat ole cuss will be made when he finds it out, won't he? Nebber mind, I'll make it up in pills, and when de flour is on dem, he won't know what's in 'em.[61]

Note, first, that the subservient Cato is not actually submissive. Despite his repeated "Yes, massa," he has not completed the work that Dr. Gaines asked of him. Moreover, he seems perfectly willing to trick Dr. Gaines rather than to do as he was told. Cato is the trickster narrator that William Wells Brown utilized in much of his writing. John Ernest writes that Brown frequently seemed to give white audiences precisely what they expected, but often in ways that commented on or undermined those very expectations.[62]

Note, as well, that Cato states he always knew he was a doctor. Cato is a doctor not because of the authority of Dr. Gaines; he is a doctor because he cannot be anything else. It is simply who he is. When Dr. Gaines entrusts him with medical duties, Gaines is only recognizing Cato's abilities, giving him permission to pull teeth, take a pulse, bleed patients, and examine tongues. Cato explains these "facts" when he flirts with a house servant called Miss Tapioca. He boasts, "Did you know, Miss Tappy, dat I is de head doctor 'bout dis house? I beats de ole boss all to pieces." Tapioca replies, "I hev hearn dat you bleeds and pulls teef." Cato states, "Yes, Miss Tappy; massa could not get along widout me, for massa was made a doctor by books; but I is a natural doctor.... So you see I can't be nuffin' but a doctor, while massa is a bunglin' ole cuss at de bissness."[63]

The fact that Cato fancies himself a doctor is intended as comedy, and it does play on the stereotypes popular in the blackface minstrel shows of the antebellum era. Cato, for example, extracts the wrong tooth from one African American patient who comes to see him. Yet despite Cato's bungling manner, his dialogue, as impersonated by Brown, poses some hard questions for the audience. What makes a doctor a doctor? Is it the ability to bleed a patient? Cato can do that. Is it the capacity to take a pulse and recommend treatment? Cato does that as well. Is it the ability to pull a tooth? Well, after his initial mistake, Cato removes the right tooth, and the patient's pain is eased. In most respects, including the appearance of respectability, Cato appropriates the role of physician in a manner that imitates his master. Cato says that he is a doctor because he was "born" a doctor, but Brown's narrative seems to indicate that Cato becomes a doctor because he imitates his master so well. Dr. Gaines does nothing in this play that Cato cannot and does not also do. Thus, if one is to question Cato's qualifications to practice medicine, then Dr. Gaines's credentials must be questioned as well. It is Dr. Gaines who first prescribes a dose of calomel (a purgative) and no cold water for all black patients, regardless of their malady. While the dialect and affectations of Brown's text seem to depict Cato as the stereotype of a black fool, the plot hints at the possibility that the white master, Dr. Gaines, is first the fool. Cato is just imitating him.

The imitation in Brown's play is multilayered. Cato, as performed by Brown, is a mimetic performance of the nineteenth-century entertainer who blacked his face to transform himself into the white image of blackness. At the same time, within the context of the play Cato imitates the behavior of his master, dressing in a long coat to "look like a doctor." This idea, that clothes can change one's appearance and alter a person's identity, is reinforced after Cato decides to abandon his master and join the young black lovers who have run North to secure their freedom. Having exchanged clothes with Dr. Gaines while he slept, Cato enters the street wearing his master's apparel. He declaims:

> I wonder ef dis is me? By golly, I is free as a frog. But maybe I is mistaken; maybe dis ain't me. Cato, is dis you? Yes, seer. Well, now it is me, an' I em a free man. But, stop! I muss change my name, kase ole massa might foller me, and somebody might tell him dat dey seed Cato; so I'll change my name, and den he won't know me ef he sees me. Now what shall I call myself? I'm now in a suspectable part of de country, an' I muss have a suspectable name. Ah! I'll call myself Alexander Washington Napoleon Pompey Caesar. Dar, now, dat's a good long, suspectable name, and every body will suspect me.[64]

Again, as in the earlier scene, this soliloquy plays on stereotypes and would probably produce laughter from Brown's audience. It is foolish to think that the change of a name provides respect or that wearing Dr. Gaines's clothes as a disguise will transform Cato into someone he was not before. Yet listening carefully to the drama reveals that this is precisely what transpired for Cato's master. In the third scene of Act II, about midway through the play, Dr. Gaines arrives home with good news. He has been elected colonel of the militia. He immediately declares to his wife that he no longer wishes to go by the title Doctor but by his new title, Colonel. "Call me Colonel, my dear. . . . If you will call me Colonel, other people will, and I want you to set the example. Come, my darling, call me Colonel, and I'll give you any thing you wish for."[65] With this bribe, Mrs. Gaines begins to call the doctor Colonel in about every third or fourth word of dialogue. In return for this favor, she demands a new watch, bracelets, a shawl, and clothing that, she says, will make her look like a proper lady. The white master has a new name, and his wife, new clothes. Both believe that they are transformed for the better by their changed circumstances.

In *Bodies in Dissent*, Daphne Brooks writes that Cato's soliloquy speaks "on dual frequencies as both captor and captive, gentleman and minstrel clown." "Cato," she says, "(re)dresses himself both in the role of the suspicious fugitive as well as the respectable master, conflating and perverting the boundaries between each role."[66] We agree in part. But while Brooks sees Cato's soliloquy as a transformation of the character from a "feckless burnt-cork puppet" into a destabilizing force in Southern culture, we contend that although he has moved from slavery to freedom, his character has not changed. He was never a "burnt-cork puppet" but only an unstable imitation of that stereotype. Likewise, despite Cato's claims at the end of the play, he is not a respectable Christian who has forsaken women, drink, and cussing. He has simply found himself in a position to imitate the manner of someone more respectable than his former master. In an imagined future Cato may become the preacher that he aspires to be on the play's final page, but we suspect that even then this fictional character would be performing yet another imitation.

To interpret Cato as a skilled imitator, another example of versatile mimesis, is not to impugn his intelligence or his agency within the world of Brown's play. It is to recognize, instead, how imitation in the nineteenth and early twentieth centuries served multiple purposes, sometimes as a tool of domination but also as a destabilizing force in racial ecology. These possibilities were not lost on the black leaders of that period. Frederick Douglass, for example, was adamant that imitation had been a strategic mode of survival for the black community. After the Civil War, he argued that imitation could teach citizenship to freedmen and women through praxis. Imitation was not a means to become like European Americans; rather, for Douglass it was, as Kirt H. Wilson states, a path to "cultural hybridity."[67] In 1877, Alexander Crummell voiced his understanding of imitation in a Thanksgiving Day sermon titled "The Destined Superiority of the Negro." People of African descent across the world possessed exactly those virtues that had sustained the great cultures of human history, he said. And what are those virtues? He declared that they were "vitality, plasticity, receptivity, imitation, family feeling, veracity, and the sentiment of devotion." He stated further that "the flexibility of the negro character is not only universally admitted; it is often formulated into a slur. The race is possessed of a nature more easily moulded than any other class of men." But while some viewed this feature as a failing, Crummell declared that imitation was a foundation on which the race's "future superiority" could be built.[68] More than this, he redefined for his audience what imitation meant. His imitation was more in keeping with at least one conceptualization of the classical theory of mimesis. It was both an individual behavior and a collective action; it was a process of refashioning the self that had widespread social implications.

Conclusion

In many respects, the racial mimesis that appeared on the public platform of the nineteenth and early twentieth centuries seemed to be precisely what supporters of segregation feared as it became an entrenched part of American life. The defenders of Jim Crow argued strenuously that white and black Americans were fundamentally different, which was why they must occupy different places in society. It was the duty of white citizens to act as the head and mind of society, while black citizens were its feet and hands. Black inferiority was a crucial part of the cultural common sense of white supremacy, but that ideology was undermined so long as black subjectivity was viewed as complex and even contradictory. Successful acts of onstage imitation were a direct challenge to any simplistic definition of blackness. It was not just that individuals like William Wells Brown or the Hyers Sisters contradicted the idea of black inferiority by their success. One can always find the rule in the exceptions. Rather, the more radical challenge that black and white racial imitative performances created was to suggest that the much-affirmed difference between the races was simply a matter of enculturation and material opportunity. In the right circumstances, black Americans could embody whiteness and white Americans could embrace blackness.

In 1913, Polk Miller, the Virginia pharmacist who became famous touring the United States with a black quartet, disbanded his small troupe. Miller would complain bitterly that he could no longer make a living as a performer because of the prejudice that Northerners felt toward African Americans. Miller was likely correct that racism contributed to the demise of his career, but we contend that he was wrong that audiences had rejected the music he played or the Old South Quartette. The interpretive insights of this essay suggest that perhaps his white audiences had become uncomfortable because they could no longer distinguish his whiteness from the blackness he performed. Standing on the stage next to African American performers, Miller was confusing. His performance did not fit the popular knowledge of the 1910s, which, by then, sustained a rigid belief that black Americans should be separate and unequal in every aspect of public and private life. Like the Hyers Sisters and William Wells Brown, Miller had become the versatile mimetic actor who undermined stable racial identities and hierarchy. Miller had become the threat to social norms that Nathaniel Shaler had warned against when he argued for a vigilance that would recognize black and white difference and keep each race in its proper place.

PART 2

DISTINCTIVE VOICES

5

A LYCEUM DIASPORA:
HILARY TEAGE AND A LIBERIAN CIVIC IDENTITY

Bjørn F. Stillion Southard

In 1845, the Liberia Lyceum was created in Monrovia as a forum for the sharing and advancement of knowledge. It thus shared a purpose with its peer institutions in the United States. Yet the membership and context of this lyceum differentiated it from its U.S. counterparts. The Liberia Lyceum comprised settler-colonists—most of whom were born in the United States—who had felt the harshness of racism in their service as slaves or their limited liberty as free persons of color and who had traveled to Liberia by some combination of force, choice, assistance, and coercion in the hope of attaining freedom.[1] The Liberia Lyceum operated within a colony, less than twenty-five years old, in which settler-colonists struggled with disease, famine, limited resources, and violent engagements with the native population.[2] At the time of the Liberia Lyceum's founding, Liberia had not yet declared its independence from the benevolent societies that established and governed the colonies since their formation in 1820, most notably the American Colonization Society (ACS). The Liberia Lyceum's commitment to knowledge and education may have resembled that of lyceums in the United States, but there can be little question that its circumstances make it a distinctive lyceum of the English-speaking world.

This chapter seeks to extend scholarship on American lecture culture by situating the Liberia Lyceum as part of a lyceum diaspora. The concept of diaspora seems fitting, as Liberia Lyceum members were geographically dispersed from the country of their birth (the United States), but they retained and transformed many of its customs and traditions. The notion of a lyceum diaspora contributes to a line of inquiry that traces how lyceums interacted with culture, broadly conceived. Such a trajectory has been charted by scholars who examine how the lyceum served as a "contact zone" for the meeting of different cultures and ideas.[3] In one sense, lyceums provided a space in which new ideas and foreign cultures could be explored without leaving one's hometown. The topics of a lecture offered some transcultural contact within the familiar confines of the local lecture hall. Woman suffrage, African American rights, Egyptian travel, and Māori culture are just a few lecture subjects that have received scholarly attention.[4] Lyceums also provided cultural connections in which Anglo-American lecture norms were reproduced and refigured. Tom F. Wright's work on the transatlantic "Anglo-American commons" explores the cross-cultural relationship between lecture cultures of the United States and Britain. Wright describes a "commons" as an investment in "traditions, practices, or heritage" by a people with the "shared resources of culture, language, and history." Wright challenges the dominant narrative that the lyceum produced a novel rhetorical model that garnered immediate adherence in the United States. Instead, Wright notes that there was "an uneasy dialectic of fascination with and rejection of such models." By examining this "uneasy" relationship through the transatlantic interactions of American and British lecture cultures, Wright argues for "an enlargement of lecturing's geographic and thematic scope."[5] Analyzing the Liberia Lyceum's participation in a lyceum diaspora further enlarges the lyceum's geographic scope while also attending to the connections (and disconnections) of disparate groups with their American origins.

In this chapter I explore how the Liberia Lyceum offered a space for settler-colonists to develop a black Liberian civic identity by rehearsing and revising American and African American rhetorical norms. Toward this end, I begin by providing a brief account of the formation of the English-speaking colonies in Liberia to show the colonies' complicated relationship with the United States. Next, I discuss the norms of the American lyceum movement of the antebellum era and the ways in which the Liberia Lyceum adopted and adapted them. I then analyze a speech by Liberia Lyceum founder Hilary Teage in which he argues for the importance of lyceums in the lives of settler-colonists. Finally, I make some concluding observations about the notion of a lyceum diaspora and the methodologies by which we might examine this concept.

The Creation of American Colonies in Liberia

The American colonies in Liberia developed as a result of the predominantly white-led movement to relocate free blacks to Africa. Thomas Jefferson discussed gradual emancipation in his 1788 book *Notes on the State of Virginia*, yet he also wrote that the two races could not coexist and later suggested "expatriation" as the solution.[6] A formal colonization organization coalesced in the waning days of 1816, counting Northerners and Southerners among its supporters.[7] The American Society for Colonizing the Free People of Colour of the United States (later shortened to American Colonization Society) aimed to "drain them off"—"them" being the free black population of the United States—for many reasons: to moralize the "benighted" African continent with Christianity, to provide African Americans with liberties that they could not receive in the United States, and to create a safer environment for the persistence of a domestic slave labor system.[8] (Of course, the framing of the movement varied depending on the advocate's outlook on slavery and his or her audience.) In 1820, the first settler-colonists arrived on the western coast of Africa from the United States as a result of the colonization scheme. By the late 1840s, the ACS had transported more than five thousand African Americans to the Monrovia colony.[9]

Settler-colonists in Liberia remained connected with the United States. Colonization did not function as a break from American life; rather, many settler-colonists saw it as an opportunity to realize more fully those rights and privileges they were unable to access in the land of their birth. Despite their freedom from plantation life, many of the settler-colonists who were manumitted slaves engaged in robust correspondence with their former masters in the United States. The letters often reported the mundane details of colonial life, asked about family and friends associated with the plantation, and requested items like newspapers, tobacco, books, tools, and rum.[10] These connections help to illustrate the problematic nature of the argument that African Americans would happily emigrate because they were being returned to their homeland. Instead, settler-colonists found themselves in a new environment, often without extended family and close friends, attempting to adapt physically, agriculturally, socially, economically, and politically. In some respects, this connection was involuntary, as the U.S.-based ACS governed the colony until 1847.[11] Yet even in the act of asserting autonomy, the influence of American traditions on settler-colonists was clear.

The Liberia Lyceum and American Lyceum Culture

The term *lyceum* often refers to a movement for popular education that developed through debating and lecturing in the early to mid-nineteenth century. Antebellum U.S. lyceums included instruction and exercises in speech and debate, activities common in organizations called literary societies.[12] Such was also the case with the Liberia Lyceum. The blurry definitional lines between a lyceum and a literary society did not negate for settler-colonists the purpose of the institution: popular education. In the United States and in Liberia, both terms—*popular* and *education*—defined the rhetorical culture of civic lyceums. The relative heterogeneity and lack of education of the audience—particularly when compared to those who attended literary societies in colleges, the long-standing loci of lecture learning—changed what one could expect of the listeners. The broad circulation of messages to a popular audience also affected the educational content. Lectures that addressed issues relevant to the locale and provided entertainment at the same time fared best.[13]

African Americans were often excluded from participating in Anglo-American lyceum culture owing to the oppressive realities of racism. Often faced with exclusion, African Americans had to adapt to white prejudice as they sought entry into Anglo-American lyceums or built their own organizations. Creating a sketch of Anglo-American lyceum rhetorical norms is essential to understanding how these norms were transferred to and translated in the Liberia Lyceum.

Beginning in 1826, but borrowing from the British tradition that came before, the American lyceum movement started as a project to promote mutual education. Josiah Holbrook, writing in the *American Journal of Education* of that year, advocated for "associations for mutual instruction in the sciences."[14] It is important to note that although Holbrook placed an emphasis on science, he listed "lectures or conversation" as the first requirement for ventures into popular education.[15] Holbrook's advocacy captured a broader sentiment that rhetoric was an implicit part of creating and sharing knowledge. As Angela G. Ray explains, "Debating and persuasive speaking were firmly fixed in the minds of many nineteenth-century individuals as an inextricable part of 'education.'"[16] Yet the expectation was that the lyceum lecturer "displayed knowledge rather than asserted strong argument."[17] Occasionally, lecturers made communication the subject of their presentation, such as Dr. A. Comstock's presentation on "Elocution, and the Cure of Stammering."[18] In the main, however, rhetorical prowess was practiced more than discussed in the lyceum.

Although not often the overt subject of lectures, rhetoric was vital to the mission of lyceums. Indeed, bringing popular education to the masses put rhetorical skill front and center. The attempts to draw the broadest possible audience—encompassing "children and adults, men and women, lawyers and blacksmiths, farmers and masons"—demanded a level of rhetorical proficiency to engage such a diverse audience while containing conflict and controversy.[19] According to Holbrook, the lyceum "aims at the diffusion of knowledge among all classes, all ages, and both sexes. Its doors are open as wide to the poor as to the rich."[20] Holbrook conceived of the lyceum as a republican institution, one that was open to the people and not, like colleges and universities, reserved for the elite. Even as the tenor of lyceums shifted "from mutual education to celebrity entertainment" in the 1840s and 1850s, the emphasis on rhetorical skill remained.[21]

The republican ideal of inclusion had its limits in the lyceum. In the United States, African American participation varied in Anglo-American lyceums. Ray explains, "The situation of enslaved African Americans was debated, abstractly, in white members' meetings; individual African Americans like Charlotte Forten sometimes attended sponsored public lectures; and other individuals were sometimes denied membership or equal privileges in these lyceums."[22] Not surprisingly, African Americans created separate lyceums and literary societies as places to learn and to participate in civic life. As Dorothy Porter notes, most black literary societies were created after 1828 and were located in larger Northern cities like New York and Philadelphia.[23] In the South, there were significantly fewer organizations, as one might expect. Still, there were some private literary, debating, and benevolence societies in larger Southern cities with free black populations, such as Charleston, South Carolina.[24] African Americans sought opportunities for rhetorical education and engagement, though these were severely limited by racism and the perpetuation of slavery.

Anglo-American lyceums faced their own obstacles, although they differed in kind and degree from those faced by their African American counterparts. Specifically, Anglo-American lyceums were beholden to newspapers for their success. Donald M. Scott argues that the popular lecture culture of antebellum America "was in many ways a creation of the world of print.... The system could no more have operated without print than the railroad could have operated without tracks." This relationship had benefits for both parties, but newspapers held more of the power. Newspapers served as the "essential instrument for turning a writer, educator, minister, statesman, journalist, scientist, or aspiring itinerant into an accepted 'professional' lecturer." The newspapers thus functioned as the certifying authority for what made a lecturer popular enough to command an audience. Newspapers received content and advertising revenue from lecture associations, but their reputation was not tied to the groups' success. By contrast, Scott claims, "When a town's newspaper withdrew its support and either attacked or simply ignored the institution, the lecture society had a difficult time surviving."[25] In the United States, there was little question that the lecture system was indebted to newspapers.

Settler-colonists in Liberia built on the Anglo-American lyceum tradition. Monrovia—the main location of the ACS-sponsored settler-colonists—supported numerous popular education and rhetorical societies, such as the Liberia Lyceum, the Union Mechanic Association, the Masonic Order of Liberia, and the Young Men's Lyceum.[26] Richard L. Hall emphasizes "how closely [the settler-colonists'] culture remained identified with that of their mother country."[27] Article 6 of the Liberia Lyceum Constitution provides a representative example: "The object of this Association shall be the diffusion of knowledge throughout the colony as the best method to advance not only general but individual improvement."[28] Similar statements could be found in the constitutions and bylaws of lyceums in the United States.[29] The creation of "mutual aid associations, debating, agricultural, and choral societies," Hall argues, offered familiar American cultural institutions in which settler-colonists could participate. These associations also provided "criteria by which settlers distinguished their culture from that of Africans around them"—yet another, though less positive, cultural trace from their American heritage.[30] The unfettered access by settler-colonists to these associations was an expression of a civic identity that they had not experienced in the United States.

Lyceums in the United States published pamphlets and newspapers, but none of those organs of information could match the significance of the relationship between the Liberia Lyceum and the *Liberia Herald*. In the United States, lyceums and black newspapers provided spaces for African Americans to assert their agency and to participate in public discourse, as Shirley Wilson Logan has shown.[31] In Liberia, the Liberia Lyceum and the *Liberia Herald* were uniquely connected.[32] The Liberia Lyceum owned the *Liberia Herald*, a reversal of power from what Scott argues was the traditional dynamic between lyceums and newspapers in the United States. On a local level, the connection between the Liberia Lyceum and the *Liberia Herald* was the only such relationship between a group organized by settler-colonists and a newspaper in Liberia during the transition from colonial to republican government (approximately 1845 to 1855).[33] During a period in which settler-colonists began asserting their political independence and crafting a new civic identity, institutions of education and deliberation became increasingly important. The paucity of newspapers in Liberia gave tremendous power to the few publications in the colonies.

As an institution, the Liberia Lyceum was built on similar principles and played a similar role as its Anglo-American counterparts. Popular education, available to the masses and circulated in voice and print, was a commitment shared across the Atlantic. Yet the context in which the Liberia Lyceum emerged had many significant differences from the Anglo-American lyceum. The settler-colonists who participated in the Liberia Lyceum were an unusual group in unusual circumstances. Their connectedness and disconnectedness to the United States took new forms as settler-colonists grappled with their identity in Liberia. These processes, distinct from what most Anglo-American lyceums were negotiating, suggest the ways the Liberia Lyceum took part in a lyceum diaspora that refracted, rather than reflected, its Anglo-American contemporaries.

The Liberia Lyceum, Hilary Teage, and African American Rhetorical Practice

The relationship of the Liberia Lyceum to Anglo-American lyceums was not only evident in the institutions that settler-colonists created but also in the speeches they gave in these forums. Very few of the speeches delivered at the Liberia Lyceum survive today. The extant texts are reprints from the *Liberia Herald* that were circulated within and beyond the colony. One of those speeches deserves sustained attention in the exploration of a lyceum diaspora. Hilary Teage—a founder of the Liberia Lyceum and editor of the *Liberia Herald*—addressed the lyceum on 21 May 1845 and published his remarks in the newspaper ten days later. Teage was part of a civically active family and a central figure in Monrovia rhetorical and political life. The subject of the speech was the importance of lyceums for settler-colonists. The combination of Teage's character and the subject of his speech yields a rare glimpse into how settler-colonists—or at least a very civically active one—perceived the role of lyceums in their community. In particular, Teage's speech expressed both support for and suspicions of the power of rhetoric for the civic identity of his settler-colonist audience. In making this point, Teage's speech interacted with norms of the Anglo-American lyceum and African American rhetorical practices. The result is a discourse that is both part of and apart from those traditions. I examine Teage's nuanced appreciation of lyceums first by delineating the journey that brought Teage and his family to Liberia. Second, I explicate Teage's speech to focus on his arguments about the virtues of rhetorical engagement in lyceums. Finally, I explore Teage's engagement with African American rhetorical norms.

Hilary Teage's Journey to Liberia

Hilary Teage's early life was marked by the exceptional drive and strong religious commitments of his family. Teage was born in Richmond, Virginia, in 1802. His father, Collin Teage, was a skilled craftsman who made saddles and harnesses. Collin and his family—which included his wife (Frances), son (Hilary), and daughter (Colinett)—were slaves in Richmond until he saved enough to purchase the entire family's freedom for $1,300.[34] The Teages attended First Baptist Church in Richmond, an integrated but predominantly black congregation. Although formally uneducated, the entire family could read and write. This literacy played a role in the Teages' emigration and would constitute an enduring part of Hilary Teage's character until his death in 1853. An account in the *Maryland Colonization Journal* tells of the elder Teage and his friend, Lott Carey, becoming interested in emigration to Liberia upon reading an account authored by the Reverend Samuel J. Mills and Ebenezer Burgess, both ACS agents.[35] The missionary element of colonization resonated with Teage and Carey, and Carey helped to establish the Richmond African Missionary Society in 1815 for the purpose of bringing the gospel to Africans.[36] After acquiring support from the ACS, Collin, Carey, and their families were among the second group of settler-colonists who removed to West Africa in January 1821.[37]

The Teages, and Hilary in particular, advocated for the rights that they believed were essential for the success of Liberia. Their assertion of their liberty as free persons and, thus, their equality to whites came early in the Teages' time in Africa. After a brief stint in Sierra Leone—when a Liberian colony was not yet viable—the Teages moved to Liberia only to face the tyranny of the ACS's colonial agent, a white man named Jehudi Ashmun. When the Teage family arrived in Liberia, Ashmun "unilaterally reassigned land on which some repatriates had built homes," "imposed two-days per week of public labor for each adult," and "threatened to cut off supplies to those who did not perform mandatory labor for the government."[38] The elder Teage was part of a group that resisted these policies, forcing Ashmun to abandon his position for nearly four months in 1826. Fighting for the rights of the settler-colonists to govern themselves did not end with Collin Teage's stand against Ashmun. Hilary entered politics, serving in 1835 as colonial secretary, the person in charge of the colonies but whom the ACS agent supervised. That same year Hilary Teage also became editor of the *Liberia Herald*.[39] Both positions were previously held by John Brown Russwurm, an African American man known for his role in coediting the first black newspaper in the United

States (*Freedom's Journal*) and, controversially, for his shift from abolitionist to colonizationist. Russwurm seemed to struggle in working as the intermediary between the ACS and settler-colonists, "hitting his lowest point of disillusionment with Liberia" in 1835, according to his biographer.[40] Teage, it seemed, was not disillusioned and did not struggle as Russwurm had. Not only did he serve as colonial secretary and *Liberia Herald* editor but he also was the convention secretary for the group that wrote the Monrovia Draft of the Commonwealth Constitution in 1838—an effort to reform colonial governance and to give more power to the settler-colonists. Those efforts failed to gain traction with the ACS, leading Teage and others to draft a Declaration of Independence in 1847. Almost immediately upon arrival in Liberia, then, the Teages played important roles in advocating for the rights of settler-colonists, and this advocacy eventually led to the creation of a free Republic of Liberia in 1847.

On the other hand, the Teages consistently faced situations in which the rights they sought were being challenged. Settler-colonists were promised freedom and liberty in exchange for their willingness to move to Liberia. Their relocation, they believed, would also serve a missionary purpose, bringing Christianity to the native African populations they would encounter. The ACS failed to deliver on these promises. At the germinal meeting of the ACS in 1816, Henry Clay had referred to the free black population in the United States as "peculiarly situated" and thus in need of resettlement to Africa to find freedom.[41] Being "peculiarly situated" did not end for African Americans upon their arrival in Liberia. In the United States, free blacks existed in a liminal social space between free whites and enslaved blacks. In Liberia, settler-colonists existed in a new, yet no less "peculiar" position; they were not free blacks in America, slaves in bondage, or natives of the area they now occupied. Thus, when settler-colonists were engaged in popular education at the Liberia Lyceum, the negotiation of this complex identity informed their proceedings.

Teage's Speech and Settler-Colonists' Relationship to Lyceum Culture

Given his role as a founder of the Liberia Lyceum, Teage unsurprisingly believed that lyceums were worthwhile organizations. Early in his May 1845 address, Teage stated, "The existence of our Lyceum indicates our conviction of the efficiency of associations." Still, Teage recognized the faults in lyceums, arguing, "It is to be regretted that in the eager strife of debate truth is too often forgotten in the anxiety for triumph." Recognizing the shortcomings of

Figure 5.1 The Liberian Senate, circa 1856. Drawing by Robert K. Griffin. Prints and Photographs Division, Library of Congress.

rhetoric—that truth is sometimes lost in an effort to persuade—might seem an odd move in a speech that aimed to support lyceum activities. Teage was not alone in these concerns, however, as his lament tapped into a centuries-old debate in the Western tradition about the role of rhetoric in civic discourse. In *Gorgias*, Plato equated rhetoric to cookery, arguing that rhetoric is harmful to the soul just as lavish meals are harmful to the body.[42] Plato sought to make rhetoric seem at best extraneous and at worst damaging to individuals and the polis. Concerns about rhetoric reveal far more than simply a distaste for eloquence. Instead, the criticism of rhetoric as harmful to truth often coincided with elites' fear of empowering the disempowered.[43] Discussions of rhetoric and truth were not merely philosophical endeavors divorced from context; they were often a reflection of power dynamics and the contestation over the right to speak.

Teage's position on this age-old controversy was to support rhetoric and debate rather than to decry it. Settler-colonists had long been kept from formal associations and institutions of deliberation; now they were free to participate in them. Teage's justification for debate was offered in terms that suggested the virtues needed for settler-colonists to assert their rights and to constitute their identity. Specifically, Teage argued that lyceums fostered a nimble mind, provided an arena for intellectual combat, and encouraged the unveiling of deception. Consistent with American lyceum culture, Teage mostly valorized rhetoric and debate as essential civic skills for settler-colonists. Yet Teage intermixed with this support a wariness of the ends toward which rhetoric and debate could be put.

Teage's promotion of a nimble mind through debate confronted the significant adaptations undertaken by settler-colonists. The process of discovering truths through debate demanded rhetorical activity. The purpose of the Liberia Lyceum, Teage argued, "is to educate and discipline" the intellectual capacity of settler-colonists through "vigorous exercise." Debating, Teage argued, "is a species of engagement in which the mind acquires dexterity of movement and elasticity of force." Teage's promotion of "dexterity of movement" addressed the novelty of the situation. Settler-colonists were in a new environment, often without their extended families and friends. They confronted new farming challenges, new diseases, and new hostilities, in addition to new freedoms and responsibilities. The novelty of the settler-colonists' situation led some to respond poorly to the challenge. Teage's framing of debate in terms of "movement" and "force" obliquely addressed a concern by many settler-colonists that some of their peers were being lazy.[44] More generally, Teage's connection of debate and a nimble mind implicitly refuted the long-standing belief by some that blacks were intellectually inferior to whites. Teage stated, "It is the possession of mind and its capacity of indefinite enlargement and improvement which imparts to man his dignity[,] for apart from mind wherein does he differ from the brute?" Teage adapted a common argument used to denigrate blacks—that they were closer to animals than whites—and used it to encourage the kind of educational experience that would disprove the supposed science of racial difference. A nimble mind would aid settler-colonists in addressing the challenges of their new life but also provide a sound rebuke to claims of black intellectual inferiority. By encouraging the development of a nimble mind, Teage provided a singular response to a variety of forces that challenged settler-colonists' efforts to define their new identity as citizens. It was in that context that Teage's evaluation of a nimble mind reads differently from a similar appeal offered in the developed confines of Boston or New York. In Monrovia, far more was unsettled than settled, a situation that created demands on its citizens not felt in the United States.

A second virtue encouraged in Teage's support of the lyceum was a masculine, gladiatorial engagement with issues. Describing the interaction of a debate elsewhere in his speech, Teage opined, "The enemy is met in the open field and grappled with hand-to-hand." Teage further extended the analogy of debate as physical competition, stating, "The conspicuousness of the theater—the gaze of congregated spectators—the fire of the eager eye in the hope of the approving award all combined wakens in the mind an ardor, and kindles in it an enthusiasm, and imparts to it an energy it can never hope to feel in the seclusion of the cloister." Here Teage provided a dialectical counterbalance to his earlier virtue of the nimble mind. One could not simply pursue knowledge without testing that knowledge against other ideas. The "dexterity of movement and elasticity of force" must be "whetted and edged" by debating others.[45] In elaborating this virtue, Teage continued to position the Liberia Lyceum as a place of rhetorical activity. Teage also continued to challenge the denigrated perception of African Americans pervading much Anglo-American discourse. Using the metaphor of debaters as gladiators, Teage associated the positive, martial characteristics of gladiators—ardor, heroism, fearlessness—with settler-colonists in the Liberia Lyceum. Perhaps most transgressive, however, was that Teage used a metaphor with violent undertones to talk about African American intellect, at a time when so many whites feared slave rebellions. The successful uprising in the French colony of Saint-Domingue and the rebellions of Gabriel Prosser, Denmark Vesey, and Nat Turner in the United States had created tremendous anxiety, rhetorical strategies of containment, and repressive laws to quell future action.[46] Settler-colonists were not slaves, and they were not beasts prone to violence; thus, in Teage's estimation, settler-colonists could be assertive, debating gladiators in the Liberia Lyceum in the fullest meaning of the term.

Teage's masculine framing of argumentation and debate aligned with the gendered public discourse that motivated support for colonization. Bruce Dorsey argues that "colonization reform assumed a masculine character from its inception." Settler-colonists' immigration to Liberia was often positioned in the same light as continental migration across the United States, and as Dorsey notes, "nothing was considered more manly in this era than westward expansion."[47] In his featured speech at the founding meeting of the ACS, Elias B. Caldwell dismissed the possibility that free blacks would be unwilling to move to Liberia. Caldwell opined, "What sir, are they not men? Will they not be activated by the same motives of interests and ambition, which influence other men?"[48] Female settler-colonists in Liberia had slightly more rhetorical agency than most women in the United States; according to

Carl Burrowes, Liberian women "engaged unhindered in public speaking and political activism especially if they were related by blood or marriage to politically active men."[49] Even with greater access to speak publicly, however, women were still denied voting rights and often discussed not as rhetorical gladiators but as what Linda Kerber calls republican mothers, women whose own education would allow them to rear the next generation of male patriots.[50] Teage's description of debate as gladiatorial combat relied on gender norms that, in Liberia as in the United States, heralded masculinity as an ideal of civic engagement.

Teage's third enumerated virtue of lyceums was that such groups provided a space to unmask deception. Abolitionists had long believed that colonization was a ruse of the slaveholders—an attempt to remove supposed black troublemakers (read: all free black persons) and to create a docile slave population.[51] Settler-colonists did not express the same level of disdain, yet the disconnections between their expectations and the realities of colonial life left many feeling deceived.[52] Teage used this sentiment as a rationale for settler-colonists to participate in debate. Engaging in the social activity of debate, resisting "the seclusion of the cloister," created a space to confront deception collectively. As Teage stated, "It is in these keen conflicts [debates] that the doublings and evasions of Sophistry are unraveled and exposed, and specious and imposing paradoxes laid bare." That is, Teage explicitly invited controversy into the lyceum. The experience of the settler-colonists demanded a sensitivity to duplicity, as a citizen could not naïvely accept the pronouncements of those in power. For, in Teage's estimation, "it is in the shocks that the sparks of truth are struck out."[53]

Teage's Speech and African American Rhetorical Practice

Teage's 1845 lyceum speech not only resonated with the norms of Anglo-American lyceums but also interacted with African American rhetorical practices. Although speaking in Liberia and living under different circumstances from free blacks in the United States, Teage engaged intertextually with African American rhetorical traditions, including the trope of the Talking Book. The Talking Book developed in the writings of African Americans in the late eighteenth and early nineteenth centuries as a way to describe their absence from public literary activities. "Talking book" figuratively described literature that was made by and for, that "talked" to, white audiences. The Talking Book trope signifies on the broader rhetorical context facing African Americans during this time. When African Americans undertook literary activities that were previously allowed only to Anglo-Americans—as when Phillis Wheatley published her poetry in 1773 or when others composed slave narratives—the presence of a black author was a significant transgression from the racialized social order. These early texts were not formally or stylistically marked as different from the work of white contemporaries but, as Henry Louis Gates Jr. explains, the simple act of participation in this previously segregated activity was crucial to African Americans' demonstrating their capacity for reason and constituting themselves as "speaking subjects" rather than commodities or objects. In essence, the Talking Book was the tropological manifestation of "making the white written text speak with a black voice."[54]

Furthermore, the Talking Book was part of what Elizabeth McHenry describes as African American "literary character." McHenry argues that an African American rhetor participating in a previously segregated rhetorical space "offered black Americans a way to refute widespread claims of their miserable, degraded position . . . with displays of black genius."[55] The key move was to operate within a white public sphere without any rhetorical difference, other than the quite significant difference of the rhetor's being black and making claims from that racial position. The Talking Book was not a move to revolutionize style, diction, tone, subject, or other traits, as such a radical departure from the norms might only serve as further evidence of difference and would, by extension, further marginalize an already subjugated race. A text thus employs the rhetorical conventions of the dominant Anglo-American culture in the service of, and authored by, African Americans.

The intertextuality and tension of the Talking Book trope come into relief when Teage's speech is compared to texts that are similarly supportive of the lyceum movement but authored by Anglo-American authors. Two decades before Teage's address, Josiah Holbrook asserted that the creation of "associations for mutual instruction" would spread "with great rapidity" and raise "the moral and intellectual taste of our countrymen."[56] Individuals would cultivate their "moral and intellectual tastes," thereby making the American nation better. Similarly, in Liberia in 1845, Teage believed that lyceums were concerned with the "indefinite enlargement and improvement" that makes a man "differ from the brute."[57] Both Holbrook and Teage extolled the virtues of the lyceum for the improvement of democratic citizens. Holbrook argued, "Every Lyceum is, in fact, a safeguard of liberty."[58] For Teage, the manner in which lyceums developed human faculties helped to temper the deleterious effects of passions on governance. Teage opined, "That apparently simplest, and certainly the most unstable of all forms of government, I mean a democracy has been ever found among an ignorant people. . . . The instability of this form of society and the evils resulting from it are undoubtedly owing to pride in ignorance. . . . The education of the people then should be an object of primary importance, as upon it depend in a very great degree their own happiness and the ability of their institutions."[59] In many ways, Teage's speech rehearsed Holbrook's justification for the creation of lyceums. Both sought broad audiences and viewed education as a necessary good for public life. The intertextual dialogue between such justifications—across time, space, and race—reinforced the connections of the Liberia Lyceum to American lyceums and of Teage to other proponents of the value of such associations.

Teage's mostly laudatory comments about lyceum activity elided discussion of racial difference until the end of the speech. Befitting the Talking Book trope, the primary marker of difference throughout most of the address was the race of the rhetor rather than the content of the message. However, Teage's conclusion brought difference closer to the surface of the text by recognizing the difficult position of settler-colonists. Teage admitted that the position of settler-colonists was "the most difficult to describe."[60] Settler-colonists "enjoyed privileges and exercised rights," he said, but only "under the patronage of the American Colonization Society."[61] Teage told his audience that it was "idle" to "enter on the discussion of right abstractedly or speculatively considered." His discouragement of speculation was tempered shortly afterward, when Teage alluded to Acts 8:1 in describing the situation facing settler-colonists: "Like wanderers from Samaria we shall find it certain death to remain here or to return to the city. Hope can be indulged only in going forward."[62] Teage discouraged the idleness of speculating about the rights of settler-colonists as citizens, but he also intimated that the path to achieving rights was akin to the journey of the wandering Samarians. It was in this juxtaposition of resisting speculation, yet acknowledging the wandering journey and the hope needed to endure it, that the complexity of Teage's address offered a distinctive black voice and pushed beyond the white referent text of the Talking Book trope.

Settler-colonists in Liberia saw value in lyceums and brought the traditions of these organizations with them from the United States. The Liberia Lyceum also provided an opportunity for settler-colonists, like Teage, to question assumptions about the value of a rhetorical education in ways that drew from their colonial experience. Despite their unique political, social, and geographic position, settler-colonists engaged with elements of the stateside African American rhetorical traditions. The movement between American traditions and Liberian revisions speaks to a process of cultural synthesis undertaken by settler-colonists and fostered within the Liberia Lyceum. Within that synthesis, rhetoric played a central role not only as a means of expressing views and creating identities but also as a force with negative potential.

Conclusion

This chapter has aimed to expand the scholarly understanding of the lyceum beyond its predominantly Anglo-American framing through the notion of a lyceum diaspora. During the heights of the lyceum movement in the antebellum United States, an English-speaking lyceum existed in Liberia. Even more, the lyceum diaspora is evident in the ways the Liberia Lyceum interacted with norms of the Anglo-American lyceum and with African American rhetorical practices. The influence of American lyceum culture was clear in the naming, purpose, and procedures of the Liberia Lyceum. Yet the Liberia Lyceum did not simply duplicate the U.S. lyceum in a new locale. Rather, distinct topics and relationships emerged to respond to a colonial context that included hardships and opportunities that African Americans did not experience in the United States. Thus, the Liberia Lyceum serves as a compelling locus from which to demonstrate the emergence of a lyceum diaspora in the transatlantic world, not in North America or Europe but in Africa.

There is much that we do not know, and may never know, about the Liberia Lyceum. We lack most of the archival resources—account books, rosters of speakers, complete speech texts, meeting minutes, or even accounts from audience members—that would allow for a fuller historical reconstruction of the institution. Such material deficiency, however, can offer an opportunity for scholars of lecture culture to develop new methods. David Kazanjian's recent work on Liberian letter writing from the mid-nineteenth century provides a powerful example of how critical methods can be refigured in the face of rhetorical and material absences. Kazanjian writes openly about wanting Liberian letters to speak in grander, more philosophical terms so that he would have something to analyze. "When will they stop writing about needing seeds and blankets?" Kazanjian recalls thinking to himself. But as Kazanjian elaborates, texts addressing these quotidian subjects required a different reading strategy than the one he was using. Kazanjian shifted his perspective, examining the "interplay between charting structural knowns and attending to failures to know."[63] The present chapter has attempted to do much the same—to understand the interplay among lyceum culture, African American rhetorical practice, and the revisions to both undertaken by settler-colonists. It is not a complete picture, but it is one that adds a fascinating dimension to the growing panoply of lyceum studies.

6

SECRET KNOWLEDGE, PUBLIC STAGE:
JOSEPH SMITH'S KING FOLLETT DISCOURSE

Richard Benjamin Crosby

Near the end of his essay "Nature," Ralph Waldo Emerson recommends a way to discern wisdom in another person. "Let us note, first, that the mark of wisdom is to see the miraculous in the common."[1] Emerson's definition captures the essential impulse of a culture of learning that swept across the United States during the antebellum era. Driven in part by altruistic democratic impulses, this culture expressed a common belief that knowledge can exalt the minds of ordinary people and, in so doing, create an enlightened—even transcendent—national community. The idea was both secular and sublime—a national project that built and sacralized the infrastructure of learning.

Understanding such a project requires a grasp of the various audiences and publics—some low, some high, some urban, some rural, some bound, some free—that constituted the national community. As this volume makes clear, there was not merely one culture of knowledge that defined nineteenth-century America's yearning for transcendence. Instead, there was a complex of knowledge cultures and subcultures, each located within what Thomas Augst identifies as a constellation of "sites and practices," and each expressing its own drive for transcendence in a rich and unique way.[2] This diversity was based in no small part on variations in access to formal education, and subcultures were often obliged to create their own definitions of and spaces for learning.[3] Thus, while the nineteenth-century thirst for knowledge was ubiquitous, variations in access dictated that the thirst would be quenched with a unique assortment of potions. For some, it would be the lyceum, the lecture hall, or the public performance of literature. For others, knowledge would come from places more hidden.

In any discussion of America's nascent intellectual life, it is easy to forget the tousled frontier, where communities just inventing themselves often lacked the educational resources of more established towns and cities closer to the East Coast. A lack of traditional education, however, did not mean a lack of learning. Rather, it meant that people took different approaches to learning, including the sort of learning that emerged from the spiritual life of a community. It would be a mistake to excise frontier and rural religious experience from a full grasp of America's culture of learning. If education is, as philosophers from Plato to Dewey have argued, a means of sustaining "the life of the group," then it follows that sustained groups will have perspectives on learning worth observing.[4]

This chapter, therefore, takes "thinking together" into the woods. Below I consider two intersecting knowledge subcultures that are rarely associated with civic intellectualism but which swept across the American landscape with considerable force during the nineteenth century: the radical democratic religious culture of the Second Great Awakening and the widespread tradition of folk magic and the occult in America's frontier communities. Although these two cultures often eschewed formal education, they produced their own ways of knowing that captured the imagination of Americans across a broad spectrum. I explore the way these two cultures blended with the more mainstream and erudite lecture culture of the period to embody a unique, complex spirit of learning.

I argue that this strange, alchemic blending of seemingly competing cultures of knowledge propelled the nation's most successful homegrown religion: the Church of Jesus Christ of Latter-day Saints, as it is officially known, or, more commonly and broadly, Mormonism.[5] Specifically, I consider the rhetoric of Joseph Smith, a poor, lowborn autodidact obsessed with religion-making and the salvific power of progressive learning. This is the same Joseph Smith who, as historians have recently learned, was deeply involved in the frontier folk magic subculture of the time and who also became a Master Mason. Smith taught that knowledge was a kind of exalting gnosis—a revelatory experience of divine mysteries—that would give human beings the power to become gods themselves.[6] This is the Joseph Smith who founded what is now the fourth-largest religious group in the United States.[7]

The example of Joseph Smith's Mormonism reveals that the American hunger for the exalting powers of education found expression far beyond lecture halls or public schoolhouses. It took root in the thick woods of upstate New York and along the American frontier—a vast region steeped in spiritualism, revolution, and the mythos of an indomitable pioneering spirit.[8] Early Mormonism, then, exemplifies a knowledge culture forced to create itself at the margins of a national community. Further, the public rhetoric of Joseph Smith reveals an extraordinarily literal interpretation of the principle that Emerson spoke of when he discussed the "miraculous in the common." Mormonism pushes this principle to its natural breaking point, invoking learning as a transcendent and sanctifying act.

To develop these themes, I focus on a sermon that Joseph Smith delivered to thousands of his followers at an outdoor meeting in the Mormon city of Nauvoo, Illinois, in the spring of 1844. This sermon is the most comprehensive statement Smith offered on the Mormon theology of knowledge and its exalting powers—a doctrine Mormons refer to as "exaltation." Although the LDS Church does not consider it official scripture, many official doctrinal statements and canonized revelations have reinforced the sermon's ideas.[9] Commonly called the King Follett Discourse, the sermon achieves an alchemic fusion of three discursive traditions: evangelicalism of the Second Great Awakening, especially its radical leveling impulses; occult mysticism and its unorthodox doctrines of knowledge; and nineteenth-century lecture culture, including a style of speech more appropriate for an East Coast lecture hall than a religious harangue in the woods. Joseph Smith regularly drew on these traditions as part of his religion-building project, and the King Follett Discourse offers what is perhaps the most sublime and radical expression of his religion's theology—namely, that a regular person, no matter how mean or vulgar, may, by the progressive acquisition of special knowledge, become the highest form of divine, even a god. The discourse also offers the radical proposition that the very God whom Christians worship followed the same pattern of intellectual and spiritual maturation available to all people. This belief represents the culmination of the Mormon revelatory enterprise, an entire religion animated by what Harold Bloom calls "a purely American gnosis."[10]

Joseph Smith, Revolutionary Religion, and the Magic Worldview

The caricature of Joseph Smith as a cheap, nineteenth-century religious huckster has bitten the dust, one can finally hope. In 2014 *Smithsonian Magazine* called him the most significant religious figure in American history.[11] Noted scholars now acknowledge his permanent impact on American culture. Calling Smith an "authentic religious genius," Bloom once said that no song or vision, not even those of Whitman or Emerson, captured the American soul with such "imaginative vitality" as did Joseph Smith's.[12] In his 2015 book *One Nation, Under Gods*, Peter Manseau writes, "Depending on one's religious sensibilities, and perhaps on one's corresponding level of cynicism, Smith was either a religious savant so dauntless in the courage of his convictions that he attracted millions around the world with his message, or he was one of the most successful fabulists in history." For Manseau, Smith's success relied on his extraordinary ability to synthesize different cultures and belief systems into a coherent and compelling whole. It was a vision for which nineteenth-century Americans yearned, a revelation that drew on the diverse cultural voices of the day and embodied "the collaborative nature of American belief."[13]

Like Manseau, Bloom links Smith's mediating capacity to an identifiably American spirit. Part of Mormonism's American quintessence, Bloom posits, is its origin in the mystical impulses of its founder, a young, eccentric daydreamer who carried talismans, hunted treasures, and claimed to have visions. This same boy declared that an angel led him to the site of ancient, buried golden plates, which he then used to launch his complete vision of a divinely restored ancient religious order and political kingdom.[14]

Smith's account of these revelatory beginnings, a personal journal now canonized as modern Mormon scripture, constitutes the rhetorically powerful origin story of Mormonism.[15] The story is oft repeated in reverent tones in every educational context within the Church—from primary lessons for young children to religious education classes for young adults, from adult Sunday school classes to general congregational meetings and massive public conferences (to say nothing of proselytizing efforts by missionaries across the globe). The story frames the adolescent Joseph Smith as a humble seeker of wisdom growing up in rural western New York, innocent of the prejudices that marked the contested religious landscape of the time. Smith reflects:

> While I was laboring under the extreme difficulties caused by the contests of these parties of religionists, I was one day reading the Epistle of James, first chapter and fifth verse, which reads: *If any of you lack wisdom, let him ask of God, that giveth to all men liberally, and upbraideth not; and it shall be given him.*
>
> Never did any passage of scripture come with more power to the heart of man than this did at this time to mine. It seemed to enter with great force into every feeling of my heart. I reflected on it again and again, knowing that if any person needed wisdom from God, I did.[16]

At this point in the story, Smith determines to seek the wisdom he so desperately lacks, not by enrolling in classes or attending lectures or even, yet, by consulting the scriptures and their related commentaries more deeply. Instead he declares, "I retired to the woods to make the attempt." Upon finding an appropriately isolated spot, he kneels and offers his prayer to God for wisdom. Immediately a dark power seizes him. His tongue is bound, and "thick darkness" gathers around him. He feels certain of his own doom at the hands of "some actual being from the unseen world." Just then, he sees a shaft of light directly above him. The light reveals God the Father and his Son, Jesus Christ, who address Smith directly, informing him that he must not join any church, for they are "all an abomination."[17]

The story has been officially titled "The First Vision," because it is the first in a series of heavenly visitations Smith received as a slow, progressive education on how to restore God's true, ancient church. Over several years, Smith would be given a series of careful instructions by angelic messengers, each testing his memory, obedience, and understanding before he could progress to the next level of instruction. He would be led eventually to buried and enchanted treasure: gilded tablets inscribed with the story of God's chosen people who had been lost to history. He would build sacred temples in which hidden wisdom would be made known, and he would reveal these great secrets to the whole world. And so he did: from finding and translating ancient golden plates into Christian scripture to adapting Masonic rituals to the cause of Mormon temple worship to challenging the theological foundations of modern Christianity by arguing that people can become gods if they attain knowledge. Smith would take the esoteric and occult to the people and carve out a fully formed, populist religion in the process.[18]

For nearly two centuries, official Mormon interpretations of Smith's story, as well as most historical studies, have situated Smith within the milieu of sectarian competition that defined rural New England and New York at the time—especially the region of western New York known as the Burned-Over District, named for the high concentration of revivalist movements it spawned.[19] And rightly so. Smith was certainly the product of a community consumed by religion in an age of democratic revolution. Populist movements led by what historian Nathan O. Hatch calls "unbranded individualists" spread out across the frontier, seeking converts to their causes.[20]

Hatch links the democratic revolutionary spirit of these religious leaders to a talent for rhetorical communication: "All were democratic or populist in the way they instinctively associated virtue with ordinary people rather than with elites [and] exalted the vernacular in word and song as the hallowed channel for communicating with and about God."²¹ Revivalism so dominated religious life along the frontier that denominational membership more than tripled between 1820 and 1860, growing rapidly among Methodists, Baptists, and other Protestant groups. The frontier was an ideal setting for such growth for a number of reasons, including the demographic reality of a population marked by poverty, low education, and a widespread religious populism—all factors that historically play significant roles in conversion rates.²²

The Mormon audience, like other audiences of the Second Great Awakening, was united not merely by its shared middle- or lower-class cultural status but by a yearning for communal transcendence. In an age of democratic revolution and religious entrepreneurialism, successful movements recognized what Hatch calls "the sovereign audience."²³ Americans who were drawn to Smith and, perhaps more to the point, those who remained his followers during hard times were people whom Richard Bushman calls "visionaries." Potential adherents to Mormonism were not only seekers who wanted a return to the New Testament church or even an ancient Old Testament kingdom but also those who yearned to wield divine authority themselves. "The greatest hunger," Bushman writes, "was for spiritual gifts like dreams, visions, tongues, miracles, and spiritual raptures," desires that were responsive to Mormonism's new, egalitarian revelation.²⁴

The appeal of this new vision was so great that it inspired Smith's followers to build cities and theocracies, even as they were exiled from state to state, moving from New York to Ohio to Missouri to Illinois. In Illinois, they finally managed to avoid harassment long enough to build a significant city, which they called Nauvoo. It quickly became the second-largest city in the state, filled with brick homes, broad streets, and, of course, the glimmering Mormon temple that stood prominently on a bluff overlooking the Mississippi River. It established its own university, administering courses in subjects ranging from English literature to mathematics, from astronomy to philosophy. The city also established a lyceum and a public school system. In this way, Nauvoo was an embodiment of Smith himself: a place driven wild by revelatory visions but tempered by a reverence for intellectual life and society. It is no coincidence that it was in Nauvoo, during the saints' longest period of tranquility, that Smith developed his theology of learning and delivered the King Follett Discourse.²⁵

Mormonism cut through the chaos of myriad sectarian movements by drawing on the fundamental rhetorical appeal of the new religious spirit—that is, its "passion for equality," its throwing down of old structures and authorities—while also setting itself apart in profound ways.²⁶ Mormonism

Figure 6.1 This lithograph depicting Nauvoo, Illinois, was created by Henry Lewis and published in *Das Illustrirte Mississippithal* (Düsseldorf, 1854–57). I. N. Phelps Stokes Collection of American Historical Prints, Miriam and Ira D. Wallach Division of Art, Prints and Photographs: Print Collection, New York Public Library.

claimed to be more than a reaction against old structures; it framed itself as a wholly new revelation with a new book of scripture, a new prophet, a new vision of a literal kingdom of Zion, and a perfect gospel fully restored from the ancient church. Over the years, the Mormon Church under Smith's direction claimed to have sole possession of the sacred priesthood that God gave the ancient patriarchs and that Christ gave the apostles. Smith thus began to experiment beyond populist appeals to the common believer, introducing a complex religious infrastructure that resembled the hierarchies and aesthetics of much older, "high" ritual traditions.

The Mormon system included multiple priesthoods; elaborate ceremonies; sacred, symbolic clothing; and esoteric signs and tokens. But it also included large, casual meetings with standard sermons spoken in plain language, and it continued to insist that the highest authority on any question of great importance was the Holy Ghost, whom anyone could access by virtue of faith. The whole framework was designed to be accessible to ordinary people. Indeed, a high priest in the elaborately ritualized Mormon temple was more likely to be a blacksmith than a scholar. Such was the distinctiveness of Smith's church. It was an exalted religious system administered by a plain body of faith. The project proved compelling. By the time of his death in Nauvoo in 1844, Smith led a quasitheocracy that included a major city with more than fifteen thousand residents and an army of missionaries gathering thousands more.[27]

If the traditional account of Smith's history seems incredible, perhaps it is because the role of magic as a source of knowledge in nineteenth-century America—and in the inception of Mormonism itself—has been so widely overlooked. In Smith's day, secret, revealed wisdom—found and sustained through elaborate private rituals, secret signs, and ancient symbols—was not wholly laughable. American aristocrats from the early eighteenth century to the mid-nineteenth century read widely in occult works and published original research affirming the viability of occult practices; the population of Freemasons grew by roughly 400 percent between 1800 and 1850; and the practice of medicine by university-trained doctors included the use of astrology and alchemy well into the 1820s.[28] But professionals and aristocrats were hardly the only ones interested in such arts.

John L. Brooke points out that the mystical, occultist teachings of Hermeticism were a regular part of some early American religious traditions and that practicing Christians fueled the rise of Masonry.[29] D. Michael Quinn adds that the alliance between magic and rural religion is especially evident in "the common believer's do-it-yourself, anti-authoritarian religion, [which] mingled Bible teachings with occult beliefs." He also notes that rural believers were slower to abandon the occult than were the classically educated elite.[30] So, while the literate and urban classes maintained an interest in esoteric and occult practices, rural populations held on to magic with tighter convictions and apparently for a longer time. In other words, Smith came from a culture that was not unfriendly to traditions of magic and that recognized a distinct relationship between the mystical, the religious, and the democratic style that this fusion of beliefs could assume in American frontier life.

In fact, nowhere was the influence of folk magic more prominent than in rural regions of New England and upstate New York—so much so that one nineteenth-century Mormon historian said that "to be credulous of such things was to be normal people."[31] For example, the use of divining rods to find treasure was no cause for universal derision. It was a known and fairly common practice.[32] But Smith's affinity for the magic worldview gradually went beyond what was common. Here I want to make a distinction between the simple folk superstitions of average communities on the frontier and the fully developed theologies and rituals of long-established secret societies and hermetic belief systems. It is one thing to be a tenant farmer at the edge of civilization who spends limited free time digging for gold with the aid of a rod that is supposedly enchanted, or to brew a home remedy for an illness based on the supposition that special plants or even chants might make the elixir more effective; it is another thing to see the world as a magically infused mystery that can be unlocked through the revelatory power of ancient priesthoods, complex ritual systems, blood oaths, and world-shattering revelatory myths waiting to cleave the veil between mortal and immortal. At some point in his young career as a magic enthusiast and prospective religionist, Smith transcended banal folk traditions and became enmeshed within a fully enchanted world, and he stood at its center as prophet, seer, and revelator who met God in the woods. It became his job to enable the flow of ancient knowledge into the world so that it could exalt the human race.

Smith's sense of calling was tied inexorably to his experience of the occult and, as he grew older, to his interest in Masonry. Clyde R. Forsberg Jr. reveals curious overlaps between the historical narrative of Smith's discovery and translation of the Book of Mormon and key Masonic traditions, icons, and legends.[33] Former LDS Church historian Reed C. Durham likewise argues that Smith's gradual pursuit of revelatory education has extraordinarily detailed parallels to the famous Masonic Enoch legend, elaborated in the ceremonies of the thirteenth, fourteenth, and twenty-first degrees of Masonry. The ceremony can be traced to the myths of ancient Kabbalah, but it was refined during the rise of modern Masonry in France in the middle to late eighteenth century. As Durham shows, a number of publications detailing the legend were available in rural upstate New York when Smith was growing up there. Much of Smith's own revelatory language seems derived from the language of Masonic rituals and legends, from the terms he used in dictating revelations to the ceremonial way that Mormon temple cornerstones were laid.[34]

Lance S. Owens's work likewise points out the Kabbalistic language of Smith's interpretations of certain biblical passages, including the account of creation in Genesis.[35] In other words, by the time Smith started the LDS Church and began revealing new doctrines and secrets to the flock, he was so steeped in the language and symbols of a magic worldview that his own life "appears to be a kind of symbolic acting out of Masonic lore" and "that to explain [the similarities] only as coincidence would be ridiculous."[36] Consider that the Mormon temple ceremony and its primary ritual, called the "endowment," is a direct symbolic parallel to its Masonic counterpart, also known as "endowment" (although the Mormon interpretation of the ceremony is markedly different).[37] It is no coincidence that Smith's development of this ritual came shortly after he was made a Master Mason himself, nor does it seem a coincidence that the "nine disciples" to whom Smith initially revealed the endowment ceremony were also Master Masons.[38] Indeed, Mormonism deeply integrated Freemasonry's traditions and symbols into its core theological system.

Smith was taking ancient knowledge and refashioning it for a new kingdom, a new Zion comprising his followers. He redesigned it to include all faithful Latter-day Saints, and he quickly set about designing an order for women, entailing what Owens calls an "androgynous new Mormon Masonry," which would endow women and men with the knowledge necessary to be ordained "priests and priestesses," "kings and queens," and ultimately gods and goddesses.[39] Smith was enacting in religion what Tom F. Wright observes as part of mainstream, mainly secular culture in the lyceums of America's urban centers—only Smith's version was cultivated within and designed for a violent, impoverished, religion-soaked frontier. The culture of lecturing and public education established, Augst says, "a contested field of cultural production, where a traditional genre of learned discourse with roots in the medieval university was democratized."[40] In other words, one of the key projects of lecture culture was to exhume special knowledge from its hidden places and share it with the broader world, and to let it be contested in the open. Ultimately, the principle of sharing knowledge meant a more edified and enlightened public.[41]

As the following analysis will show, Smith's rhetoric represents an especially revolutionary example of the relationship of learning and religion in the tumultuous religious landscape of the Second Great Awakening. Smith, consistent with his role as an antebellum preacher in a nation of learners and religionists, saw regular folks as no less qualified than the nobility or the clergy to receive wisdom in an effort to realize a transcendent destiny. They, too, could access hidden knowledge and translate it into sanctifying, even exalting, powers. His controversial King Follett Discourse is a prime example of this principle.

Analysis

The King Follett Discourse has nothing to do with royalty. King Follett was the name of a member of the church in Nauvoo, a common laborer who had been crushed by a falling tub of rock while working in a well. Smith was fond of Follett personally, and Follett's outdoor funeral in April 1844 drew a crowd of about twenty thousand, mostly in anticipation of a eulogy from Smith himself. Smith used the opportunity to elucidate the latest mysteries that had been unlocked to him via prayer and revelation concerning the nature of the dead as well as the character of God.[42] In the discourse, Smith links biblical teachings with gnostic philosophies of knowledge and the democratic revolutionary spirit of the early American republic. Brooke calls the sermon "the most definitive and authoritative synthesis of [Smith's] cosmology."[43]

The most authoritative version of the King Follett Discourse comes from a transcription compiled from the notes of three of Smith's lieutenants who were present at the event. The transcription was then printed in *The Documentary History of the Church*.[44] My reading of the discourse shows how it blends the knowledge cultures of lecturing, magic, and democracy.

Lecture Culture

The discourse styles itself a lecture, not unlike the kind of lecture one would expect to hear in a civic hall or schoolhouse or in a more mainline religious service. Consider the way Smith begins: "Beloved Saints: I will call [for] the attention of this congregation while I address you on the subject of the dead. . . . I feel disposed to speak on the subject in general, and offer you my ideas." The occasion suggests a eulogy, but the opening lines imply a restrained sermon or even an instructional lecture. Other elements within the discourse indicate that the audience is hearing a revelation directly. The King Follett Discourse blends genres, consistent with Smith's self-presentation as a rhetor-prophet who mixes cultures and systems of learning, heedless of any rules that would limit what can be done, or how.

Smith continues with the same didactic tone: "I will make a few preliminaries, in order that you may understand the subject when I come to it." He is using a traditional, classical organizational pattern, with an *exordium*, *narratio*, *divisio*, and a series of proofs, which are broken into sections by topics. In other words, he is doing what other Americans with any exposure to nineteenth-century rhetorical education might do. He offers an introduction, outlines the goals of the speech, provides an argument in defense of those goals, includes evidence, and divides his ideas into digestible sections fit for an audience of students. A classical reading of the discourse also reveals that Smith has adopted the plain style of speech, which, Cicero claimed, is best designed for educational instruction.[45] Smith himself is explicit on this point. In the introduction, he remarks, "I do not calculate or intend to please your ears with superfluity of words or oratory, or with much learning; but

I calculate to edify you with the simple truths of heaven." His auditors are clearly hearing a lecture. Smith's stated intentions do not suggest a bombastic sermon or an excited performance, but they do suggest a rhetoric of simple instruction in which new, edifying knowledge will be shared. This passage bears the markers of the general culture of learning recognizable to Americans even on the margins (both geographically and culturally) of national society. The lecture is designed to reveal simple, clear principles of knowledge, the end of which is to stretch the listener to higher realms of civility and experience. Smith acknowledges King Follett and the occasion of his death in the second sentence of the discourse, but thereafter he keeps silent about the man himself. The occasion becomes no more than a jumping-off point for elucidating new doctrines.

The plain, instructive style remains consistent throughout most of the discourse. For instance, as Smith transitions to revelations of the anticipated mysteries, he uses a restrained enthymematic structure, establishing premises from which he derives ostensibly logical conclusions. As Smith transitions from introductory content to the major parts of the discourse, he states, "In order to understand the subject of the dead, for consolation of those who mourn for loss of their friends, it is necessary we should understand the character and being of God and how He came to be so; for I am going to tell you how God came to be God." Also in this section, Smith begins to introduce rebuttals, another standard element of the classical pattern: "We have imagined and supposed that God was God from all eternity. I will refute that idea, and take away the veil, so that you may see." This moment is a critical turning point, because while the discourse remains entrenched in a plain rhetorical style, Smith begins to advance the radical doctrines for which the sermon is known. The audience reaction here is impossible to isolate, but it seems clear that the discourse is building a sense of heightened anticipation. The plain style as a container for such a profound claim creates a tension within the text. The restrained, plain structure begins to interact with a radical and subversive content—the promise to a baited audience of a transcendent outflow of new knowledge from a divine source. The effect is to make the provocative mystery into a plain truth elucidated in a plain way—in effect, to take away its mystery.

Shortly thereafter, Smith acknowledges that some people may find his ideas incomprehensible. "But," he protests, "they are simple. It is the principle of the gospel to know for a certainty the character of God." Such an idea is already provocative in that it rejects the long-held belief that God is unknowable, an inexorable mystery according to ancient creeds. But Smith goes even further: "We may converse with Him as one man converses with another, and . . . he was once a man like us; yea, . . . God himself, the Father of us all, dwelt on an earth." Thus Smith introduces a radical new doctrine, which fundamentally challenges the structure of accepted Christianity, as a "simple" principle—within the second clause of a compound sentence. It appears as if it is an afterthought or, at most, no more or less important than the notion that human beings can converse with God.

In some sense, it is puzzling that such a radical notion—that God was once human—is embedded so deeply within the syntax of an otherwise relatively uncontroversial statement. The order suggests that Smith saw little distinction between one's ability to talk with God and one's eternal co-equality with God. That is to say, given that people can talk with God as if he were a person, it naturally follows that he may be, in some sense, a person. Smith elaborates on this unusual doctrine later in the discourse. Here the plain structure acts as a vehicle for one of the most cosmologically unorthodox statements on Christian doctrine known in American religious traditions.

Cultures of Magic

Cosmologically unorthodox though Smith's teachings may have been, they were not created out of nothing. Instead they were an organized patchwork of different religious and mystical ideas that long predated Smith. A close reading of the King Follett Discourse reveals how Smith drew on magic and occult influences as inventional material for the founding revelations of his public, Christian religious movement. Brooke identifies several parallels, for example, between Mormonism's doctrine of exaltation—or theosis—and the philosophical claims of alchemy and Hermeticism.[46] With these parallels in mind, consider some of Smith's more controversial declarations in the discourse:

> God himself was once as we are now, and is an exalted man, and sits enthroned in yonder heavens! That is the great secret. If the veil were rent today, and the great God who holds this world in its orbit, and who upholds all worlds and all things by His power, was to make himself visible—I say, if you were to see him today, you would see him like a man in form like yourselves in all the person, image and very form as man; for Adam was created in the very fashion, image and likeness of God, and received instruction from, and walked, talked and conversed with Him, as one man talks and communes with another.

The idea of an anthropomorphic God and, by correlation, theomorphic humans is not an invention of Joseph Smith. Among other places, it can be found in parts of the Hebrew Bible and, to some extent, in the story of Enoch in the teachings of Kabbalah.[47] Enoch walked with God and talked with God, and he was eventually taken up into heaven to be restored to his preexistent state as simultaneously God, angel, and man. The notion is also hermetic in that it captures the principle of transmutation inherent within alchemy as well as human perfection. Just as tin may be made gold by the application of secret ritual knowledge practices, so humans may become gods by the same sort of magic.[48]

This familiarity between God and humans may derive in part from Smith's own sense that the stuff God and humans are made of is the same essence and co-eternal. Smith's name for this substance is intelligence: "The mind or the intelligence which man possesses is co-equal [co-eternal] with God himself.... The intelligence of spirits had no beginning, neither will it have an end." Smith does not belabor the point with mounds of scientific or theological evidence. He simply declares its reasonability: "This is good logic. That which has a beginning may have an end.... Intelligence is eternal and exists upon a self-existent principle. It is a spirit from age to age and there is no creation about it." Like a good populist theologian, Smith concludes this section of the address by linking his new and highly controversial doctrine of intelligence to the yearnings of his audience: "All the minds and spirits that God ever sent into the world are susceptible of enlargement." He returns to the miraculous in the common, making the miraculous seem less mystifying. Ordinary people may partake in the divine power only by a process of gradual enlargement.

According to Brooke, the language and the content of the King Follett Discourse are unmistakably hermetic.[49] Creation, Smith declares, was not ex nihilo. It was instead an act of organization. The elements preexisted the act of creation. Likewise, human spirit is made of fine matter and has always existed, even before God did. Smith describes the act of creation as a progressive, alchemic organization of existing materials, which, once organized, become sublime in potential. Furthermore, the revelation of this knowledge, though radically unorthodox, should not pose too much of a challenge, because it is "good logic." The implication of Smith's declaration here, especially when taken in light of other discourses he offered prior to King Follett, is that the heavens are filled with an infinitude of gods, each having achieved her or his godhood the same way. (Smith believed women were equally capable of deification.)

Consider Smith's penultimate proof:

> God himself, finding he was in the midst of spirits and glory, because he was more intelligent, saw proper to institute laws whereby the rest could have a privilege to advance like himself. The relationship we have with God places us in a situation to advance in knowledge. He has power to institute laws to instruct the weaker intelligences, that they may be exalted with Himself, so that they might have one glory upon another, and all that knowledge, power, glory, and intelligence, which is requisite in order to save them in the world of spirits.

For Smith, the miracle of exaltation is inseparable from the miracle of learning itself. As he says in a separate discourse, eternal progress is not a sudden and mysterious flash but a progression, "line upon line, precept upon precept."[50] Exaltation, the great mystery of the heavens, is not a gift bestowed as a consequence or statement of faith or a life of self-denial and dogmatic obedience. One *learns*. God himself became God by recognizing his own intelligence and desiring to share it.

One imagines, as Brooke puts it, a heaven "where a tiered pantheon of gods progressed through infinite stages of divinity, powered by succeeding generations of saints-becoming-gods."[51] Smith's appeal to his listeners, therefore, is not merely to teach them the principle but to urge them to live it: "Ye have got to learn how to be gods yourselves, . . . the same as all gods have done before you, namely, by going from one small degree to another, and from a small capacity to a great one."

Radical Democracy

The democratic impulse was powerfully at work in the King Follett Discourse. In a nation that had revolted against a monarchy by an appeal to the inherent equality of "all men," Smith's doctrine seemed almost natural. If the people are divinely created to rule their own world, then are they not divinely ordained to rule their own heaven? According to Smith, God's impulse, once he recognized he was more intelligent, was not to command and subjugate but to teach, to "institute laws to instruct the weaker intelligences, that they may be exalted with Himself." This is the American educational project writ large. There is no distance between the farmhand or the garment worker and God, other than the learning process itself. And if this process is pursued and achieved, the result is transcendent indeed. Smith declares, "They might have one glory upon another, and all that knowledge, power, glory, and intelligence, which is requisite in order to save them in the world of spirits." The power to save, according to Smith's logic, is inextricably tied to principles of knowledge and intelligence. There is no discussion, at least not in the King Follett Discourse, of confessing Jesus and awaiting his grace.[52] True religion is about learning, advancement, and eternal power.

Smith also implies a God who is subject to unchangeable natural laws. Just as God cannot create spirit or intelligence, so he cannot advance himself any faster than the process of learning and progression will permit. Such a god does not respect persons, because he regards them all, including himself, as subject to the same laws. Smith accordingly notes, "I have intended my remarks for all, both rich and poor, bond and free, great and small. I have no enmity against any man." Smith, an abolitionist and a believer that the families of gods in the heavens included men and women, saw, as Emerson put it, "the miraculous in the common." His version of this particularly American gospel took the matter to new heights—heights that sent American religious history in radically new directions.

Yet Smith's ideas are deeply familiar; they emerge from the roots of America's egalitarian, revolutionary, work-driven cultural history. As if to punctuate this point, Smith offers what initially seems like a disjointed transition to this personal avowal: "I never did harm any man since I was born in the world. My voice is always for peace. . . . I never think evil, nor do anything to the harm of my fellow-man." The statement seems out of place, coming after a long discourse on the nature of God. But it is consistent at least in one way with the main idea of the discourse. Smith sees in each person the potential to become a god. To think ill of or to harm a person would be a great sacrilege.

Conclusion

Joseph Smith's statements on learning have become aphoristic in Mormon culture: "A man is saved no faster than he gains knowledge."[53] "The glory of God is intelligence."[54] "Whatever level of knowledge a man attains in this life, it will rise with him in the resurrection."[55] One wonders: if Emerson had been born a poor, semiliterate tenant farmer on the American frontier, what would he have made of himself? Emerson the philosopher may not have agreed with the Prophet Joseph's radical and shockingly straightforward interpretation of the exalting power of knowledge and learning; but if

Emerson had been handed Smith's lot, what might he have said instead of his friendly quip about the miraculous and the common? Had he lived in the powder keg of poverty and revolutionary religion that scorched the upstate countryside, maybe Emerson, rather than one of the Church's later prophets, would have come up with Mormonism's famous chiastic couplet: "As man is, God once was. As God is, man may become."[56]

I have argued that America's lecture culture and Smith's Zion were parallel cases of the same act of alchemy, pouring the esoteric and learned into the popular and quotidian, then pouring the popular and quotidian back into the esoteric and learned in a kind of ritual of communal refinement toward some perfect end. Such is Mormonism's American quintessence, a vibrant balance of contradictions enchanted by a drive for godliness and a willingness to do. For a rural mystic like Joseph Smith, true knowledge was revelatory and experiential. It could be complemented by the intense study of texts and languages, as Smith himself would do during his time in Nauvoo, but its ultimate source was the intelligence, co-equal and co-eternal with God and therefore able to recognize the Holy Ghost. In his King Follett Discourse, Smith called the Holy Ghost "the oldest book in the world," because it made learning a whole-souled experience. It is the radical religious version of William James's move to put experience at the heart of the "American Theory."[57]

I began this chapter with evidence of Smith's religion-making as an exercise in a strange but rich patchwork, a blending of diverse ways of thinking and knowing. From lecture halls to secret societies to backwoods tent meetings, Mormonism organized its own revelation for an eager audience. In this way, Smith managed to introduce different knowledge cultures to one another, creating his own radical version of thinking together—or thinking differently, together. His audience comprised regular people from across a broad spectrum of experience, united by a vision of spiritual power that they could wield themselves.

Today, Mormons remain what Terryl Givens calls a "people of paradox," trying to reconcile their radical progressive roots with a new culture of conservative orthodoxy.[58] But Mormonism is still a movement defined by "a knowledge-hungry religious zealotry."[59] Smith did not have the luxury of much formal education. Still he was obsessed with learning and knowing. He took the fragments of culture he could grasp from the world in which he was steeped—a world of popular education, religious enthusiasm, democratic revolution, and mystical tradition. From these raw resources of intelligence, he made his own knowledge and organized his own world, even if it meant digging it out of the earth.

7

THE "PERFECT DELIGHT" OF DRAMATIC READING: GERTRUDE KELLOGG AND THE POST–CIVIL WAR LYCEUM

Sara E. Lampert

Sallie Joy White was not enthusiastic about the debut of another dramatic reader. "I have a horror of new readers," she explained in her column "Matters in Boston" in February 1878. She had, after all, "heard every reader of note who is before the public." White expected merely to "assist . . . at the obsequies of the aspirant." But Gertrude Kellogg's entrance, unattended, her quiet but "straightforward" stride to the stage, roused White. Here was something different. "As she commenced to read," White recalled, "she fairly bound her audience."[1] As was customary in this form of entertainment, Kellogg delivered her readings from memory, standing in the middle of a platform adorned by little more than floral arrangements. The power lay in the reader's performance alone, with no scenic enhancement or costuming, though Kellogg was fashionably attired, wearing a black velvet dress with blue satin trim.[2] For White, Kellogg was Cassandra-like in her "magnetism" yet seemed completely unaffected. Perhaps this was the source of her power. Kellogg's reading of "Charles Edward at Versailles" was particularly "thrilling." Her selections and delivery suggested "a woman of more than ordinary mental ability." Kellogg, White thought, was worth hearing.[3]

White was well prepared to evaluate individual readers. After all, she had seen many aspirants come through Boston in recent years. In the immediate post–Civil War period, an expanding cohort of young women launched platform careers with a skill that as children they had learned and practiced in the common school and probably also performed as a parlor entertainment for family and friends. As adults, they would pursue further study, hoping to parlay the art of recitation into a career. In the late 1860s, the formation of the first lyceum bureaus—commercial management agencies that represented platform performers, principally lecturers and then dramatic readers and musicians—contributed to the resurgence of platform entertainment.[4] The appeal of dramatic reading as a form of employment and a vehicle for renown meant that within a decade the platform reader (or elocutionist) had become ubiquitous enough to be considered tiresome to audiences. Kellogg's reading entertainment was not a novelty; she was an emerging performer in a popular, and consequently quite saturated, genre of platform entertainment.

This genre was strongly associated with young women. Consider the platform performers advertised by the Redpath Lyceum Bureau, which served as Kellogg's agent for the 1878–79 season. Through the Redpath Bureau, local lyceums could book courses or individual engagements, drawing on a roster of forty-six lecturers, three of whom were women; fifteen musical acts; three novelty entertainments; and twelve readers, eight of whom were women.[5] Since the founding of the Redpath Bureau in 1868, the overall ratio of male to female lecturers consistently favored men—fewer than one in six lecturers in a given season were women and in most cases one in ten. The Redpath Bureau represented far more lecturers than readers, usually at a ratio of ten to one; however, readers were more evenly divided between men and women. By the end of the 1870s, the number of dramatic readers represented by the bureau had increased, and the ratio of lecturers to readers shifted significantly in favor of the latter. Likewise, the category itself had become overwhelmingly female.[6] In 1892, both the presence of dramatic reading in the lyceum and dramatic reading's status as a gendered genre of performance held strong: the 1892 list boasted forty-eight lecturers, of whom five were women, sustaining the one in ten ratio of the last twenty years; twenty-one readers, seventeen of whom were women; and nineteen other "entertainers."[7]

The popularity of dramatic reading as Gilded Age entertainment intersects a number of questions—about the nature of oratory as a cultural form, the cultural work of the platform, and the cultural work of the platform in relation to the nationwide "woman question." As scholar Nan Johnson has argued, the gender politics of rhetorical culture in the late nineteenth century were largely conservative: rhetorical pedagogy reinscribed the domestic as woman's appropriate rhetorical sphere. Johnson builds this argument from her analysis of elocution manuals, speakers (books of recitation), and conduct manuals. She argues that women who became orators did so against the larger messages of this rhetorical culture. Great oratory that had the power to move the public remained the province of men.[8]

But what to make of the increasingly visible cohort of women, largely white and middle class, who not only sought formal instruction in elocution but also launched careers as itinerant platform performers? And indeed, how to account for the numbers cited above? A closer examination of these women's careers suggests that the women who became dramatic readers did so *through* the gendered terms of contemporary rhetorical culture. As dramatic reading grew in popularity over the 1870s and '80s and became a mainstay on lyceum lists and in lyceum courses, it simultaneously became a major entry point for women onto the platform.

Both numbers and commentary tell the story of a market saturated by "young ladies." In an 1882 issue of *Lyceum Magazine*, the Redpath Bureau's new owner, George Hathaway, published a "warning . . . to sound ladies" about the challenges and improbability of achieving success as readers. Hathaway described a seemingly endless stream of letters from "ladies in various parts of the country," each hoping for a place on bureau lists and "almost begging us to procure engagements for them, as 'reading' is their only means of obtaining a subsistence." Hathaway warned that scarcely "one in a hundred can ever earn more than the merest pittance." While a noted few had achieved success and contributed to the "erroneous impression" that such a career would put a "large fortune within their grasp," Hathaway explained that for every successful engagement "there are at least fifty struggling aspirants." He urged applicants to seek a "livelihood" in a less competitive field and, for those with the means, to study elocution mainly as an "elegant accomplishment" rather than a "profession." Hathaway's admonition highlighted women's aspirations only to dismiss them as superfluous and their energies as misdirected.[9]

But as closer examination of the career of Gertrude Kellogg makes clear, for the women who became dramatic readers, it was personally empowering to identify something that one was truly good at and to have a goal toward which one could work. Likewise, the ability to earn good money with this skill made a degree of independence possible. Kellogg's diaries help us to see the post–Civil War platform as a site around which women imagined, performed, and were exposed to shifting models of public womanhood.[10] As the first half of this chapter demonstrates, the possibilities of a platform career built on and enlarged components of middle-class girlhood, allowing white middle-class women to achieve a purposeful, fulfilling, independent womanhood.[11]

The performances themselves, however, conformed far more carefully to normative racialized and class-based gender ideals, as the second part of the chapter shows through analysis of repertoire and promotional literature. Indeed, the appeal of dramatic reading both as an entertainment and as a profession was connected to its particular gendered performance, which looks very much like the ideal of "real womanhood,"[12] a set of gender expectations identified by historian Frances Cogan as a contemporary alternative to the "cult of true womanhood" explicated by Barbara Welter. "True womanhood" celebrated woman's moral superiority while anchoring her influence to the domestic sphere and submission to male authority.[13] As scholars have pointed out, these ideals supported white middle-class women's reform work and pursuit of education, yet Cogan argues that this was by no means the only model of femininity open to women. Rather, between the 1840s and the 1880s, didactic and sentimental literature offered an alternative image of an American girl who was intelligent, physically active, self-reliant, economically self-supporting, and "careful about marriage"—although the domestic orientation of American womanhood was hardly challenged by this alternative.[14]

Analysis of the repertoire of dramatic readers, audience response as conveyed through published criticism, and the terms according to which readers were praised or panned underscores how, as dramatic reading was feminized, it became a major site in the construction and policing of a normative, white, middle-class feminine ideal that can be readily identified as Cogan's "real womanhood." Dramatic reading also embodied these ideals with far more consistency and stability than did lecturing, which permitted a wider variety of appearance and age and offered women the opportunity to engage and shape a national conversation about women's civil and social role.[15] The appeal of the feminized dramatic reading entertainment was also highly racialized and nationalistic. Through her performance of sentimental poetry and prose that included regional vernacular fictions, the platform reader became the feminine embodiment of an imaginary white, Anglo-Saxon, Protestant nation emerging out of the Civil War—an embodiment, an agent, if not yet an author.

Becoming a Reader

In 1864, twenty-one-year-old Gertrude Kellogg could not decide whether she wanted to be an actress or a dramatic reader. She was clear, however, on one point: "I love to . . . read I guess it is my chief talent perhaps my only one."[16] She had just started taking reading lessons from a woman in New York, beginning her study with recitation of popular dramatic roles. Thus her first recitation achievement of the year was as Julia from *Hunchback*, a part written for Fanny Kemble in 1829 that was standard repertoire for actresses. She continued her study with *Fazio*, yet another play made famous by Kemble. Kellogg's list of purchases for the year, the plays *A London Assurance*, *Ion*, *Lady of Lyons*, and *The Stranger*, suggest an ambitious course of study that built on a public school education in which she would have learned to recite prose and poetry. It is likely that Kellogg, like countless other schoolchildren, gave public readings for her community at end-of-year exercises. However, when Kellogg began to study elocution in 1864, she did so with a stated goal of becoming a professional performer on both the platform and the dramatic stage.

Kellogg's engagement with the platform and the stage, both as a consumer and a laborer, followed from the transformed status of theater as a legitimate and popular form of middle-class amusement that, after midcentury, was successfully being marketed to middle-class women.[17] Her career highlights changing middle-class leisure practices and women's growing participation in new forms of entertainment culture that, in turn, opened up theater as a legitimate site of employment for women not raised within the profession.[18] Her diaries demonstrate how closely her professional ambitions were linked to her middle-class upbringing and participation in this expanding world of commercial leisure.[19]

Kellogg had enjoyed a comfortable middle-class childhood in Carroll Gardens, Brooklyn. Her father, Charles, worked out of New York as a produce commission merchant, while her mother, Demis, fulfilled the contemporary ideal of domestic maternal femininity. Demis raised three children—Gertrude, her younger sister Fanny, and their elder brother Peter—and maintained the comforts of the family's two-story home with the support of domestic servants. The Kellogg children probably attended a local public school. Gertrude's diaries, which commenced in 1863, when she turned twenty, document the thriving social world and leisure activities of her young adulthood—activities that also nurtured her command of and passion for performance arts. Kellogg and her siblings gathered with their Brooklyn friends and a rotating cast of visiting cousins to play music and create tableaux vivants, mount amateur theatricals, and attend theater, readings, lectures, and concerts in Brooklyn and New York. Both Gertrude and Fanny took music lessons and acquired their own private pupils.[20] What began as requisite accomplishments for a middle-class girl became the foundation on which Gertrude Kellogg imagined and pursued her platform and stage careers.

Kellogg began formal study of dramatic reading at twenty-one, but several years would elapse before she pursued a professional stage career. It is unclear what exactly prompted Kellogg to seek out instruction in elocution. She was a regular theatergoer, although in her diaries she rarely commented at any length on plays or performers. She also went to hear lecturers and dramatic readers with growing frequency as the decade progressed, because of her growing ambitions and the increasing popularity of these entertainments. It is possible that Kellogg's immediate inspiration for her new vocation came from her obsession with the Italian actress and opera singer Felicita Vestvali, who toured the United States in 1864. Kellogg noted that she was "completely fascinated" with Vestvali and, on another occasion, "bewitched." She wrote Vestvali, asking for her autograph, and dreamed that she could "know her."[21] It was within a month of first seeing Vestvali that Kellogg made arrangements to take reading lessons for two dollars a session with Miss Winship in New York.

It seems that Kellogg would have considered trying to be a lecturer if she had had more confidence in her intellectual abilities. Following a mass meeting for woman suffrage in 1869, where she heard such oratorical luminaries as Olive Logan, Frances Park, Henry Ward Beecher, Frederick Douglass, and Phoebe Couzins, she wrote, "If I had the brain to write a lecture as I have the power to deliver it when written, I would take the field and try to do some good."[22] Kellogg's education may not have nurtured confidence in her unique intellect, but dramatic reading was a skill she might master and from which she might even profit. She concluded her 1864 diary by reflecting on the "new source of perfect delight" that was "opened to me . . . in the study of Dramatic Reading. It is meat and drink to me. I hope to make it a source of profit before another year passes."[23]

It would take several more years before Kellogg was able to transition out of the amateur world of the middle-class parlor. In 1867 and 1868 she began taking on her own elocution students and then set up her first paid reading engagements. These early engagements were somewhat ad hoc. Following tests of her abilities at private functions, Kellogg was invited to give a reading in 1867 at a Christmas festival at the local Baptist church. The experience was equally unnerving and invigorating. She wrote in her diary the following day, "It was I think I may say really my first appearance in public, certainly I never spoke before so many people. It seemed pleasant but strange and very *exciting*. Opera glasses leveled at me for the first time at any rate. I was scarcely nervous at all. I am *very glad* I tried myself."[24] Another year would pass before Kellogg had any regular reading engagements. Her first engagements were local, at churches and with the Franklin Literary Society in early 1869. Through social connections, she secured an opportunity to read in Buffalo for the Young Men's Association course. By 1870, this was one of several recurring gigs. Yet she was frustrated that reading engagements remained few and far between and that theatrical engagements, which she sought with stock and touring companies, were rarely longer than a single production; she could not seem to secure a season contract.

Kellogg was doggedly persistent, however. She insisted that managers accommodate her reading engagements, and she continued to look for new venues and connections to advance both facets of her career. In late 1877 a dramatic role took her to Boston. She used local connections to book a reading at the Music Hall and devoted the ensuing months to careful study and preparation. This was the reading performance in February 1878 that so captivated Sallie Joy White. Fresh from the laurels of her Boston success, Kellogg approached the Redpath Lyceum Bureau, also based in Boston. With both Redpath representation and an independent agent, Cotton Clark, she would find the 1878–79 season to be her most successful to date.

Lyceum bureaus like Redpath's were a key agent for the profusion of dramatic readers in the 1870s, the majority of whom did not have theatrical careers. Prior to the Civil War, dramatic readers were usually established actresses and actors who got up reading entertainments, often because they were out of work or hoped to expand their paying public. In the 1830s and '40s, for instance, readings by members of the theatrical profession appealed largely to those who did not go to the theater. Reading entertainments also functioned as handy advertisements for private elocution lessons.

The changing context for dramatic reading as well as changes in Northern white middle-class culture between the 1840s and the 1870s can be illustrated by comparing Kellogg's career with the earlier example of Anna Mowatt, a member of the New York elite. In 1840, Mowatt organized a public entertainment of dramatic readings in Boston to support her husband, who had lost everything after the Panic of 1837. While Kellogg would enjoy the support of family and friends, Mowatt's move onto the platform drew condemnation. Mowatt would later write in her *Autobiography of an Actress* about the social costs of capitalizing on her genteel accomplishments, first on the platform and then, in 1846, on the dramatic stage.[25] Genteel girls of the next generation, such as Kellogg, enjoyed far more independence and physical mobility, including access to a much broader world of leisure. The changing relationship between middle-class culture and commercial leisure created the context in which girls of the 1860s could imagine and pursue careers on both platform and stage.

Figure 7.1 Gertrude Kellogg. Portrait by Armstrong and Company, Boston, from *The Redpath Lyceum, Season of 1878–79*. Kellogg Family Papers, box 11, image #93220d, New-York Historical Society. Photography © New-York Historical Society.

By the 1860s, dramatic reading had come to occupy its own space within a broad spectrum of entertainments, connected to but not entirely defined by its not being theater. This cultural shift helps to account for the proliferation of women as platform readers after midcentury—although as Kellogg's career makes clear, it was just as likely that a woman might pursue the stage as well. The appeal of dramatic reading as profession and entertainment was certainly connected to broader antitheatricalism in American culture, expressed through aversions to theater as a morally dangerous space and perceptions of acting as a morally bankrupt profession. As the century progressed, this would remain true even as theater managers became more successful in marketing theater as a respectable middle-class amusement.[26] In fact, dramatic reading was among the many "paratheatrical entertainments" that vied for nineteenth-century audiences, including lantern shows, blackface minstrelsy, concerts, and lectures.[27] These amusements could be put on in a range of venues and with low overheads. They were also competitive with the cost of a theater ticket, ranging from twenty-five cents to the rare extreme of one dollar. After the Civil War, the bureaus that formed to manage lecturers expanded to incorporate more of these other platform entertainments, including dramatic readers, musical soloists and ensembles, stereopticon views, ventriloquists, opera combinations, and even the occasional theatrical performance.[28] The post–Civil War lyceum and the place of the dramatic reader within this evolving and increasingly corporate institution participated in a long and varied nineteenth-century practice of paratheatrical platform performance.[29]

Rarely was the platform the elocutionist's only sphere of labor, let alone an end in itself. It was a somewhat ad hoc genre of performance pursued by retired or out-of-work actors and actresses and by "professors" (men) and "teachers" (women) of elocution who were advertising for students and adding to their income—or perhaps trying to leave the schoolroom behind them permanently. Much like lecturing, dramatic reading should be considered an "act in the construction and conduct of . . . professional or intellectual careers."[30] Dramatic readers were often pursuing careers in education or literature as well as the dramatic stage. This is where significant patterns in the careers and marketing of dramatic readers in the 1870s break down according to gender. Men who offered readings on the post–Civil War platform were more likely to be marketed as experts, either in the art and science of elocution or in a particular category of literature. Professors of oratory like Moses T. Brown of Tufts College used the platform to extend their careers in higher education, performing their expertise.[31] An emerging group of dialect humorists like William Andrews used the lyceum to showcase their own work.[32] In contrast, women writers like Grace Greenwood and Julia Ward Howe, who found employment on the platform, lectured on gendered topics, exemplified by Howe's 1873 offerings, "Is Polite Society Polite?" and "Men's Women and Women's Women."[33] Women rarely performed their own literary productions.

Many of the readers who found work on the post–Civil War platform were also pursuing stage careers or were veteran stage actors. English tragedian George Vandenhoff, who was in demand by lyceums for his Shakespearean recitations, had been offering reading entertainments for the past thirty years. For women in particular, going on the platform as a dramatic reader was often linked with broader ambitions for the dramatic stage. But notwithstanding the Shakespearean reading—an enduring entertainment that had grown in popularity following Fanny Kemble's wildly successful 1849 tour and was offered by both men and women—the majority of women who went on the platform as readers in the 1870s offered a miscellaneous entertainment of prose and poetry. While men also gave miscellaneous entertainments, women rarely presented single-author entertainments and never offered interpretive lectures. Women's interpretive abilities were to be found in the literary performance itself. In short, the feminization of dramatic reading in the 1870s was connected with the miscellaneous entertainment.

More significant still in understanding the feminization of dramatic reading is the place that both platform and stage occupied relative to more limited and comparatively underpaid professional employment opportunities for middle-class women.[34] Here, the rough contours of Kellogg's career are representative. Platform reading, like lecturing, increased the earning potential of educated white middle-class women and made marriage more choice than necessity. Dramatic readers like Kellogg were the daughters of upwardly mobile middle-class strivers. A career on the platform furnished financial independence while allowing these women to sustain their class identity.

Like many a son who uses his father's business connections to obtain a trade, Kellogg found in the material and professional support of her family an enhancement of her professional ambitions, although some of this attention may have reflected the closer control they expected to exert over an unmarried daughter. Kellogg lived in the family home at Carroll Gardens until her death (but her brother inherited the house). This arrangement offered vital material security as she faced the uncertainties of life as an entertainer. Her father facilitated some early connections with managers and agents.[35] In the 1860s and '70s, Kellogg often traveled with her mother or sister, but they accompanied her less frequently as she grew older and more successful.

Were Kellogg's parents aware of her stated determination, at age twenty-one, that she would "live and die single"?[36] Perhaps this was the defensive posture of a girl who, unlike several of her friends, had not yet enjoyed any romances or offers of marriage. But over the next decade, as Kellogg navigated two serious attachments, ultimately turning down both her suitors, she seems not to have faced any strong pressures from her parents to choose matrimony over career ambitions. Instead, Kellogg was able to defer and ultimately to avoid marriage while pursuing her youthful dream and earning an independent income.

It is clear that Kellogg's earnings were hers to dispose of, but she may have used them to supplement the family income. Money was often tight at home, particularly in the hard times of the 1870s, and Kellogg's income could help the household sustain middle-class comforts. Overall, she seems to have enjoyed a significant degree of independence and support. Kellogg had long recognized the importance of financial independence in the careers of other women in the lyceum. Upon seeing lecturer and journalist Kate Field deliver "Woman in the Lyceum" in May 1869, Kellogg wrote, "I hope Kate Field will coin for herself fame, and what is more essential for comfort in this world—money."[37]

As Kellogg's trajectory demonstrates, George Hathaway was missing the point when he urged girls to stop trying to be professional readers and instead to pursue reading mainly as a genteel accomplishment. Rather, young women could parlay this accomplishment into fame and fortune—or at least into a modicum of financial independence and personal autonomy. Reading was appealing as a profession not only because it drew on components of middle-class education and domestic leisure but also because it was a form of performance that attracted audiences *through* the white middle-class feminine ideal.

Her "Wonderful Power of Word-Painting"

On 1 February 1870, Gertrude Kellogg "woke up to find myself the subject of a most cutting criticism in the Tribune"—and for her first paid performance at that.[38] She had read the evening before at a benefit for a church in New York. Dramatic critic William Winter, who reviewed the debut for the *New York Tribune*, was disappointed. He may have been the wrong man for the job, since he held a low opinion of dramatic reading as entertainment. Although Winter granted that "many ladies and gentlemen . . . read with feeling and taste," Kellogg, he said, did not "show . . . dramatic talent . . . on this occasion." Her selections were either "weak" or delivered poorly. She performed John Greenleaf Whittier's "Barbara Freitchie," Winter said, "without characterization and without fire." "Sheridan's Ride" by T. B. Read and Robert Browning's "How They Brought the News from Ghent to Aix," both verses chronicling the exploits of heroic messengers in time of war, were "not in Miss Kellogg's line."[39]

Kellogg did have redeeming qualities, Winter wrote. She was pretty, a "blonde, with a slightly aquiline face," and she spoke in a "smooth, pleasant voice." She had all the requisite training: her "enunciation is pure; her gestures are easy." Winter concluded that like most "public readers," Kellogg possessed the "sensibility to appreciate" literature but lacked the "power to interpret or the magnetism to thrill." Although she was adept at "mild satire" and had an appealing "relish for fun," the performance amounted to little more than "respectable mediocrity."[40]

This review was hardly encouraging, but Kellogg determined "not [to] let it trouble me."[41] She redoubled her efforts, increasing her lessons so that she would not disappoint at a forthcoming engagement in Buffalo. It seems that Kellogg also took some constructive advice from Winter: in Buffalo her renditions of Read's and Browning's works seemed "too violent and impetuous at times," according to a reporter for the *Buffalo Courier*. The entertainment, however, was unquestionably successful. Although Winter had endured an expected evening of sober mediocrity, the *Courier* reporter was surprised to discover that the "debutante" was an accomplished "*artiste*."[42]

Tellingly, the Buffalo writer identified the same qualities enumerated wearily by Winter but gave them a different spin. Kellogg spoke with "a voice of great compass and fine quality . . . under admirable control." She was "easy and natural in gesture and graceful in her bearing." Her selections and delivery indicated "an industrious and intelligent student." The reporter expected "a brilliant career."[43] Winter, on the other hand, merely expected her to "maintain a rank among the ordinary readers of the day."[44] This juxtaposition of reviews, one from a theater critic who did not consider dramatic reading worthy of its growing popularity, the other from a critic eager to recognize and praise a promising new performer in a worthy line of work, helps us understand the terms according to which readers were judged and the standards whereby they were seen to excel.

The most consistently valued quality in a reading entertainment, noted by Kellogg's Buffalo critic, was her ability to move between "interpretation of passion and sentiment."[45] Effective elocution was affective. As one midcentury elocution manual explained, "whenever a good elocution exhibits itself in the speaker," the audience is able to "feel the overwhelming power of his eloquence."[46] A speaking manual from the turn of the twentieth century elucidated many of the same principles. Elocution was the "art of conveying thought, sentiment and emotion in the most natural and effective manner" in such a way that "his hearers see, hear, and *feel* the unquestioned truth of his statement."[47] Although the application of these principles to oratory may be more readily apparent, midcentury platform publics eagerly sought and delighted in the affective experiences that dramatic readers provided. Audiences attended these entertainments expecting an emotional journey brought about through performance of familiar and beloved literature. And literature, in turn, might achieve its full artistic and affective potential through the delivery of an accomplished reader.

A typical reading program from the 1870s alternated the pathetic, dramatic, and comic. In this variation Kellogg was highly representative, alternating pathetic or dramatic verses with a comic poem or prose monologue. The handbill for a series of readings in Plattsburgh, New York, in March 1878 under the auspices of the Young People's Association suggests how she structured her entertainment. The performance consisted of two acts of three or four selections, with each act followed by musical entertainments (and probably separated by an intermission). All her pieces were rich in visual imagery, the poems often plot-driven, conveying sentiments heroic, patriotic, pathetic, and occasionally tragic. Kellogg consistently began her readings with one of two narrative poems: Browning's "The Pied Piper" or T. B. Macaulay's epic of ancient Rome, "Virginia." Browning was the lighter fare, its chilling story of children spirited away by the vengeful Pied Piper captured through fanciful and, at times, comic imagery.

At Plattsburgh, the remainder of the evening's first act alternated the pathetic with the comic: Browning was followed by Trowbridge's "Darius Green," then T. B. Aldrich's "The Face Against the Pane" about little Mabel watching for her "fisher lover . . . out there in the storm." The act concluded with an energetic tale of a hunt, Adam Lindsay Gordon's "How We Beat the Favorite." In the second act, two sober epics positioned the audience for a rapid and exhilarating shift in mood as Kellogg closed the evening with the dialect monologue "Kitty Maloney on the Chinese Question" by Mary Mapes Dodge.[48] Kellogg always ended her evenings with laughter.

Kellogg's alterations to the program for her second performance the following day suggest the care she took in pacing the evening's affective journey while working from a consistent and contained repertoire. She had planned to open her second program with "Virginia" but switched it for Whittier's "Barbara Freitchie," thus opening her program with a stirring anecdote of female bravery that could instill national pride.[49] Kellogg kept the mood bright with Oliver Wendell Holmes's "The One Hoss Shay," about the Deacon's indestructible buggy, which also offered a lesson about the pitfalls of pride. The heroic and patriotic nostalgia of Alice Cary's "The Young Soldier" called back to Whittier, while also setting up Macaulay's "Virginia," ending the act on a more sober note than originally planned. Audiences might dwell on the account of a Roman farmer's sacrificial murder of his daughter to save her from enslavement and the sexual designs of the corrupt patrician Claudius. This was a heavy program, followed by humor and heroic exploits: the second act began with a Yankee vernacular performance of J. T. Trowbridge's comic monologue poem "Old Simon Dole" and ended with a series

Figure 7.2   Recitations by Miss Gertrude Kellogg, broadside for a reading in Plattsburgh, New York, March 1878. Kellogg Family Papers, box 11, image #93219d, New-York Historical Society. Photography © New-York Historical Society.

of monologue excerpts from the comedy of manners *A London Assurance*. Browning's "How They Brought the News from Ghent to Aix" balanced the humor with some fast-paced heroism.[50]

By the late 1870s, Kellogg was in full command of her powers. She excelled at humor. Her rendition of Trowbridge's "Darius Green and His Flying Machine" (featured by many readers) remained a favorite, with reporters consistently commenting on her "rare facility with humorous delineation."[51] Her powers with the pathetic had likewise grown. As Sallie Joy White explained in a piece for the *Lowell Courier*, also excerpted in Kellogg's Redpath circular, "I really believe she made everyone in the house forget there was any but the reader and herself in the hall. I know I was perfectly oblivious to my surroundings, and I think she brought the tears to my eyes."[52] Lyceum-goers eagerly sought these experiences. Kellogg's circulars from the 1870s comprised excerpts from the press that enumerated her pleasing appearance and qualities of voice and identified the emotions her performances would elicit. However, as reviews likewise suggest, the reader's physical appearance and gendered performance of class as much as her powers of elocution made possible this kind of affective experience.

Dramatic reading aligned readily with genteel white feminine ideals. Physical beauty was valued highly in platform readers, but beyond the aesthetics of facial features, hair, figure, and costume, readers were also expected to demonstrate qualities that communicated gentility and naturalness. White described Kellogg as a "slight, graceful figure, earnest face, and honest blue eyes" and "prettily dressed too, in a trailing black velvet dress, trimmed with pale blue silk." The long description captured the fall of her lace jabot and hair, "which waved without the aid of crimping pins." Kellogg's Plattsburgh reviewer commented approvingly on qualities that aligned with a gendered performance of class: "pleasing address, perfect self-possession, tasteful attire, graceful proportions and gestures, and comeliness of feature."[53] The resounding sameness of language in reviews of readers like Kellogg underscores the qualities that enabled these women successfully to claim a lyceum public and to move an audience.

Although cultured genteel femininity was itself a carefully curated performance, its effect was enhanced by the appearance of being unaffected. When Sallie Joy White gushed about Kellogg's "straightforward walk, with no mincing or absurd airs" and explained that it "gave me faith in her at once," White was in effect describing an appearance of artless gentility. This was a quality prized in other readers as well. Compare the terms used to describe Kellogg with the language praising another Redpath reader, Laura Dainty: Dainty possessed a "rare and cultured talent" (Kansas City, Missouri) and a "highly cultured" voice (Jackson, Michigan) but was "spontaneous and unaffected" (Peru, Indiana), more charming for her "artistic artlessness" (Logansport, Iowa) and her "naturalness" (Adrian, Michigan).[54] Dainty was also an aspiring actress and former public schoolteacher in Illinois. Her career resembled Kellogg's inasmuch as dramatic reading produced income and renown that ultimately supported her career as a thespian. But both women, though known to their lyceum publics as aspiring actresses, delivered performances on the platform that audiences and critics identified as distinct from the embodied performance of acting. The appearance of artless gentility was key to this differentiation.

Promotional material drew a clear distinction between the reader and the actress, drawn around the quality of "artistic artlessness" that distinguished elocution. Even as readers were praised for effectively subsuming their own individuality in the characters they "bring to life," this kind of performance could not be found in theaters.[55] The *Buffalo Express* considered Kellogg to be "our ideal of true and pure dramatic elocution, marred by no mannerisms of the stage."[56] The importance of the distinction had to do less with a perception of acting as a disreputable profession that might compromise a reader's claim to her public and more with an understanding that the dramatic reader remained herself throughout her performance. While the actress transformed herself into a character, the dramatic reader moved through a profusion of characters. The actress's virtuosity involved sustaining an illusion of total transformation, whereas the reader's virtuosity involved an array of moods and characters, particularly characters that she could not herself become. In short, the appeal of dramatic reading operated through juxtaposition of a naturalized ideal of white feminine gentility and the performance of a range of literary scenes and characters. The performance showcased her elocutionary art, even as the reader was presumed to be artlessly genteel, or genteel by virtue of her artlessness. So concluded a Milwaukee reporter about Laura Dainty: "She is nature itself, apes no one, does not endeavor to please, or strain for applause, but forgets self and surroundings in her sympathy with the subject. Her voice is superb, her presence bright and pleasing, her carriage graceful, and her entire freedom from affectation wins her audiences wherever she goes."[57] Yet when critics praised readers for their artlessness, they were responding to a highly effective performance of genteel white femininity.

The effectiveness of dramatic reading was likewise presented in highly gendered and classed terms, aptly illustrated by the opening anecdote in

Dainty's 1878 promotional booklet about a gratis reading before convicts at a prison in Lincoln, Nebraska. When this "brave little woman" delivered Anna Stansbury's poem about a Charleston slave who saved St. Michael's Church from burning, her "wonderful power of word-painting aroused in the imaginations of the men their slumbering ideals of heroism" and caused the "rigid lines of the hardened criminal [to] relax and soften."[58] The transformative effect of the poem was made possible by the genteel femininity of the performer, her body and interpretation of literature credited with the power to awaken a dormant desire for virtue. This account of her visit to the prison connected the power and appeal of dramatic reading with woman's civilizing influence. But the transformative power of the reading was also based on a conviction among her auditors that she remained in some way herself.

This was the key to understanding the platform appeal of regional dialect literatures, a type in "special demand" in the 1860s and '70s. Their popularity was closely connected with national economic integration achieved by innovations in technology and corporate capitalism in the Gilded Age, as well as the fraught processes of postwar recovery and reconciliation. Tales of provincial places told in vernacular voices promised to capture regional cultures that seemed to be under threat. In the context of the fraught work of reunification, regional vernacular literature implicitly positioned reimagined "local cultures" within a historical narrative of national progress.[59]

Performances by dramatic readers enhanced the broader cultural, nationalistic, and racial work of this "local color" literature. In "Old Simon Dole," for example, Kellogg spoke in the voice of a geriatric Yankee farmer reminiscing to his widowed sister about the vagaries of his fifty years of married life. Dole delivered what might have been perceived at the time as a comparatively quaint notion of gender roles. The performance, however, could either reinscribe these gender roles or poke fun at them and signal progress. Much depended on the interpretive choice of the reader, but different messages could be heard by members of the same audience. Dole ranted, "I hate / a women 'at wears the breeches; an' so, / Mebby, by tryin' to stan' too straight, / When she'd have bent me a little, I fell / Over back now an' then,—do'no'; can't tell." Dole had no patience for his wife Mary's middle-class pretensions, such as her scheme to "Give Simon a college education." Dole also complained that Mary "Teased me to send our secon' dotter / (She snowed 't would cos' like all creation!) / To boardin'-school, an' have a pyaner." He doubted that all this "education" would help the girls "fin' good husban's" or "make good wives." Here was the folk response to mainstays of modern middle-class life. Through the voice of the old timer, the poem conjured up a powerful domestic and gender ideal in the face of modernity.

It also referenced ongoing demographic transformations. Simon Dole and his auditor, his sister, were all who remained, while the children were "doin' re'l well, out West." The poem, meanwhile, connected its auditors to that imagined world of simple, sensible, hardworking Yankee farm folk, who also dispensed useful wisdom for the new generations. Dole had choice words to say about the institution of marriage: "Men tock o' divorce,—that never 'd be needed, / If all drah'd true in the yoke as she did." The poem concluded with a stirring affirmation of a time and type of family that never existed, speaking reassuringly to the changes of the day—or the backwardness of the past.[60]

The reading surely heightened the emotional effect of the poem and likewise showcased Kellogg's mastery of the Yankee dialect as well as her interpretive abilities. Through the recitation, Kellogg was able to conjure scene and character, joining the familiar poem with her new interpretation and producing among her audience an intersubjective emotional experience. Further, the contrast of Kellogg's comparative youth and femininity intensified the particular humor and poignancy of Dole's lines. She was physically, socially, regionally, and culturally distanced from her character, and yet as a young woman, she was readily aligned with the feelings of nostalgia for home and family that the poem inspired in its auditors. It is also worth considering how the performance of first-person pieces like "Old Simon Dole" allowed a young woman to develop a characterization that would never have been open to her on the dramatic stage. Yet both the entertainment form and its performative context, the platform, preserved the reader's social status, in contrast to the increasingly popular genre of burlesque, which afforded women a different avenue for developing comic vernacular portrayals of both male and female characters.[61]

The opacity of much nineteenth-century criticism makes it difficult to imagine the dramatic textures of these performances. One wonders what vocal acrobatics, facial expressions, and gestures led a Brooklyn reporter to single out Kellogg's "peculiar method of interpreting" the character of the Irish domestic Kitty Maloney, which "invested it with new interest" and "afforded abundant evidence of the artist's veracity."[62] And yet, consideration of the expressive elements necessary for performance of vernacular dialect literature, particularly humor, is our most productive means of imagining the varieties of vocal and physical expressiveness in the dramatic reading performance, thinking through conflicting claims about its distance from acting, and asking whether there were more subversive elements to some of these entertainments than critics allowed. A reviewer of Kellogg's 1878 Plattsburgh reading singled out her voice as well as her "wonderfully mobile features," no doubt connected with her "rare faculty for humorous delineations."[63]

Early reviews of Kellogg suggest that in the process of developing their skills, readers struggled to achieve the right degree of intensity—for example, in more suspenseful or plot-driven pieces. Vocal tone, flexibility, and control were paramount, but audiences also scrutinized the reader's movements; skillful delivery should combine dramatic effect of voice with the appearance of ease in gesture and use of the body.

It is less clear from reviews how much readers were expected to perform with the face and body—or in what ways they actually did. Kellogg clearly used the performative skills from her parallel acting career to enhance her affective powers on the platform. Likewise, Kellogg's memorization of her program meant that she also could deliver it without a desk or lectern, which created more opportunities for physical expression. But when the Plattsburgh critic noted that Kellogg's profusion of genteel qualities aided "her audience" in "overcoming their repugnance to any eccentrics of manner or otherwise," was he referring to choices that stretched the acceptable contours of the genteel performance? Were some aspects of these performances too jarring a contrast with the carefully cultivated gestalt of genteel white American womanhood that appeared on the platform? A conservative reading of the sources supports a qualified conclusion: as women dramatic readers carved out space on the platform through a normative gender performance, the cultivation of this ideal made possible their performance of a range of contemporary literatures. These texts likewise helped to reinforce a genteel feminine ideal invested with domestic and sentimental virtues, even as the presence of young, middle-class white women became firmly established on American platforms, serving as a new model of public womanhood.

Conclusion

One wonders whether Kellogg would have recognized herself in Elizabeth Cady Stanton's "coming girl," an idealized figure at the center of Stanton's lyceum lecture "Our Girls." In an 1880 version of this lecture, Stanton imagined that the "coming girl" would be raised to "have an individual aim and purpose in life" like any boy, with the ability to support herself and to depend on no man. In contrast to this "coming girl," Stanton described a "beautiful girl just eighteen" who was told, despite her "strong steadfast desire for years to be educated for the stage," that it was "not respectable." This Stanton found absurd and no longer true, although she wanted women to look even beyond the stage for a career. Stanton asked, rhetorically, "What do the guardians of this girl propose for the sacrifice they ask? Can they substitute another strong purpose?" Instead, like most girls of the day, she would discover that her anointed purpose was to "fulfill [her] man-appointed sphere" and that she was to have "no individual character, no life purpose, personal freedom, aim or ambition" otherwise.[64]

Kellogg, on the other hand, embarked on what was largely a journey of personal fulfillment, able to act on her "strong purpose" while enjoying the support of family and friends. However, she was impatient for success, even turning down a position in the auxiliary corps of Edwin Booth's theater in 1868 because she wanted to star. Rather than preparing Kellogg for "blasted" domesticity, as Stanton described it, if anything Kellogg's upbringing supported what may have been unrealistic expectations about the route to stardom.[65] But the path that she carved out over the 1870s as dramatic reader and actress allowed her to nurture her "individual character" and "life purpose," achieving "personal freedom" as well as financial self-sufficiency—all qualities Stanton hoped for in her "coming girl." Kellogg's close relationship with her sister, brother, and sister-in-law also meant that the comforts of middle-class domesticity surrounded her even though she forswore marriage. Thus Kellogg's career manifested a cultural shift that had led to a profusion of women platform performers and actresses out of the homes of the white middle class. For these women, both platform and stage became legitimate vehicles for achieving an independent livelihood, but their performances built on core features of middle-class girlhood, including a set of ideals that historian Frances Cogan has characterized as "real womanhood" and that Stanton likewise built on to construct her "coming girl."

Certainly Kellogg's life illustrated these ideals, yet stories like Kellogg's are rarely found in scholars' investigations of changing gender roles of the post–Civil War era. We have been more likely to focus on lecturers like Stanton, who used the platform to participate in a broader set of conversations about women's changing roles in society, while her career as a lecturer enacted these new possibilities.[66] Dramatic readers enacted and performed these possibilities, even as their performances reinscribed a highly racialized and classed feminine ideal. Indeed, dramatic readers constructed careers on the platform through these norms. Their carefully honed, racialized, and gendered performances of gentility facilitated their move onto the platform, effecting the feminization of the dramatic reading entertainment from the 1870s on. Through this new form of public womanhood, the dramatic reader became a feminine embodiment of an imaginary white, Anglo-Saxon, Protestant nation emerging out of the Civil War.

8

TALKING MUSIC:
AMY FAY AND THE ORIGINS OF THE LECTURE RECITAL

E. Douglas Bomberger

"Where words leave off, music begins." This famous aphorism attributed to Goethe captures the tension between music and language that was keenly felt among performers, audiences, and music critics in the nineteenth century. The tension is illustrated by the contrast between the prominent German composers Felix Mendelssohn (1809–1847) and Richard Wagner (1813–1883). Mendelssohn distrusted words so much that he preferred simply to play his music rather than explaining it. He believed that the meaning of a musical composition was too specific to be described in language. His rival Wagner, however, was known for lengthy verbal explanations of his music, as well as for composing both the texts and music for his operas, an unusual practice in any era.[1] The nineteenth century also saw the growth of the new field of musicology, an explosion in the number of journals devoted to writing about music, and the publication of several foundational reference works in the field. Following the example of European authors, John Weeks Moore published the *Complete Encyclopaedia of Music* in Boston in 1854, the first comprehensive dictionary of music issued in the United States. A generation later, British scholar George Grove reshaped musical scholarship in the English language with his four-volume *A Dictionary of Music and Musicians*, published in London between 1879 and 1890.[2] These publications supported the Wagnerian view that music—and particularly instrumental music—was more deeply appreciated when listeners were educated about its structure and meaning.

The nineteenth century also gave birth to a new form of lecture that, in the right hands, could illuminate and clarify instrumental music in ways that enhanced an audience's appreciation. What is now known as the lecture recital—a performance of music accompanied by verbal explanations designed to deepen the audience's understanding of the music—was pioneered in the late nineteenth century by an American pianist seeking to reinvigorate her languishing career. When Amy Fay introduced her "piano conversations" to Chicago audiences in the spring of 1883, she created a model that not only ensured her own professional success but also inspired countless imitators. The success of her innovation, which continues to thrive in the twenty-first century, proves that her idea was suited to an era when audiences were eager not only for entertainment but also for education.

Fay's Musical Education

Amy Muller Fay (1844–1928) was born in Bayou Goula, Louisiana, but she spent her childhood in St. Albans, Vermont, before moving to Cambridge, Massachusetts, in 1862. Her parents fostered an intellectually stimulating home environment filled with art, music, and literature. Like most American women of the middle class, Fay took music lessons as a child. She was unusual, however, in aspiring to a professional career in this field. The last two decades of the nineteenth century would produce more female professional performers than ever before, but Fay was ahead of this trend in the 1860s.[3] As a young adult in Cambridge she studied piano with Otto Dresel, a German immigrant pianist and composer who had been a pupil of Mendelssohn and Schumann in Europe, and she attended lectures on musical topics by John Knowles Paine, the first professor of music at Harvard University. She became a close friend of poet Henry Wadsworth Longfellow, nearly forty years her elder, who would later be a crucial mentor in her publishing efforts. Her older sister Melusina "Zina" Fay Peirce, who married the philosopher Charles Sanders Peirce in 1862, was a noted feminist writer who advocated a system of cooperative housekeeping that would afford middle-class women more time for intellectual pursuits. Zina was one of the first-wave feminists who, along with other prominent woman's rights advocates, laid the groundwork for later political, legal, and social activism.[4] The two sisters were very close, and it is clear Zina's progressive ideas influenced Amy's desire to stretch the limits of gender restrictions in her profession.

In 1869, at the age of twenty-five, Fay traveled to Berlin to pursue advanced music studies. Music, like athletics, is a profession that requires not only intellectual understanding but also years of intense physical training. It is typical for professional musicians to begin serious studies at age four or five

Figure 8.1 Amy Fay, circa 1870s. Preston Tuttle Collection, Institute for Studies in Pragmaticism, Texas Tech University.

and to arrive at a highly skilled level in their early teens. Most nineteenth-century conservatory students were teenagers, as conventional wisdom held that beyond a certain age it was too late to pursue advanced training, both because of the physical requirements and because of the mental demands of this rigorous pursuit. Fay was unusual because she was much older than the typical music student, but she compensated through her dogged determination. In Germany she devoted long hours to practicing the piano, overcoming the skepticism of some of her teachers who doubted whether she could master the necessary skills.

Although her age was unusual, her choice to study in Germany was not. The perception in the United States at this time was that no schools in the nation could offer adequate preparation for a professional career in music. Germany had a rich array of top-notch schools in Berlin, Leipzig, Stuttgart, and other cities that attracted Americans who could afford to travel and live abroad for an extended period. At least five thousand Americans studied in Germany's musical conservatories between 1850 and 1915.[5] Amy Fay stayed in Germany from 1869 to 1875, a period when the aftermath of the Franco-Prussian War of 1870–71 led to dramatic economic expansion. Her presence in Germany during this vibrant period allowed her to study with pianists Carl Tausig, Theodor Kullak, Ludwig Deppe, and most famously Franz Liszt (1811–1886). The elderly Hungarian pianist, whose virtuoso performances in his youth had conquered Europe in a wave of "Lisztomania," spent his summers in the sleepy Thuringian town of Weimar teaching master classes to a small group of aspiring pianists. He did not teach piano lessons in the traditional manner of systematic technical instruction over the course of many years. Instead, he met twice weekly with a select group of young pianists whose prior training and professional aspirations made them especially receptive to his advanced but unsystematic teaching. His classes were famous for attracting future concert pianists to an atmosphere where the competition was fierce and his insights were highly prized. Fay was apprehensive about her chances of acceptance, but she played well enough at her audition to be accepted into his class in 1873, and her lessons during that spring and summer formed the defining experience of her musical career.[6]

Fay as an Author

During her six years in Germany, Fay maintained an active correspondence with family and friends at home. Her letters to her family described in engaging prose the challenges of music study and the frustrations of cross-cultural interactions. An 1873 letter contrasting the performances of pianist Franz Liszt and violinist Joseph Joachim is characteristic:

> Like Liszt, [Joachim] so vitalizes everything that I have to take him in all over again every time I hear him. I am always astonished, amazed and delighted afresh, and even as I listen I can hardly believe that the man *can* play so! But Liszt, in addition to his marvellous playing, has this unique and imposing personality, whereas at first Joachim is not specially striking. Liszt's face is all a play of feature, a glow of fancy, a blaze of imagination, whereas Joachim is absorbed in his violin, and his face has only an expression of fine discrimination and of intense solicitude to produce his artistic effects. Liszt never looks at his instrument; Joachim never looks at anything else. Liszt is a complete actor who intends to carry away the public, who never forgets that he is before it, and who behaves accordingly. Joachim is totally oblivious of it. Liszt subdues the people to him by the very way he walks on to the stage. He gives his proud head a toss, throws an electric look out of his eagle eye, and seats himself with an air as much as to say, "Now I am going to do just what I please with you, and you are nothing but puppets subject to my will." . . . In reality I admire Joachim's principle the most, but there is something indescribably fascinating and subduing about Liszt's willfulness. You feel at once that he is a great genius, and that you *are* nothing but his puppet, and somehow you take a base delight in the humiliation! The two men are intensely interesting, each in his own way, but they are extremes.[7]

This passage illustrates Fay's ability to humanize world-famous celebrities. Although she is awed by the accomplishments of each man, her awe does not impede her ability to describe in vivid, analytic prose their distinctive qualities.

Throughout the course of her six years in Germany, Amy applied this astute observational skill to a range of topics, from the profound and rarefied world of the concert artists she admired to the petty annoyances of living in a German boardinghouse:

> I shall relish a good dinner when I come home, for this is the land where what we call "family dinners" are unknown. They have *parts* of meals five times a day, but never a complete one. The meat is dreadful, and I never can tell what kind of an animal it grows on. They give me

two boiled eggs for supper, so I manage to live, but O! *has* beefsteak vanished into the land of dreams? and *is* turkey but the figment of my disordered imagination? They have delicious bread and butter, but "man cannot live by bread alone." Mr. F. says that where *he* boards they give him "pear soup, and cherry soup, and plum soup!"[8]

Zina admired the style and the content of these letters so much that she arranged to have excerpts published anonymously in the *Atlantic Monthly* in 1874, while Amy was still in Germany.[9] An explanatory footnote at the start of this compilation shows the care that Zina took to hide the identity of both author and editor: "The reader will please to note the dates of the letters, which, as well as those from Weimar about Liszt, were written home without a thought of publication. One of A.F.'s friends wished to print extracts from her letters, and though she would not say 'yes,' she did not say 'no.' With this negative permission they were arranged for The Atlantic without her supervision, and are given almost *verbatim* as they left her rapid pen."[10] The motivation for this note may be interpreted on the one hand as humility, but on the other as a desire to avoid the risk of criticism in this public forum. Amy Fay's biographer Margaret McCarthy points out that Zina's claim to have published the letters "almost *verbatim*" is not entirely true, since she exercised "a heavy editorial hand" in excising anything of a personal nature that would shed light on the author.[11]

Despite Zina's efforts to excise her sister's most obvious personal observations, it was the author's personality that most appealed to readers in the excerpted letters published in 1874. Fay's ability to make astute assessments of famous European musicians while also retaining a sense of naïve wonder at their discovery proved to be a winning combination. After her return to the United States in 1875, Fay's friends urged her to expand on the letters published in the *Atlantic Monthly* by publishing a compilation of her letters in book form. With Longfellow's support, her sister Zina compiled and published a book of Amy's letters in 1880 under the title *Music-Study in Germany*. She selected letters that balanced her sister's personal observations of living conditions in Germany with information on music educational practices and concert life in the country Americans considered to be the epicenter of musical culture. Amy's writing and Zina's editing created a vivid literary portrait of contemporary Germany and the welcome that a young American had found there.

This book exceeded the expectations of even her most optimistic friends. The first edition, published in Chicago in 1880, was an immediate popular success. The book went through well over a dozen American editions during her lifetime, it was translated into German and French, and it has never gone out of print. More important, it inspired thousands of American music students to follow her by studying in European musical conservatories. By 1890, more than half the students at the Leipzig Conservatory were international students, a pattern repeated at many of Germany's leading music schools. Ethelbert Nevin, a composer contemporary to Fay, called *Music-Study in Germany* "The Book of the Age."[12] This was no doubt hyperbole, but it helps us to understand the book's widespread cultural significance.

The success of Fay's book created an ongoing interest in her writings. Among the music periodicals that often featured her essays were *The Etude* (Philadelphia) and *Music* (Chicago). In addition to offering reflections on musicians she had known in Europe and America, she wrote extensively about piano technique and teaching. She became America's leading advocate for the method of Ludwig Deppe, the last teacher with whom she had studied in Germany. She published not only journal articles advocating the Deppe system but also a collection of his exercises for use by piano students.[13]

Fay as a Pianist

Although Fay would be best known as an author, the goal of her European studies had been to prepare herself to be a concert pianist, a career traditionally dominated by men. The short list of successful European female pianists included Clara Schumann (1819–1896), widow of Robert Schumann; Marie Pleyel (1811–1875), daughter-in-law of an important Paris piano manufacturer; Sophie Menter (1846–1918), Liszt's favorite female student; and Annette Essipoff (1851–1914), who toured the United States in 1876. The even shorter list of American women pianists who made careers on the concert stage included Venezuelan Teresa Carreño (1853–1917) and Cincinnati native Julie Rivé-King (1854–1937), who had studied with Liszt in Weimar at the same time as Fay.[14] By the early twentieth century, more American women would make careers as concert pianists, including Fannie Bloomfield-Zeisler (1863–1927), Amy Beach (1867–1944), and Olga Samaroff (1882–1948), but in the 1870s Fay had few models.

She made a successful concert debut in Cambridge on 19 January 1876. The audiences for her concerts in her hometown were uncritical, and newspaper critics were supportive. On 16 February she was heard for the first time in Boston, in a concert at the Horticultural Hall for the benefit of St. Luke's Home for Convalescents. The concert featured performances by a variety of local musicians, but her appearance was highly anticipated, as noted by the

Boston Globe: "She comes of a Cambridge family, and is already well-known by reputation to many Boston people. Her first appearance here was therefore the subject of the most vivid interest, and it is scarcely too much to add that the expectations of music lovers have been quite fulfilled with regard to her talents. She has had the advantage of the best of training and is said to be ardently devoted to her art. . . . Her touch is vigorous and masculine, yet elastic and assured in style, and her reception yesterday was most gratifying."[15] Nineteenth-century Romantic performance style demanded a full range of emotional expression, from poetic sensitivity to dramatic power. Contemporary stereotypes of women ascribed to them the former rather than the latter because of physical strength on the one hand and perceptions of emotional frailty on the other. When a reviewer called attention to a woman's vigor and masculinity, he signaled to readers that she displayed a noteworthy emotional range. After Fay's successful concerts during her first winter in Cambridge, she established herself as a piano instructor and continued playing solo works in concerts throughout the greater Boston area, most often in the suburbs.

In February 1877, during her second winter back in the United States, she had the opportunity to play the Chopin F-minor piano concerto with the Theodore Thomas Orchestra at the Sanders Theatre in Cambridge. The German-born Thomas was the most renowned American orchestral conductor of the late nineteenth century, and performing with his orchestra was the goal of every American pianist. In February 1877, the Thomas Orchestra played nine concerts in the Boston area, including two in the Sanders Theatre concert series. It is not clear how Fay was chosen to perform with the orchestra, but this was a major step for her advancing professional career.[16] A concerto is a large-scale work that pits a soloist against an orchestra, requiring the pianist to play with more power, volume, and endurance than is typically the case in solo repertoire. The concert reviewer for *Dwight's Journal of Music* was one of the first to refer explicitly to a problem that would detract from Fay's playing in years ahead:

> The pianist Miss AMY FAY, of Cambridge, made her first appearance hereabouts with orchestra. A certain nervousness appeared to check the free motion both of hands and spirit in the opening *Maestoso*; and in this condition it was no wonder that she had to learn the lesson of the danger, to which any mortal memory is liable in some degree, of playing in concerted music without notes, as we inferred from one or two otherwise unaccountable "flashes of silence" in the orchestra. She gained courage, and with it freedom, however, as she went on; the

broad *recitative* in the *Larghetto* movement was well emphasized, and the rapid finale was played firmly, brilliantly and clearly. Yet it is the brilliant rather than the poetic side of Chopin that she represents. The effort was heartily applauded.[17]

A concert pianist needs not only physical skill, intellectual understanding, and expressive ability but also the presence of mind to play a long composition flawlessly by memory without losing her place or getting out of sync with the orchestra. In this case, Fay's nervousness undermined the performance of the first section of the work before she recovered her composure and finished with aplomb. It is not surprising to learn that the slower maestoso opening was where the problem occurred, or that she played the rapid finale confidently. When a player lacks confidence it is often the slower passages that allow her doubts to surface, while the rapid finger work of a fast passage allows no time for such thoughts to arise. As early as 1871 she had acknowledged in a letter to her family, "I am such a nervous creature . . . that the least thing gives me a violent headache, or robs me of sleep; even a call upsets me, if the person is animated or excited."[18] The problem was exacerbated when she attempted to establish a career in the United States and felt the pressure inherent in performing publicly.

Among middle-class women in the Victorian era, female hysteria or "nervousness" was a common diagnosis. As noted by Diane Price Herndl in *Invalid Women*, the second half of the nineteenth century gave rise to "an unprecedented increase in the diagnosis of 'nervous' illnesses." These illnesses came with a panoply of symptoms and were the fashionable affliction of upper-middle-class women. Many physicians believed that professional women were especially susceptible to these illnesses because their brain capacity was not adequate for complex thought.[19] Fay was not alone in suffering debilitating bouts of nerves, which in her case presented itself as performance anxiety, or stage fright. On some occasions she played well and was much appreciated, as in her appearances in Milwaukee, Des Moines, and other smaller Midwestern cities. But when the stakes were highest, she was unable to produce her best performances. Reviewer George P. Upton summarized a series of 1879 concerts in Chicago, where she had moved in 1878, with these words:

> She has true musical feeling, a remarkable memory, an exquisite taste, a thoroughly intelligent grasp of composition, and a good technique. She is in every respect a highly cultivated musician, well versed in the

rules and traditions of the schools. If to these she joined the requisite repose and concentration of a virtuoso, she would achieve great results in the concert-room, but in this regard she is deficient. Physical nervousness, when it cannot be controlled, will mar the best efforts, and no one can be more painfully aware of this than the player.[20]

Readers familiar with golf, baseball, and other sports requiring precise fine-motor skills will recognize Fay's affliction as "the yips." Whereas Dwight had described her lapses in the 1877 concerto performance in Cambridge as primarily mental, Upton observed that her nervousness manifested itself in uncontrolled physical motions. Pianists, like golfers, demand precision of their muscles, but that precision can vanish inexplicably under the pressure of performance. Despite her excellent training and years of practice, her public performances seldom measured up to her expectations, leaving her disheartened and uncertain. The published compilation of her letters from Germany was an unqualified success, in large part because of the unstudied spontaneity of her writing, but she longed for a similar triumph in the field for which she had trained and studied.

Talking (About) Music: The Piano Conversation

In the spring of 1883, Amy Fay scheduled a series of four performances in Chicago that she called piano conversations. She apparently got the idea from her maternal uncle Jerome Hopkins, who had conceived similar programs in New York years before, but without creating a lasting impact on concert life there. In 1883 the concept was still so novel that Fay's announcement of her series attracted significant advance attention from the press. *Brainard's Musical World*, with a large national circulation, stated, "Miss Amy Fay announces 'Four Piano Conversations' in Chicago, beginning March 3d, and continuing every other Saturday afternoon. Each piece is described by the pianist before it is performed."[21] The concept was clearly a new one that required explanation. The *Chicago Inter Ocean* noted that she had experimented with the format in a workshop in Goshen, Indiana, the previous summer, which had been so well received that she was emboldened to replicate it in Chicago. The article explained, "They are called 'Piano Conversations,' because before each piece the pianist describes its character, and tells what she thinks may have been in the mind of the composer when writing it. These viva voce comments have been so much enjoyed by

Miss Fay's audiences in smaller places that she has decided to introduce this feature into her city recitals as well."[22]

Simply put, the programs were recitals covering a wide range of classical and modern piano repertoire with the addition of brief explanatory comments before each piece. Fay typically began with eighteenth-century music by Bach and Beethoven, proceeded to early nineteenth-century music by Mendelssohn, Schumann, Liszt, and Chopin, and concluded with several works by recent composers like Anton Rubinstein or Carl Tausig, and usually works by living American composers. Over the course of the four concerts she presented an extensive and varied list of solo piano works. The recitals were presented in Hershey Hall on Madison Street, an auditorium that was known to be well suited to chamber music. According to the *Chicago Tribune*, "The hall itself is a cosy, comfortable auditorium, with a small gallery and generous stage, capable of seating about 800 people, very neatly ornamented, and with good acoustic qualities."[23] The ticket price of one dollar was not cheap, a sign that Fay's target audience was sophisticated listeners accustomed to the ticket prices of opera and symphony concerts.

The first piano conversation on 3 March drew a capacity crowd curious to see what the format would be like, and the positive reports of this recital ensured equal interest in each of the subsequent programs. The ad that appeared in newspapers before the second concert in the series described the format as "popular," capitalizing on the positive word of mouth that followed the first concert. Fay's comments were not long, but they provided just enough information to give listeners a context for the performance that followed. In a sense, the "conversations" were similar to program notes, but in oral rather than printed form. The comments ranged from historical background on the circumstances of a work's composition to descriptions of the imagery that Fay wished to convey in the performance to thoughts on the composer's biography. As the series progressed, public interest grew rather than diminished. After the third concert, the *Chicago Tribune* noted, "Miss Amy Fay's third 'piano conversation' was held in Hershey Hall yesterday afternoon and was very well attended. These 'conversations' have been very popular and have drawn excellent audiences."[24] The critic for the *Chicago Inter Ocean* confirmed this assessment in a review of the same concert:

> Miss Amy Fay, a lady of whose musical accomplishments Chicago may well be proud, has been giving a series of Saturday evening piano conversations that have proved to be most instructive and enjoyable. Each programme of the series presents a historical view of music, commencing with Bach and Beethoven, coming through Mendelssohn, Chopin,

Liszt, Rubenstein, and Tausig. . . . Miss Fay is a brilliant interpreter of Beethoven as shown by her disposition of the Sonata in C major, which is replete with technical difficulties. . . . These entertainments gain a varied value from Miss Fay's comments upon the numbers of the programme prior to performing them. She is a charming conversationalist, and has a vast fund of information as to the subject in hand.[25]

This was the sort of praise Fay had seldom received before. It is noteworthy that the reviewers were commenting not only on a novel format but also on her abilities in the two different skills it required.

Chicago newspaper reviewers noted that her playing was more confident. In the words of one reviewer of the first concert, "As a pianist Miss Fay is intellectual rather than emotional, but grows upon her audiences as they become familiar with her style. It is a good sign of musical progress in the city that Miss Fay ranks higher every season."[26] The *Chicago Weekly Magazine* described her playing with visual images: "Her touch and style have a marked individuality. There is nothing brilliant or abrupt in either, but there hangs about her performance a softness and an atmosphere that are as poetic as they are unusual. Like the pictures of Corot and Millet upon the eye, her playing melts upon the ear by sympathy, and is so little startling or sensational that at first one hardly realizes how rare the art is. Its sentiment is often profound."[27] One of the most positive reviews came from Upton, who had been so dismissive of her playing four years previously:

Miss Amy Fay . . . is giving a series of what she terms piano conversations in which she and the piano converse together and with the audience. In other words, [she] explains her programmes, the character of the numbers and the ideas of the composers, and then interprets them at the piano. The conversations are proving very attractive and drawing very large houses. Miss Fay's high ability as a musical student, and her European experiences peculiarly fit her for this style of work and she evidently has no difficulty in making the talk both of herself and her piano interesting and agreeable to her audiences. It is a common criticism on musicians that they know nothing outside of their playing. Miss Fay is evidently not one of that sort.[28]

The format was uniquely suited to Fay's personality and skills. From childhood she had been immersed in a broad range of literature, and she was known as an avid conversationalist. The piano conversations allowed her to put herself and her audience at ease through her comments, thus minimizing the effects of nervousness on her playing. As Upton astutely noted, her conversations with the audience carried over into her playing, allowing the auditors to imagine that she was conversing with the instrument as she played. She was skilled at knowing exactly how much information to provide, how to balance explanation with personal anecdotes, and how to leaven her presentation with just the right amount of humor. The authorial voice that had made her memoir so irresistible proved to be an ideal enhancement of her piano concerts, and although we do not have transcripts of any of her piano conversations, the reviews make it clear that their tone and content was similar to her writings. In the opinion of Upton after the series was concluded, "It is not often an audience is treated to such a program as this, thoroughly explained and commented upon. It is a pity more of this kind of work is not done. Probably the reason is that so few pianists are competent to describe what they are playing, even if they understand it."[29] The *Chicago Tribune* summarized the series thus: "Miss Fay's conversations have been largely attended and have excited much attention among musicians—professional and amateur. Students have taken a special interest in her explanations of the various themes treated of, and her practical illustration of their meaning and the difficulties involved in their representation."[30]

The news of this unique series of programs was reported throughout the country, and Fay immediately reaped the benefits of her experiment. She signed an agreement with the Chicago Amusement Bureau, and within months the agency had scheduled a series of piano conversations for the following year. These proved to be just as popular in Omaha, Indianapolis, Minneapolis, New Orleans, and other cities as they had been in Chicago. She often remarked that audiences asked her for more talking because they enjoyed her observations so much.[31] The fame of her piano conversations also increased her demand as a teacher, as the *Musical Visitor* of Cincinnati reported in November: "Miss Amy Fay, the popular pianist and teacher, is very busy, having more pupils than she can attend to."[32] Even as her performance opportunities increased, Fay kept piano teaching at the center of her career.

Fay in New York

In 1890 Fay moved to New York. The piano conversations continued to be an important part of her professional life, as she performed them throughout the Northeast and in the metropolis itself. An 1896 brochure advertising her availability as a lecturer-pianist listed eight different programs she was prepared to play. The repertoire ranged from the Baroque era to the late nineteenth century, encompassing some shorter pieces of a popular nature but mostly difficult works by European masters. The shorter works featured descriptive titles like Joachim Raff's *Fairy Story* or dance titles like Tausig's *Valse Caprice*. Among the serious works were Beethoven's Pathétique, Moonlight, and Waldstein Sonatas; Schumann's Sonata in G Minor, op. 22; and the Chopin Ballade in F Minor, op. 52—all of which are challenging virtuoso works. Fay played relatively little American music, but six of the eight programs contained at least one piece by the following contemporary American composers: John Knowles Paine (1839–1906), William Mason (1829–1908), Louis Moreau Gottschalk (1829–1869), Edward MacDowell (1860–1908), Jerome Hopkins (1836–1898), and W. C. E. Seeboeck (1860–1907).[33]

Like many artists before and since, Fay discovered that New York reviewers could be severe. When she introduced the piano conversation format for the first time in Chickering Hall in June 1891, both the *Times* and the *Sun* were sharply critical. Reviewers were unimpressed with her playing, and they thought the verbal comments were unenlightening for an educated audience. According to the *Times*:

> The unsuspecting music lover who attends one of these entertainments expecting to have his store of information increased or his imagination quickened would, judging from yesterday's performance, meet with disappointment. Miss Fay's talk about Schumann's personal history was almost impudent in the amount of ignorance which it presupposed the audience to possess. Her remarks about his G minor sonata were ridiculous in their brevity and lack of suggestiveness. However, after hearing the lady's performance of the composition, there is no room for wonder at her inability to say much about it. In order to make the record complete, it may as well be added that Miss Fay does not speak any better than she plays.[34]

The probable author of this review, W. J. Henderson (1855–1937), was part of the old guard of New York critics who saw themselves as gatekeepers of America's cultural capital. Henderson was especially noted for his harsh criticism of women. In the words of Mark N. Grant, a historian of music criticism, Henderson "left his own negative stamp on his profession: the legacy of the art of epigrammatic cruelty."[35] Henry E. Krehbiel of the *New*

York *Tribune*, whom Grant calls "the most esteemed and influential newspaper music critic America had yet seen," took a more balanced view of Fay's efforts.[36] He pointed out a feature that we can easily forget in our era of ubiquitous air conditioning: "The entertainment which Miss Amy Fay . . . gave at Chickering Hall yesterday afternoon would have served its purpose better had it been given earlier in the season, before interest in pianoforte music had become fagged and the temperature of the concert-room such as made simple attendance a weariness of the flesh." He also noted that Fay's decision to include one of her piano students and a young dance student on the program detracted from the seriousness of the event.[37] These negative reviews reflected the New York critics' role as cultural arbiters for the country. Their snobbishness was characteristic of the reception that Henderson, Krehbiel, and their colleagues often gave to first-time performers in the city.

Fay found perhaps the ideal audience for her piano conversations in the New York public schools, when the school board contracted her to bring programs to a broad range of neighborhoods, including those serving the impoverished tenement dwellers of the Lower East Side of Manhattan. This quarter was the most densely populated real estate in the world, where immigrants lived in squalor in crowded tenements.[38] Despite the efforts of Jacob Riis and other reformers to expose these conditions over the previous decade, the problems persisted, and most Americans were not fully aware of the life-threatening situation. Fay was warned that the students in these districts could be a tough crowd, but she found them to be among her most attentive audiences. The repeated invitations to perform indicate that the Board of Education found her presentations worthwhile. A letter to her sister Zina, describing a piano conversation at a school on the Lower East Side in 1901, is enlightening both for what it tells us about social conditions in New York and as an example of her lively writing style.[39] In describing this event to her sister, she treats it as a cross-cultural experience: "Last night I played down in East 5th St., between Avenue C. & D. You would not recognize *New York* over *there*! The signs on the shops are many of them in Hebrew characters, the women are hatless, & there is no evidence of the 'four hundred' [the city's social elite] in *that* part of the city. I was told that the Polish women wear *wigs*, as it is a law that they must 'cut' their hair when they marry, to prevent them from being attractive to other men. I did not see any, however." She goes on to describe the reputation of the students in this school and the warning she received from the principal. His negative comments about his students prepared her for the worst, but as she had done since her youth, she overcame the situation through sheer determination. Her letter, then, offers the most detailed extant description of the content and circumstances of her piano conversations:

> I went to this school with some trepidation, as I was told by Mr. Beers, the principal, that the crowd was a very lawless one, & the janitor had to clear them out with his club at a lecture with steryopticon [sic]. He said they chipped the desks, & stole the pictures, &c, & that he "just *dreaded* when the lecturers came there." I said, "perhaps they will behave better at my Piano Conversation." He grunted, & replied, "it don't seem much use to put *music & art* before *these* people." My audience, however, did not turn out as he said, & was composed of young men & girls, the *men* largely predominating. One working woman, in a short red skirt & bundled up in a shawl, of the lower classes, sat in one of the front seats, a Jewish Pole probably. Four toughs, & one "*athlete*" came in. Mr. Curtis, the teacher in charge, remarked, "those fellows have come in to make trouble. I had to force them to *leave* at the preceding lecture." They sat in the back of the hall, & reminded me of the bad boys in your choral school in Cambridge who used to hang around so. . . . I began to talk punctually at eight oclock. You can imagine I felt some trepidation to play the [Beethoven *Sonata*] *Pathétique* before this audience. I expected there would be talking & laughing so that I could not hear myself think. Do you know, they were as quiet as mice, *all through*, except when they were *laughing out* with amusement at my remarks! At the close, they applauded like everything, & then they crowded up around me on the stage, & begged to know "*when* I was going to play to them again?" . . . Mr. Curtis escorted me to the car, & he said "the concert was a success." He was a cultivated & well mannered young man. The four toughs gave no trouble, & seemed as much interested as all the rest. . . . Well, it was lots of fun down there, & I enjoyed myself like everything. It quite inspired me to talk to that audience, it was so responsive!

This passage demonstrates Fay's openness to cultural differences. For the daughter of a privileged New England family, this predominantly poor immigrant audience was far from her own personal experience. She overcame the differences not only through the strength of her personality but also through the firm belief that music could bridge cultural differences. Her success with the "toughs" earned the respect of the "cultivated & well mannered" Mr. Curtis. Her enjoyment of this challenge and her willingness to tackle such challenges again was a validation of the progressive ideals she shared with her sister.

Echoes of Fay's Piano Conversations

If imitation is the sincerest form of flattery, then Fay must have felt gratified by the spread of her innovation. Almost immediately, others adopted various versions of her format. When she performed her first series of piano conversations in the spring of 1883, for instance, the Boston pianist William Sherwood was in Chicago for a series of his own concerts. After witnessing the success of Fay's conversations, he announced in the press that when he returned the following year he would enhance his concerts with introductory remarks on the pieces he played. The report in *Brainard's Musical World* makes his intention to imitate Fay explicit: "The most cheerful result of his visit is the announcement that he will come again, next season, for a series of recitals, which will be accompanied by running explanations, after the style of Miss Amy Fay's recent 'Conversations,' which, by the way, he complimented very highly."[40] Sherwood and many other pianists experimented with Fay's format, but it soon became clear that few could match the appeal and appropriateness of her verbal comments.[41] Yet Fay's innovation spread, and two artists in particular devoted much of their careers to presentations like hers. Both artists adopted *lecture recital* as a preferred term to describe their presentations, thus emphasizing their authority as scholar-performers rather than the folksy appeal of Fay's "piano conversations."

Edward Baxter Perry (1855–1924) was an American pianist who was blind since the age of two. Like Fay, he studied in Europe with Kullak and Liszt, and returned to the United States to establish a performing career. He adopted the piano conversation format in the mid-1880s, shortly after Fay introduced it, and he eventually performed more than 3,300 lecture recitals over the course of a long career.[42] In a December 1894 article in the journal *Music*, critic W. S. B. Mathews stated that these programs were vitally important in a country where music was more widely appreciated than understood. Of Perry he wrote, "The recital-lecturer fills a place peculiarly his own. Mr. Perry, in particular, is to be praised not alone for the magnitude of the works which he presents, and the generally able manner in which he plays them, but still more for the moderate way and generally tasteful character of his introductory remarks."[43] Since the Chicago critic Mathews was familiar with Fay's presentations, his comments on Perry's moderation and taste may have been a subtle jab at the more effusive Fay.

The format reached its largest audiences at the hands of Walter Damrosch (1862–1950), conductor of the New York Symphony. In 1887, four years after Fay's first piano conversations, he began presenting public lecture recitals on Wednesday afternoons before the public rehearsals of his orchestra. The format allowed him to explain the week's program and to educate audiences about symphonic music in general. These events were so popular that he expanded them the following year and introduced a series on the operas of Richard Wagner. During his first season he gave sixty lecture recitals on Wagner, followed by 110 the following year. Over the course of his career he gave thousands of public lecture recitals, sometimes sitting alone at the piano and sometimes enlisting the services of orchestral players. Like Fay, Damrosch used a combination of verbal skill and musical knowledge that made him very popular, and he found his ultimate audience with the introduction of radio in the 1920s. This medium was still in its infancy when he began broadcasting lecture recitals in 1923, but he clearly saw the potential for reaching more listeners via the airwaves than he ever could in person. With an easygoing yet informative style, he soon became a fixture on weekly radio. After years of broadcasting to adults, he created the *NBC Music Appreciation Hour*, an educational program that aired during the school day and reached millions of children between 1928 and 1942.[44]

Damrosch also discovered that explaining and popularizing classical music was not universally applauded. Just as Fay had been attacked by Henderson in the 1890s, so Damrosch became the target of an infamous critique by philosopher Theodor Adorno. Music on the radio, according to Adorno, reinforced elitism and class domination, while Damrosch's benevolent explanations for children consisted of "erudite babbling" that undermined the intellectual vitality of classical music.[45] Despite the enormous popularity of Damrosch's broadcasts and the millions of children who were introduced to orchestral music through them, Adorno's scathing critique tainted them in the eyes of many music scholars.

Damrosch had capitalized on the new technology of radio to bring lecture recitals to a mass audience, and conductor Leonard Bernstein (1918–1990) used the same strategy with television. On 18 January 1958, two weeks after assuming the musical direction of the New York Philharmonic, Bernstein conducted the first of fifty-three Young People's Concerts. These televised concerts, which appeared from 1958 to 1972, allowed him to introduce musical works and concepts in a format that would have been familiar to Fay. A gifted speaker, he introduced music that would be performed on upcoming concerts in language accessible to children but not condescending. The New York Philharmonic played the works in masterful style, creating an unforgettable experience. The video recordings of these concerts have been rereleased on DVD, and the texts of his commentary were compiled in book form, making them available to successive generations of students.[46]

Conclusion

As is often the case with innovators, the person who initially popularized the new idea did not benefit as much as those who came later and modified the form. The *Musical Courier* summarized Amy Fay's reputation in 1917: "Miss Fay, as a pianist of broad experience, originator of the 'Piano Conversation,' and one of the real Liszt pupils, has established a name and fame which are unique among American instructors of the piano."[47] Despite this acknowledgment of her importance to American piano teaching, Fay's later years were marked by restricted financial circumstances when her engagements declined in number. She began to experience serious health problems in the late teens, leading her to retire from teaching in 1919. Her siblings placed her in a nursing home after she began to develop dementia, and she died there on 28 February 1928. She had two noteworthy pupils: John Alden Carpenter was a prominent American composer, and Almon Kincaid Virgil developed a silent keyboard and an accompanying practice method that were highly successful. Fay's book *Music-Study in Germany* continued to be widely read long after her death, and her innovation of combining performance with verbal explanation was profoundly influential.

Amy Fay's piano conversations were designed to highlight her personal strengths and minimize her weaknesses, but they had a lasting impact on concert life in the United States. Today the term *lecture recitals*, used by Perry and Damrosch, is preferred. These programs are still heard widely, especially in universities that have music performance programs. At Michigan State University, Boston University, the University of Houston, the Eastman School of Music, and the College-Conservatory of Music at the University of Cincinnati, for instance, all students pursuing Doctor of Musical Arts degrees in music performance are required to present a public lecture recital. At many other schools the lecture recital is not obligatory but may be substituted for one of the required standard recitals at the discretion of the degree candidate. Like Amy Fay's first series in 1883, the format today is a hybrid one, and its success depends on the performer's ability to balance speaking with playing.[48] In the right hands, the commentary and playing become a seamless whole, enhancing the audience's understanding of the music in ways that neither a lecture nor a concert can achieve on its own.

9

HINDUISM FOR THE WEST: SWAMI VIVEKANANDA'S PLURALISM AT THE WORLD'S PARLIAMENT OF RELIGIONS

Scott R. Stroud

A significant moment in the history of American oratory and comparative religion in the nineteenth century happened not on North American shores but at the rocky headland at India's southernmost point. In late December 1892 a young ascetic monk arrived at Cape Comorin. The monk, later to become renowned as Swami Vivekananda, had completed a herculean journey across India—mostly on foot—and finally reached the sea. From the Himalayas to the cities, he had seen India and its problems. Poverty, lack of education, British control and oppression, and harmful interpretations of religion seemed to conspire to hold back his fellow Indians from a life free of suffering. Vivekananda swam across a channel to a small rock island off the Cape, and he meditated on this barren rock for three days. Here he had a life-changing experience, which he would later recount in an 1894 letter to a fellow monk, Swami Ramakrishnananda: It was no use, he said, to continue as his fellow monks had always done things, "wandering about, and teaching the people metaphysics." Instead, he would make his religious teachings practical, aiming to alleviate the problems and challenges of India's suffering poor. Of course, he would need money to do this work, but he was staring across the ocean toward the financial solution. Vivekananda would travel to North America and exchange his riches of religious knowledge for monetary contributions to help poor Indians.[1]

Not long after this insight, Vivekananda heard about the perfect venue for sharing his religious knowledge: the upcoming World's Parliament of Religions.[2] Convening in Chicago at the World's Fair, the Parliament was to be a large gathering of representatives of religions from across the West and the East. He seemed to think of attending the Parliament as his destiny, as he relayed to another monk: "I am going to America. Whatever you hear of as happening there, [it] is all for this"—striking his chest to indicate that he was "this." "For this alone," Vivekananda prophesied, "everything is being arranged."[3] While this may have been an aspirational way to look at the purpose of the Parliament, it is true that the event in Chicago clearly and decisively established Vivekananda as the face of Hinduism in the United States, propelling him on a lecture tour across the country that lasted more than two years. As one biographer, Sister Nivedita, has claimed about Vivekananda at the Parliament, "When he began to speak, it was of the religious ideas of the Hindus; but when he ended, Hinduism had been created."[4]

This chapter links the story of intercultural lecturing and learning with discussions of the American public stage. Vivekananda is important as he represents a form of diversity beyond what scholars often associate with nineteenth-century U.S. lecture culture: he was an Indian monk speaking enthusiastically and successfully to an American audience—and to other international visitors—about the millennia-old religious traditions of India. Yet Vivekananda faced a significant challenge. Immigration from India to the United States was virtually nonexistent up to the end of the nineteenth century, and by 1920 only a little more than six thousand immigrants from South Asia had arrived on American shores.[5] What American audiences knew of India and Hinduism came from Christian missionary reports, and as Stephen Prothero explains, these "typically denounced living Hindus as heathens."[6] How was Vivekananda able to captivate such audiences—interested in religious matters and pluralism, yet likely to be skeptical of Indian culture and religion—in his addresses at the 1893 World's Parliament of Religions? The source of his success on this grand stage, as well as the smaller stages of his subsequent lecture tour, relates to his ability to think with his audience and to encourage them to recognize a valuable form of Hinduism emerging from his addresses. How was he able to build identification with his audiences in a way that furthered his goals of creating a non-pejorative image of Hinduism in the United States, all the while not alienating his largely Christian audiences? This chapter explicates Vivekananda's work at the 1893 Parliament and, along the way, affirms his significance in late nineteenth-century lecture culture.

Getting to the Stage of the World's Parliament of Religions

Vivekananda's path to Chicago was not straightforward. In fact, Swami Vivekananda, as such, did not exist until the eve of his departure for the

Parliament in 1893. Before he chose that name at the behest of one of his royal benefactors, he was known by various other monastic names. Preceding these was his given name, Narendranath Dutta. Young Naren was born into a family in Calcutta of the Kayastha caste, neither the lowest nor the highest caste in that social setting.[7] His early education was thoroughly English in scope and content. He studied at the Presidency College in Calcutta in 1879, then at the General Assembly's Institution, later known as the Scottish Church College. It was during this time that he read such European philosophers as John Stuart Mill on religion and utilitarianism, and Auguste Comte and Herbert Spencer on social evolution and science. Amiya Sen notes that Spencer shook Vivekananda's worldview, causing him to question his trust in Hindu systems of priestcraft.[8] During these years his religious tendency mingled with a youthful enthusiasm, and he joined a modern Indian theistic movement known as the Brahmo Samaj. This faction mixed Indian traditions with Christian Unitarianism and focused on reforming Hindu social and religious customs such as caste oppression. It also advocated the abandonment of the millennia-long polytheistic tradition of Hinduism. Importantly for Naren's later thought, the Brahmo Samaj strongly rejected idol worship and its associated imagery.[9] In the place of idol-worshiping traditions, the Brahmo Samaj attempted to craft an abstract, monotheistic practice of religion that could accommodate diverse believers. This pluralistic search for unifying religions would remain central to Naren's life.

In November 1881, Naren met the religious leader Gadadhar Chattopadhyay, more commonly known as Ramakrishna, who embodied a concern for non-sectarianism and religious tolerance that Vivekananda would later extol and modify in his own religious teachings.[10] Ramakrishna inspired Naren, and upon the elder guru's death in 1886 Naren turned to the life of the wandering monk. He was torn between spreading Ramakrishna's teachings around India and supporting his brother monks—all students of Ramakrishna—at their home monastery. It was this tension that spurred his journey to Cape Comorin in December 1892. Through dreams, discussions, and meditations, Naren resolved to present his vision of Hinduism to the West. Assuming the name Swami Vivekananda, he departed Bombay for the United States on 31 May 1893, stopping first in China, Japan, and Canada on his way to the Chicago Parliament.

Vivekananda arrived in Chicago an unknown foreigner. Furthermore, his arrival was soured by the fact that his supporters in India had assumed he could simply walk up and take part in the Parliament. Vivekananda reported to the Chicago office set up in advance of the Parliament and learned that all delegates had to have been invited through a recognized religious organization and that the time for invitations and credentialing had long passed.[11] After poking around the cultural and technological exhibits of the Columbian Exposition for ten days, spending much of his money in the process, Vivekananda followed up on an offer he had received from a fellow passenger on the train journey from Vancouver to Chicago. On this trip Kate Sanborn, a woman of social and financial means from Metcalf, Massachusetts, had invited him to visit her after his Chicago duties ended.[12] Vivekananda had heard that Boston was the "Athens of America" and that it would not strain his disappearing funds as much as Chicago, so he traveled to Sanborn's home, Breezy Meadows, in mid-August.[13] It was in Massachusetts that Vivekananda gave his first talks to American audiences and met Harvard professor John Henry Wright, who helped him to obtain entrance to the Parliament. Wright was so impressed by Vivekananda's vision of Hinduism that he supposedly exclaimed, "To ask you, Swami, for credentials is like asking the sun to state its right to shine!" Convinced that Vivekananda had an important message to share, Wright wrote to the Parliament's organizers and secured delegate credentials for the Hindu monk. "This is the only way you can be introduced to the nation at large," Wright said.[14] Vivekananda returned to Chicago in time for the opening of the Parliament on 11 September 1893.

Lecturing, Listening, and Learning at the World's Parliament of Religions

The World's Parliament of Religions was part of a much larger event, the World's Columbian Exposition, which celebrated the quadricentennial of Columbus's discovery of the "New World." The Exposition was dedicated in October 1892, but it did not open until the summer of 1893. It was an explicit attempt to highlight the latest technology of American and European design as well to showcase cultures from around the world. As Richard Seager notes, the Exposition can also be seen as an attempt to buttress American culture against worldwide surges of immigration in the 1880s and 1890s.[15] The Exposition was located at two sites in Chicago. One was called the White City because of its gleaming reproductions of classical architecture. This site included the Art Institute of Chicago, which would host the Parliament. The other main site of the Exposition was a scene of cultural excitement and chaos—the Midway Plaisance. This latter location featured a huge array of putatively authentic re-creations of settings and scenes from different cultures. Organizations such as the Harvard Peabody Museum and the Smithsonian Institution brought in people from other countries in an elaborate effort to represent life in foreign locales. Even though the United States was a land of immigrants, visitors to Chicago were still thrilled to see the exotic settings of a Java Village occupied by more than a hundred Muslims and Hindus, or the Chinese Joss House with its representation of culture in China.[16]

The Exposition featured not only a pluralistic urge to present other cultures to American audiences but also a tendency to proselytize on behalf of Christian religious traditions and American worldviews, extolling Europe's colonial activities in the "New World." Buildings in the White City had classical columns inscribed with verses from the New Testament, highlighting the special place that Christian tradition held in the eyes of organizers. The Exposition thus blended inclusion of world cultures and an emphasis on a hierarchical ranking of civilizations and religions, with Christian America at the apex.

A slew of auxiliary events and congresses were connected to the Exposition. One was the World's Parliament of Religions, organized by Charles Carroll Bonney, a prominent lawyer in Chicago. Bonney had proposed as early as 1889 a series of conferences highlighting the cultural achievements of human civilization alongside the Exposition's display of technological marvels.[17] Another organizer was the Reverend John Henry Barrows, who saw the promise in Bonney's ideas and the novelty in summoning a truly worldwide gathering of religious leaders to speak about their faiths. Barrows and Bonney both took an active part in shaping and running the Parliament. In opening the Parliament, Bonney spoke of pluralistic motives: all of the world's religions deserved a place at this historic event, he said, since "the finite can never fully comprehend the infinite, nor perfectly express its own view of the divine."[18] Each person must approach the divine through his or her own cultural lens, a point Barrows made when he declared to the assembled crowd, "Each must see God with the eyes of his own soul. Each must behold him through the colored glasses of his own nature. Each one must receive him according to his own capacity of reception."[19] There was an educative and social value in assembling representatives of the world's religions, and listening audiences would gain from the experience.

More than pluralism played out on this grand stage, however. Some Christian leaders had already refused to take part in the Parliament, since the event, they claimed, positioned non-Christian religions as equal to Christianity. For instance, the archbishop of Canterbury declined to attend, indicating that such a worldly event presumed and justified "the equality of other intended members and the parity of their positions and claims."[20] Christianity would not be presented as the universal religion, in other words. Bonney and Barrows tried to appease all sides. They persisted in inviting delegates from non-Christian traditions. Yet each day the Parliament started with a reading of a text described as the "Universal Prayer"; it was the Lord's Prayer from the New Testament. On the most important days a Catholic bishop presided over the discussions. In the written accounts of the Parliament, Barrows summarized the event in a decidedly pro-Christian fashion: "The Parliament has shown that Christianity is still the great quickener of humanity, that it is now educating those who do not accept its doctrines, that there is no teacher to be compared with Christ, and no Saviour excepting Christ." He bluntly concluded that "there is no assured and transforming hope of conscious and blessed immortality outside of the Christian Scripture, and that all the philosophies do not bring God so near to man as he is brought by the Gospel of Christ."[21] On his account, other religions deserve attention because they offer the value of meliorative criticism of Christian practices. They do not, however, hold any cognitive or religious values of their own. The pluralism of the event, thus, was caught between a cosmopolitan respect for the many cultures of a growing world and the power struggles needed to sustain Christian dominance. Thus the Parliament extended the tension at the heart of the Exposition—celebrating Western achievements, culture, and religion, while still including non-Western traditions in a respectful and serious manner.

The Parliament was held in the grand, and newly constructed, Art Institute of Chicago. Its largest halls could accommodate three to four thousand people, and it had smaller rooms for panels held in conjunction with the "scientific section" examining religion. On the fifty-foot stage in the Hall of Columbus sat the main delegates, assembled in front of hanging Japanese and Hebrew scrolls and flanked by large statues of Demosthenes and Cicero. An ornate, wrought-iron chair dominated the stage, and it was occupied on the first day by Cardinal Gibbons, archbishop of Baltimore, the highest-ranking Catholic priest in the United States.[22] Delegates on stage hailed from various Christian denominations as well as vastly different traditions from the East, such as Confucianism, Taoism, Islam, and Zoroastrianism. Counting all the sessions, the Parliament heard a total of 216 papers, including sixteen from Buddhists, thirteen from Hindus, and eleven from Jews.[23]

The seventeen-day Parliament started on 11 September with the singing of the Christian Doxology and a recitation of the Lord's Prayer. After a few speeches of welcome in the morning, the stage was turned over to the main

Figure 9.1 Swami Vivekananda (*seated, second from right*) on the stage at the World's Parliament of Religions, Chicago, 1893. Courtesy of the Vedanta Society of St. Louis.

delegates of the different faiths. The audience was excited to engage certain speakers; they applauded various Christian representatives vigorously, and they loudly cheered the Chinese Confucian representative, Pung Kwang Yu, as the perception among many in attendance was that China had not been treated kindly by Western powers.[24] Indeed, Barrows expressed hope that the U.S. government would curtail Chinese exclusion.[25] One by one, the delegates read prepared statements discussing the origin and the virtues of their religious traditions.

Vivekananda sat quietly and let pass each opportunity for him to speak. The ascetic monk from India had not addressed a crowd this large: close to four thousand individuals crowded the floor and balcony in the Hall of Columbus, and another three thousand listeners overflowed into the neighboring Hall of Washington.[26] Eventually Vivekananda stood to introduce himself, announcing, "Sisters and Brothers of America." This opening line brought the house down: "There arose a peal of applause in acknowledgement of the originality of the salutation, and perhaps not less as testifying interest in the personality of the speaker."[27] Romain Rolland would later describe this opening statement as "a tongue of flames" and deem Vivekananda "the first to cast off the formalism of the Congress and to speak to the masses in the language for which they were waiting."[28] Vivekananda thus began his illustrious career as a nationally and internationally known orator who would speak to the American public directly about one of the most elusive and abstract religious traditions devised by any culture—his version of Advaita Vedanta.

Vivekananda Speaks About Hinduism to the Masses

Vivekananda, like the other delegates from the East, noted the Christian slant to the Parliament's structure, audience, and operation.[29] The audience, while excited about the diversity of religious leaders, was still clearly Christian in its orientation. As the *Chicago Evening Journal* stated in an editorial on 14 September, "Very few people in this country have any knowledge of the religions of the Orient. . . . The common impression is that the natives of India, China, and Japan belong to semi-civilized races and worship idols."[30] Despite these perceptions, Vivekananda had his listeners standing and applauding from the moment he uttered the words "Sisters and Brothers of America." What accounts for this reaction? Part of his oratorical power on the stage came from his persona and delivery style. Unlike the other delegates, Vivekananda almost always spoke without a prepared text. Thus he seemed to speak from his heart, and the spontaneous-but-organized remarks connected with the audience. A man named Frank Rhodehamel, upon hearing Vivekananda speak on a later trip to Northern California, highlighted the power of this style: "As a lecturer he was unique: never referring to notes, as most lecturers do. . . . He seemed to be giving something of himself, to be speaking from a super-experience."[31] Sister Christine, a German American follower of Vivekananda, also emphasized his remarkable presentation and attributed it to a spontaneous source from inside the swami. "When asked what preparation he made for speaking," she recalled, "he told us none—but neither did he go *unprepared*. He said that usually before a lecture he heard a voice saying it all."[32] Others connected this spontaneity not simply to the authenticity of his message but also to his oratorical power. Martha Brown Fincke, upon hearing Vivekananda speak at Smith College shortly after the Parliament, recalled that "he personified Power."[33] Thus his spontaneity of delivery showed that he believed deeply in what he was saying, and the passion with which it flowed forth gave his listeners a sense of his power. Kate Sanborn, Vivekananda's friend from Massachusetts, later connected his style to his familiarity with Western content: "He spoke better English than I did, was conversant in ancient and modern literature, would quote easily and naturally from Shakespeare or Longfellow or Tennyson, Darwin, Muller, Tyndall; could repeat pages of our Bible, was familiar with and tolerant of all creeds.... He was an education, an illumination, a revelation!"[34]

At the World's Parliament in Chicago, his message went well beyond his captivating style. He was both an advocate and missionary for his variety of Hinduism, yet he masterfully sought ways to achieve identification with his American audience. The audience was engaged with the Parliament from the opening addresses, yet it was by no means familiar with Hinduism, at least beyond the information and misinformation that funneled by missionary channels back to American shores. Vivekananda, after his rousing opening statement, proceeded to do something remarkable: he began to delineate a version of Hinduism that respected the Christian heritage of many in his audience. Thus he followed his opening line by thanking his audience "in the name of the most ancient order of monks in the world; I thank you in the name of the mother of religions; and I thank you in the name of millions and millions of Hindu people of all classes and sects."[35] Vivekananda's persona was that of the sole, authoritative representative of Hinduism who invited the audience to learn the religion directly from him. Speaking spontaneously, he foregrounded the notion of tolerance as an entry point for Hinduism into the Parliament's discussion of religions. He did this by thanking the speakers before him "who, referring to the delegates from the Orient, have told you that these men from far-off nations may well claim the honour of bearing to different lands the idea of toleration."[36] Vivekananda thus drew attention to Western delegates who spoke of toleration, thereby lending legitimacy to the activities of the "pagan" delegates from the East.

He then went further by linking the toleration that Western delegates spoke of to the toleration that had long defined his religion: "I am proud to belong to a religion which has taught the world both tolerance and universal acceptance."[37] In this statement, Vivekananda made an important distinction that would prove vital to his advocacy of Hinduism to the audiences of the Parliament. Because Hinduism believes not only in "tolerance" but also in "universal acceptance," Hindus not only tolerate other religions but, he continued, "accept all religions as true."[38] To demonstrate universal acceptance as a Hindu trait, Vivekananda quoted two passages on pluralism from Vedic and Hindu sources—the *Rig Veda* and the *Bhagavad Gita*. This form of Hinduism, he intimated, is clearly opposed to "sectarianism, bigotry, and its horrible descendant, fanaticism," which "have filled the earth with violence."[39] Vivekananda would eventually use this form of pluralism as a way to encourage his audience to reject fanaticism in their own religious traditions. Ultimately, Vivekananda's introductory remarks enabled him, in subsequent addresses, to reconstruct Hinduism as something unique and, he hoped, acceptable to non-Hindu audience members at the Parliament.

From the recollections of other participants, we know that Vivekananda became so popular that the organizers put him on potentially boring panels to attract an audience, or even manipulated his speaking times to maintain a crowd. The Jain delegate, Virchand Gandhi, recalled after the Parliament the consequences of Vivekananda's finishing a speech: "At least a third and sometimes two-thirds of the great audience of Columbus Hall would make a rush for the exits when a fine orator from India had closed his speech."[40] To save the noise and loss entailed by more than a thousand people leaving the hall, organizers placed Vivekananda's speeches toward the end of the day. Across these sessions, even with relatively minor speeches, he developed a significant reputation. His introductory remarks were brief but popular. As early as the third day of the Parliament he appeared as a chairperson for a potentially dull panel involving three orthodox Christian ministers.[41] Vivekananda did not deliver a formal—or lengthy—address until a week into the Parliament, on 19 September.[42] He was such an intriguing and popular figure, however, that he was asked to give a special response to the topics discussed on the afternoon of 15 September. Amid presentations on the comparative study of religions and on Confucianism, Vivekananda began to address one of the most important, but unstated, conflicts in the Parliament: the issue of resolving plurality into agreement, or at least respect, among adherents of various religions.

In a short speech Vivekananda worked to combat the bigotry that prevented Eastern traditions, including his own, from receiving a hearing in the West. He also responded to the tensions building on the Parliament's stage. As the Unitarian minister J. T. Sunderland put it in a report, Vivekananda's address followed "a particularly narrow paper by a Catholic theologian, claiming for his Church the possession of the one only divine religion of the world."[43] In response to "the eloquent speaker who has just finished," Vivekananda announced, "Let us cease from abusing each other." He then offered a parable about religious differences—one that defended his journey and Hinduism itself. The parable was a story of a frog who traveled from the ocean and fell into a well inhabited by another frog. The well-locked frog, incredulous when the oceangoing frog maintained that the ocean was larger than the well, reacted with hatred and exclaimed, "Nothing can be bigger than my well; there can be nothing bigger than this; this fellow is a liar, so turn him out."[44]

Vivekananda adapted this story to explain the "difficulty" of religious dialogue. Personalizing the story for his audience, he claimed that, as a Hindu, he sat "in my own little well . . . thinking that the whole world is my little well." Christians and Muslims, he continued, do the same thing in their "wells." He then rather abruptly moved from this analogy to the Parliament itself: "I have to thank you of America for the great attempt you are making to break down the barriers of this little world of ours, and hope that, in the future, the Lord will help you to accomplish your purpose."[45] Differing from the version preserved in Vivekananda's collected works, Sunderland's recollection of this speech ends in a slightly different way. He remembers that Vivekananda concluded with an appeal to all to "climb up out of our dark wells, and see how large and glorious is the real world of God and humanity and truth and religion!" According to Sunderland's version, Vivekananda related this transcendence of limited religious points of view to a cessation of interreligious argument and strife: "Then, I am sure, we should cease to quarrel. Then I think we should begin to act like brothers."[46]

Either conclusion to Vivekananda's remarks would have promoted identification with the audience. Everyone in attendance was in a position similar to Vivekananda's because each inhabited a well, while a vast ocean spread beyond all wells. Thus Vivekananda began to build common ground with his audience through this humble parable of pluralism. Yet the logic of the story is curious, as there is a potential difference in the status of the religious thinkers and traditions Vivekananda analogized. Unlike Christianity or Islam, Hinduism gave Vivekananda the conceptual room to incorporate other faiths and their limited perspectives. In a sense, Vivekananda, like the oceangoing frog, had a superior frame of reference within which judgments of comparative religious worth could proceed. This universal claim would become a hallmark of his advocacy while on the stage of the Parliament in the following days. Vivekananda would build common ground with his American audiences in an attempt to establish respect for Hinduism, but he would also construct a version of Hinduism as a universal religion—one that could tolerate and accept other religions as true paths to enlightenment, but on its own traditional terms.

Vivekananda's first official address at the Parliament—not counting shorter presentations in side "congresses" or at offsite churches—was by all accounts his longest and most significant statement in Chicago.[47] Delivered on 19 September and titled "Hinduism," this rare prepared lecture marked

Vivekananda's first extended and sustained discussion of the view of Hinduism that he wished to present to his American audiences. Before he could explicate his own religion, however, he had to respond to the various pro-Christian speeches that preceded him. The Parliament was still reeling from the exclusionary remarks of the imposing and well-known Protestant lecturer, the Reverend Joseph Cook from Boston. On the fourth day of the Parliament, Cook offered a heated diatribe against non-Christian faiths, making the "platform tremble with the weight of three hundred pounds of orthodoxy," according to one commentator. Another reported, "It was a humiliating fact to the liberal and tolerant Christian to find that the first discordant note sounded at the Parliament of Religions—the first manifestation of bigotry and ill-will—was made, not by a Pagan . . . but by a Christian."[48]

On the ninth day, after other speakers had made similar pro-Christian appeals, Vivekananda issued his reply. In defending the value and legitimacy of his faith, he knew he had to avoid the aggressive, polemical tone of the Reverend Cook. Vivekananda thus emphasized transcendence in the creation of common ground, which maintained Hinduism's value. As he explained to the audience, he and others "have sat here day after day and have been told in a patronizing way that we ought to accept Christianity because Christian nations are the most prosperous."[49] He then challenged the assumption that prosperity is of utmost value, regardless of how one attains it. To the extent that wars and bloodshed preceded European colonial expansion, he noted, "Christianity wins its prosperity by cutting the throats of its fellow men. At such a price the Hindoo will not have prosperity."[50]

After this stunningly direct assertion, Vivekananda then moved into his prepared, full-throated explication of Hinduism. Of course, Hinduism is a complex collection of often contradictory or independent sects, traditions, and ritual practices; Vivekananda was in reality presenting *his* view of Hinduism. But he aimed to show that Hinduism was simultaneously similar to and different from Christianity. To that end he connected his tradition with other long-standing religious traditions including "Zoroastrianism and Judaism."[51] However, Vivekananda maintained, Hinduism is the oldest and most resilient of these ancient religious traditions. Its strength is clear in its consonance with modern science—a point Vivekananda made especially for the technologically advanced West. At the same time, he said, Hinduism eschews the talk of idolatry and barbarism that Western traditions use to condemn it.[52] Hinduism, in fact, can enfold it all: "From the high spiritual flights of the Vedanta philosophy, of which the latest discoveries of science seem like echoes, to the low ideas of idolatry with its multifarious mythology, the agnosticism of the Buddhists, and the atheism of the Jains, each and all have a place in the Hindu's religion."[53] Vedanta is one of the more prominent schools of Indian philosophy, arising after the earlier sacred texts known as the Vedas and Upanishads, and after their critics such as the Buddha. As its name signifies ("end of the Vedas"), Vedanta aspires to be a completion or fulfillment of the inner meaning of these earlier texts. As is evident in his addresses, Vivekananda's construction of Hinduism privileged a Vedantic reading of the progression and telos of Indian philosophy and Hinduism.

In his speech, Vivekananda proceeded to construct for his rapt American audience a vision of Hinduism that was an intellectual companion of modern science, friendly to Christianity but distinctively Indian in source and scope. This vision was based on religious principles codified—but not exhausted—by the ancient Indian Vedas. These laws, he recounted, were discovered by ancient "Rishis, and we honour them as perfected beings. I am glad to tell this audience that some of the very greatest of them were women."[54] Vivekananda was building on the unusual inclusion of women in the planning of the Exposition (in the Board of Lady Managers), as well as the twenty-three women who would speak on stage at the Parliament.[55] He quickly returned to his presentation of the core views of his Vedantic Hinduism—that God, and the created world, are eternal. If either compromised the other's perfect absoluteness, it would impugn the majesty of God, Vivekananda claimed, suggesting that in such circumstances "God would die, which is absurd. Therefore there never was a time when there was no creation."[56] Thus God and the world, he said, are immutable and permanent. This was a stunning split from the Christian worldview of ex nihilo creation familiar to his American audience.

Vivekananda's next point concerned the self or body. Whereas Christian members of the audience were primed to see the soul as individuated from other souls or prepared by science to see an individual as a material creature, Vivekananda insisted, "I am a spirit living in a body. I am not the body."[57] Vivekananda then reaffirmed the immortal "soul," a concept that likely repelled materialists in his audience but captivated Christians familiar with the idea. In all likelihood, Vivekananda was referring to the concept of *atman* (self) in Vedantic thought. In the Upanishads, the atman merges with the Self of all selves, a monistic entity. Vivekananda then posited that God was eternal and infinite, and if humans become perfected, they could become one with this eternal state: "He enjoys infinite and perfect bliss, having obtained the only thing in which man ought to have pleasure, namely God, and enjoys the bliss with God."[58] In a nod to materialist, scientifically minded audience members, he quickly translated his monism into the vocabulary of "unity," admitting that "science is nothing but the finding of unity." Hinduism thus respected the ethos of science and built it into the nature of true religion: "The science of religion [would] become perfect when it would discover Him who is the one life in a universe of death, Him who is the constant basis of an ever-changing world. One who is the only Soul of which all souls are but delusive manifestations."[59]

Using these translational techniques, Vivekananda created identification with his audience to assuage potential worries that his vision of Hinduism might be anti-Christian or opposed to science. The Yale philosopher Filmer S. C. Northup later commented on Vivekananda's communicative skill in this regard, noting, "To convey Hindu meanings in English words is exceedingly difficult. The difficulty arises from the fact that the reader inevitably reads modern western, rather than ancient Hindu, meanings into the English words."[60] Vivekananda, speaking in powerful English prose, used this tendency to his advantage. When he was not eloquently translating the meaning of Hindu terms into English, he used common terms such as *soul* to encourage listeners to view Hinduism as non-foreign. This was simply his entry point for advancing a radical sort of religious pluralism under the label *Hinduism*. De-emphasizing polytheism and idol worship, Vivekananda instead positioned Hinduism as an overarching explanation for the value of all religions, as each allowed apprehension of the "divine nature" of the human being.[61]

After establishing common ground with Christian and scientifically minded audience members, Vivekananda connected his Hinduism to the view of each religion as a path toward the unity of God. The pluralistic vista he opened was grand in its intellectual scope, showing every religion, including Christianity, as one path, but positioning Hinduism as the organizing core of inclusivity. Using the *Bhagavad Gita*, Vivekananda linked all religions with Hinduism by quoting Krishna, the earthly avatar of Vishnu and the divine, all-encompassing Self of all beings: "The Lord has declared to the Hindu in His incarnation as Krishna, '*I am in every religion as the thread through a string of pearls. Wherever thou seest extraordinary holiness and extraordinary power raising and purifying humanity, know thou that I am there.*'" Yet he quickly delivered a blow against the charge of ethnocentrism, referring to the mythic sage Vyasa, composer of Hindu epics, and his claim that "*we find perfect men even beyond the pale of our caste and creed.*"[62] This version of Hinduism would become increasingly popular in the twentieth century, as it emphasized monism while respecting other religions as equally viable paths to the same goal.[63] At the World's Parliament, Vivekananda taught his audience about Hinduism and enunciated a form of engaged pluralism rooted in the Vedic tradition that encompassed, respected, and subordinated other religious traditions. All religions, on his reading, made sense in relation to one Indian goal: "the great central truth in every religion, to evolve a God out of man."[64]

Difference in Unity, Unity in Difference

The most impressive accomplishment of Vivekananda as an orator at the 1893 World's Parliament of Religions was his ability to promote a radically novel vision of Hinduism as multilayered, pluralistic, and inviting. His religious tradition could not be reduced to Christianity, for such a reduction would render his country, his religious teachers, and his beloved Vedic texts superfluous. Yet he could not directly refute Christian doctrine, for such refutation would repel both his audience and his own sense, derived from Ramakrishna, that there are many effective paths to religious realization. The goal of all these efforts in religion, however, is firmly placed and explained in and through his Hindu religious tradition. Thus his speaking activity at the Parliament spanned a range of goals. In his address on Hinduism and in his extemporaneous comments on the parable of the frogs, he sought to build a place for Christianity within the framework of his Hindu monism.

As the Parliament wound down, Vivekananda shifted his pluralistic manner of lecturing about Hinduism and other religions into specific attacks on missionary activities in India. He welcomed religious interaction, but he would not suffer the mind-set of many Christian missionaries that Indians must be converted before they could be helped to meet basic physical needs. On 20 September Vivekananda was called on to give an extemporaneous comment on speakers discussing missionary activity. He pulled no punches, stating, "You Christians, who are so fond of sending out missionaries to save the soul of the heathen—why do you not try to save their bodies from starvation?" Vivekananda then exclaimed to the Christians on stage and in the assembled audience, "You erect churches all through India, but the crying evil in the East is not religion—they have religion enough—but it is bread that the suffering millions of burning India cry out for with parched throats."[65] Clearly, his respect for Christianity as a path among other religions did not preempt him from criticizing the specific tactics of Christian missionaries. Such an assessment evinced a sophisticated notion of charity, one that surely his audience could sense was lacking in missionary appraisals of India and Hinduism, which typically reduced Hinduism to idolatry and barbarism. Christianity was worthy of respect, according to Vivekananda, and this was exactly why he worked to ameliorate its missionary flaws.

Vivekananda's urge to build bridges among religions and religious believers, while maintaining his own religious identity as a Hindu, extended to other Indian traditions. For example, in an evening panel on the "Defense of Buddhism" on 26 September, the Buddhist delegate from Sri Lanka, Anagarika Dharmapala, turned to Vivekananda and asked him to offer some criticisms of Buddhism.[66] Vivekananda obliged, but his criticism was far from a negation of the Buddhist critique of Vedic Hinduism. Instead, Vivekananda opened his extemporaneous criticism by claiming, "I am not a Buddhist, as you have heard, and yet I am." He quickly recontextualized Buddhist criticisms of the Vedic tradition by arguing that "our views about Buddha are that he was not understood properly by his disciples." Instead of seeing Buddha as overturning the early Vedic tradition, Vivekananda offered an analogy suitable for a Western audience: "The relation between Hinduism (by Hinduism, I mean the religion of the Vedas) and what is called Buddhism at the present day is nearly the same as between Judaism and Christianity. Jesus Christ was a Jew, and Shâkya Muni [Buddha] was a Hindu." Drawing further on the Judeo-Christian narrative, Vivekananda explained that the Buddha, "like Jesus, came to fulfil and not to destroy. Only, in the case of Jesus, it was the old people, the Jews, who did not understand him, while in the case of Buddha, it was his own followers who did not realise the import of his teachings." Doctrinal criticism is due to interpreters. "As the Jew did not understand the fulfilment of the Old Testament," Vivekananda said, "so the Buddhist did not understand the fulfilment of the truths of the Hindu religion." Simply put, Buddha was not a critic but an agent of Hinduism: "Shâkya Muni came not to destroy, but he was the fulfilment, the logical conclusion, the logical development of the religion of the Hindus."[67] Complementing his inclusion of Christianity in the Hindu story, Vivekananda masterfully constructed a sense of identification with traditions such as Buddhism that might be seen as offering an indigenous critique of Hinduism.

The final half of the Parliament's concluding day, 27 September, was reserved for Western orators who tended to praise the Christian mission, as they saw it, of the diverse international gathering. The delegates from the East, however, got their final say that morning. Vivekananda continued his strategy of constructing Hinduism as a bridge among religions. He thanked the American audience and organizers, as well as a vaguely Christian "merciful Father."[68] Even though he had been laying the groundwork for a pluralistic orientation—grounded in Hindu tradition—for the respect of all religions, he said he would refrain from speaking on one goal that many had posited for the Parliament—searching for "the common ground of religious unity."[69] Why did he strike this seemingly discordant note? Vivekananda surely sensed that one way of searching for the "universal religion" was to reduce all sects and traditions to one. Indeed, the final talk that afternoon was scheduled to be given by the Baptist minister George Dana Boardman of Philadelphia on the topic "Christ the Unifier of Mankind."[70] Vivekananda did not want to endorse this approach to religious unification. Instead, he criticized those who sought unity through destruction of opponents and differences: "But if any one here hopes that this unity will come by the triumph of any one of the religions and the destruction of the others, to him I say, 'Brother, yours is an impossible hope.' Do I wish that the Christian would become Hindu? God forbid. Do I wish that the Hindu or Buddhist would become Christian? God forbid."[71] Vivekananda believed deeply that the message of the Parliament was that religions could be unified, if given the right unifier and orientation. He saw himself as that unifying figure and conceived of his tradition in terms of inclusion and respect. Thus he could proclaim himself a Hindu and tell his audience that the activities on the diverse and sometimes raucous Parliament stage "proved to the world that holiness, purity and charity are not the exclusive possessions of any church in the world, and that every system has produced men and women of the most exalted character."[72] Instead of religious exclusivism, Vivekananda would, in the following years, build on the foundation of identification he exemplified in Chicago, working tirelessly to forge a living vision of Hindu thought and practice that remained Indian yet also lived up to his concluding lines at the Parliament: "Upon the banner of every religion will soon be written, in spite of resistance: 'Help and not Fight,' 'Assimilation and not Destruction,' 'Harmony and Peace and not Dissension.'"[73]

Conclusion

The Parliament decisively established Vivekananda as an advocate for Hinduism and Indian thought in the United States. It turned an unknown monk—one who was denied entry to the Parliament at its start—into a speaker in demand across the country. After this grand series of successful speeches in Chicago, he undertook a two-year lecture tour of the United

States, organized by the Slayton Lyceum Bureau and others.[74] Rapt audiences heard him speak about Hindu thought and culture—including the treatment of women in India—in cities such as Buffalo, Boston, Cambridge, Baltimore, Washington, New York, Memphis, Indianapolis, Minneapolis, Iowa City, and Detroit. He sometimes delivered twelve to fourteen lectures in the span of a week, in his trademark extemporaneous style.[75] He took his powerful style to the American countryside and proselytized Hinduism to attentive, mainly Christian audiences large and small, urban and rural. He eventually gained a coterie of American disciples who would power the fledgling Vedanta Society in the United States after his death in 1902.[76] All these events featured Vivekananda building connections with his American audiences while maintaining a strong sense of his Hindu identity.

Beyond the sheer scope of his lecturing and organizational activities is the rhetorical accomplishment of the pluralism he built. Vivekananda did not speak of Hinduism as one religion among many; he continued to paint the picture he began to sketch at the Parliament, one that portrayed Hinduism as a universal religion that did not exclude or demean any other sect or tradition. Like his patriotism, this pluralistic religious system remained distinctly and proudly Indian in its origin and specifications. If one's self (atman) was really the self of all beings and all people, then love and charity for others was the strong commandment for one's life. Love of others, in Vivekananda's Hindu monism, was an extension or conflation of the idea of self-care. He could assert his version of Hinduism to the American public as a religion that comprehended and embraced all other religions and that yet retained for India the special privilege of having originated such pluralistic engagement.

Much more can be said about the lecturing activities of Vivekananda on his extended American tour, as well as the lectures he gave to Indian audiences upon his triumphant return to India in January 1897.[77] All of these showcased his pluralistic reconstruction of Hinduism, albeit with varying emphasis placed on building up an Indian tradition and attacking Western chauvinism. This chapter represents a beginning of such a study, one that promises to include India and its orators in scholarly accounts of public lecturing and learning in the nineteenth and twentieth centuries. The story will inevitably foreground the unique, occasionally tense mixture of religion and pluralism so engrained in the Indian tradition.

CONCLUSION:
PLACING PLATFORM CULTURE IN
NINETEENTH-CENTURY AMERICAN LIFE

Carolyn Eastman

If there is one thing that divides our own experiences of most spoken-word performances from those during the long nineteenth century, it is that we have—for the most part—lost a precise sense of the magic of public assembly.

When nineteenth-century Americans talked about the power of public speech, they often described it as a mystical form of electricity that tied people together. This metaphor imagined the orator's power working on two levels. First, it emanated outward from the stage via the speaker's words, gestures, facial expressions, and vocal tones, electrifying each individual audience member: exciting the mind, bringing tears to the eye, raising goosebumps. But this combination of corporeal, intellectual, and emotional exhilaration was not the only way that the power of public speech functioned. It also worked collectively among audience members, as if the electric "energy and force" gained in power as the attendees became aware of one another's reactions, producing static or friction that ricocheted around the room and built in force.[1] In a nineteenth-century culture still mystified by electricity, what could be a more powerful metaphor than to describe spoken-word performances as exciting an electric reaction among their audience members? Listening together, reacting together, hearing one another gasp or murmur, and *thinking* together, however ephemeral such moments may have been—this idealization of oratory's galvanizing force helps us to understand why public speech mattered in nineteenth-century American culture.

As scholars of various forms of media, we often point to print culture as a primary force in an era when literacy rates rose rapidly and a newly efficient post office transported printed goods swiftly throughout the nation. News, information, printed images of fashion plates, gossip columns, racy novels—all now circulated with a speed rightly celebrated by many scholars during the past forty years. There is no doubt of the significance of print, yet our scholarly preoccupation with that medium has overshadowed and diminished our explorations into the vibrancy and importance of public speech. In part, this emphasis has lingered from older scholarship that stressed the developmental centrality of print at the expense of orality—a form of technological determinism that posited that human cultures move *from* orality *to* literacy and that, specifically, orality waned in the increasingly literate long nineteenth century. That older framework has been roundly undermined, most substantively by scholars who point out the increasing prominence of oratory and platform culture during the nineteenth century that emerged in tandem and in productive tension with print.[2]

Nothing better captures the creative dynamism of public speech than the essays in this volume. Indeed, it would be easy to come this far in *Thinking Together* and feel overwhelmed by the variety of lecturers and cultures of the nineteenth century. Listening audiences might encounter an Irish diaspora or a refined discussion and performance of Liszt. An Indian man advocating for the universal acceptance of Hinduism or a white religious visionary describing how his encounter with an angel led to a new form of American religion. Women disrupting gender norms by offering educational lectures on geography and history or performing dramatic readings using men's narrative voices. Moreover, the range described here represents only the tip of the iceberg. This tremendous variety, together with the many ways that these performances played with and against social expectations by race, nationality, class, and gender, has brought scholars back repeatedly to the subject of lecture culture. Nor does this field of research appear to have exhausted the available resources: far from it. In many ways, scholars in a variety of disciplines have just begun to explore and assess the broader meanings of public speech during more than a hundred years of complicated, contradictory cultural movements and political change.

Thus, it is worth spending a little time widening the lens to consider the place of these many forms of speech performance in the context of the time. My comments here seek to step back from the specifics to survey platform culture during the long nineteenth century—to place it in a broader context, as well as to consider what we mean when we discuss those audiences "thinking together" as they encountered the lecture culture of their day.

The first important context to consider is that orality was becoming more important to many institutions and cultures, and in ways that emphasized the importance of the *persuasion* of audiences rather than a top-down vision of cultural transmission. Nineteenth-century lecture culture rose to prominence in American life at a specific moment in time when the spoken word, and oratory in particular, occupied a primary place in public life. Many social, religious, educational, and political movements, both long established and upstart, utilized oratory at the center of their organizations in ways that looked far different than during earlier centuries. To be sure, orality and oratory had long been the central media of these institutions and movements; even with the rising importance of print, orality remained the primary mode of communication, in many cases throughout the eighteenth century and possibly through the nineteenth as well. I do not seek to portray a sense of opposition between the media of print and oratory, for this emphasis on persuasion rather than coercion affected print in similar ways. Rather, the crucial distinction I draw here concerns the particular understanding of the relationship of power between leaders and followers, ministers and congregations, writers and readers, teachers and students. What changed over time was a sense of the relative power of audiences.

These historical changes took time, for the members of audiences had to learn and adopt new roles, which required new forms of cultural literacy in the West. When radical Protestants during the Reformation began to argue that ordinary Christians did not need a learned intermediary to help them access religious faith, or when some seventeenth-century Britons began to argue that a government's legitimacy comes from its representation of its citizens, the relative power of the people began to change. With the translation of the Bible into vernacular languages, increases in literacy, and the growth of the newspaper press came a gradual democratization of knowledge. The growing sense that ordinary believers and citizens required information suggested along the way that they ought to make up their own minds about matters of dogma or governmental action. Slow changes such as these altered how speakers addressed their listening audiences and how writers sought to persuade their readers. Over time we see not only a profound change in modes of persuasion but also the increasing importance of persuasion and a heightened attention to the rhetorical and performative techniques best designed to capture an audience's attention, appeal to their reason, and engage their emotions. By the middle of the eighteenth century, schools and colleges emphasized that knowledge was inert on its own and needed rhetorical persuasion to make it meaningful within human affairs. An argument might be logical and correct, but without rhetorical flourishes, metaphors, humor, and the speaker's own gestures and facial expressions, it could not be truly effective. If speakers and writers could once assume authority due to their social position and/or educational prestige, by the eighteenth century they sought to use a battery of persuasive methods that implicitly understood reading and listening audiences as more skeptical and independent minded. Over the course of time, the new importance of the public, public opinion, and the persuasion of audiences altered the concept of authority.

This historical context helps to situate the optimism behind the American lyceum and other platform oratory of the long nineteenth century, for it conditions our understanding of the concept of "thinking together" laid out in this volume. It is vital to recognize that the importance of audiences and public opinion had grown significantly by the era described here, and that these developments coincided with the gradual democratization of education, politics, print culture, and religion.

In addition, we should keep in mind that the lecture culture described in such detail here constituted only one aspect of a long nineteenth century during which oratory played a major role in American life. Religious revivals and movements placed the spoken word at the center of the task of salvation, of which we see only hints here in the essay on Joseph Smith's oratory to his Mormon followers. Political oratory utilized new rhetorics amid the waves of democratic movements as well. American presidents and senators would make their marks on history not merely for their deeds but for the stirring words that brought about new political systems. In many ways the nationwide preoccupation with formal deliberative oratory rested on the great speeches by these figures, some of which—like Abraham Lincoln's Gettysburg Address—became required for memorization and recitation in schools for more than a century. Contrasting with lofty words like Lincoln's, but equally influential, was "stump speaking," gradually accepted as an aspect of the electoral process. Whereas political figures once derided the frontier candidates who had the temerity to advocate for themselves—and to do so outside, among whiskey-soaked audiences, with florid and improvised speeches—by the late 1840s such advocacy had become an accepted part of the process of democratic elections. American politics spilled over into the realm of social reform, another area in which public speech became central. From the abolitionist speeches of Frederick Douglass to the temperance oratory of John B. Gough, who dramatically told a tale of a reformed drunkard, to the labor agitation of Lucy Parsons, Emma Goldman, and others, reform rhetoric became one of the most dynamic engines of change in the long nineteenth century. The spoken word likewise played a central role in American education at all levels, from the youngest children through college students, as they tested their knowledge through the recitation of memorized facts as well as literary declamation. Beyond the formal schooling that remained resolutely rhetorical during this era, ad hoc literary and debating societies provided men and women with further educational experience in public speaking and discussion. Finally, it remains difficult to separate many kinds of oratorical performances from the theater. The oratorical guidebooks that taught youth how to read and speak invariably included theatrical speeches and dialogues alongside canonic orations by the classical greats. Pedagogical training in oratory was indistinguishable from training as an actor, calling for the same attention to bodily performance and manifestation of the passions.

If at one time many scholars of oratory focused on a canon of "great speeches" like Lincoln's, the disciplinary range of the contributors to this volume signals that the study of the spoken word in history is a truly interdisciplinary field. It features contributions from scholars in history, literature, religious studies, performance, and communication, to name only the most prominent. The disciplinary mixing bowl has brought many new methods and theories to our analyses, but this interdisciplinarity has also resulted in a dispersion of our work, such that it often gets missed by scholars who might benefit from it. This volume places side by side the work of scholars educated in American studies, anthropology, communication, English, history, musicology, philosophy, and rhetoric—and invites readers to engage them together, even as the chapters speak across disciplinary difference.

Altogether, this book mounts a powerful argument for the continued exchange of ideas about lecture culture and wider cultures of public speaking in the long nineteenth century. Indeed, we begin to show here that understanding the spoken word during this era is vital for understanding American culture, for it functioned as a primary medium for the articulation of ideas, as well as an explosive and innovative site for performance, criticism, deliberation, debate, and the embodiment of those ideas in the form of new speakers who challenged conventions of gender, race, and class.

Thinking Together

When we call this volume *Thinking Together*, what do we mean by "thinking"? Or to be more specific, to what extent, and in what ways, were nineteenth-century lecture cultures oriented to intellectual and deliberative aims—versus, for example, pure entertainment?

For the women lecturers of the early national period who sought to earn a living from their performances, the transmission of knowledge was crucial even as it came wrapped in an entertaining package, as Granville Ganter shows. Indeed, women like Eliza Harriot O'Connor and Anne Laura Clarke earned their authority from their experience in the classroom and their close association with formal schools. "She was no common puffer or entertainer," Ganter tells us about O'Connor. "She positioned herself as one of the new nation's elite, engaged in a serious educational project with civic purpose."[3] Likewise, Clarke supplemented her extensive lectures on history and anthropology with charts and maps, visual guides that illustrated everything from biblical history to styles of clothing throughout the world. To buy a ticket for one of these women's lectures was to express a commitment to supplementing one's knowledge of a topic. Like the lecturers who delivered talks to mechanics' associations and local lyceums beginning in the 1820s, these women participated in a national culture that privileged the acquisition of education in addition to formal schools. The historian Joseph F. Kett has called this an early form of adult education, given particular cachet in the nineteenth century because this pursuit of knowledge was often acquired under difficulties: squeezed in during those rare hours away from work or family, and with tickets purchased using limited discretionary income.[4]

A more potent combination of education and entertainment manifested itself closer to the end of the century in the lecture recitals of Amy Fay, as E. Douglas Bomberger shows. Foiled in her effort to become a traditional concert pianist, Fay borrowed a format conceived by an uncle: recitals of a wide range of pieces together with explanatory or biographical comments about the composers, amounting to "piano conversations." This format allowed her to demonstrate her musical interpretation of each piece, but it also gave her listeners resources with which to hear those pieces and to find new meaning in them. Altogether, she impressed her audiences with her "charming conversationalist" skills that demonstrated the "vast fund of information as to the subject in hand."[5] Information that appealed to the mind, aural musical pleasure that appealed to the emotions, and Fay's own feminine charm and considerable musical talent—even more than the lectures of Ganter's early nineteenth-century female entrepreneurs, such performances blurred the boundaries between thinking and pure enjoyment. Fay popularized a format that took advantage of the limited opportunities for female musicians. When she asked her audiences to think and feel along with her as she framed their understanding of any given piece of music, she positioned herself as a conduit for both knowledge and artistic enjoyment.

Both examples—the earlier female lecturers and Amy Fay, spanning almost a century between them—show the extent to which educational knowledge played an important role in nineteenth-century lecture culture, even when individual performers might sweeten it into something more like *edutainment*, like the twenty-first-century TED Talk or the Great Courses. But these examples also open broader horizons beyond the essays in this volume regarding the nature of "thinking together." As Angela G. Ray showed us a decade ago, the American lyceum placed heavy weight on its capacity to popularize knowledge in an expanding nation; and as Paul Stob demonstrated in his book on William James, major American thinkers of the long nineteenth century used public lecturing as a way to shape their ideas and to craft their philosophical positions rhetorically.[6] To emphasize the give-and-take between speakers and their successive audiences—the gradual, mediated articulation of ideas and their reshaping or repackaging over time—is to reconsider the role of spoken-word performance in the shaping of American thought from the Transcendentalists to the Pragmatists. Although it is common to think of authors' lectures as mere presentations of the ideas they codified in print, figures like James used those talks as a means of developing their ideas and texts over time. In short, the thinking that took place in lecture halls *between* speakers and their attendees, as well as from one venue to the next, exemplified an important, process-oriented aspect of the development of major American ideas that has only recently been recovered by scholars of public speech.

Nineteenth-century lecture culture could also advocate for modes of thinking that emphasized ecstatic experience and alternate knowledges that rejected Enlightenment- or science-based concepts of knowing. Upstart evangelical religions and their innovative rhetorical and oratorical forms had profound effects on the religious scene as a whole and on American culture at large, as many scholars have shown. In this volume, Richard Benjamin Crosby demonstrates that when Joseph Smith delivered his King Follett Discourse, he dwelled on the widespread evangelical ideal that believers "produced their own ways of knowing" religious truth, separate from well-educated and highborn religious mediators who sought to tell the people what to think. To advocate for these other ways of knowing was to insist that ordinary believers had the power to determine their own truths, "that a regular person, no matter how mean or vulgar, may, by the progressive acquisition of special knowledge, become the highest form of divine, even a god." As a result, as Crosby shows, Smith conveyed to his listeners a powerful message of unity and a promise of the possibility of transcendence that connected Mormonism to other ecstatic evangelical faiths of the era. Perhaps the same kind of alchemy that produced Americans' idealistic accounts of transformative orators and the "magic" and electricity of the lecture hall also infused Smith's relationship with his Mormon auditors.[7]

One final mode of thinking as exemplified in these essays allows us to step back from the specific content of nineteenth-century lectures and to think about how speakers encouraged audiences to think about broader matters—most notably when the lectures were delivered by women, people of color, foreign nationals, or figures who otherwise stood apart from the elite white men who rose to assume the roles of oratorical heroes during this era. In this regard, it is important to remember how much public speech usually epitomized a hierarchical arrangement of social power. In general—and as had been true for centuries in the Anglo-American context—the role of the orator was filled by men who held authority in a variety of ways, most notably by their high social status, whiteness, and gender. Nor was that hierarchical social power limited to the subject position of the speaker. Highborn male orators had long geared their speech to persuade those listeners who "mattered," hence directing their arguments primarily toward the white male citizens with the capacity to cast votes or voice opinions. Though this was rarely an exclusive mode of persuasion, during the nineteenth century it remained the case that the overwhelming majority of public speakers, whether religious, political, educational, or entertainer, was white, male, and of high station.

Yet consider some of the exceptions to this rule. We have already touched on the female lecturers of the early republic as well as Amy Fay and her piano conversations—women who positioned themselves as authorities capable of educating their audiences in ways that did not conflict with their performance of feminine roles or lead attendees to question their characters. Even more clearly, the experiences of the dramatic reader Gertrude Kellogg during the 1870s illustrate how much female public speakers might challenge audience members to think differently about conventional arrangements of gendered public power. As Sara E. Lampert shows, the format of dramatic reading attracted ambitious, talented women to the lyceum circuit in the postbellum United States, making it possible for at least some of them to enjoy lucrative public careers. In other words, these "genteel young women" helped to expand popular understandings of appropriate female work.

How fascinating, then, that the very nature of dramatic reading entailed such complex performed identifications and impersonations. Kellogg was beautiful, white, refined, and middle-class, but during her performance she sustained "an illusion of total transformation," whether as J. T. Trowbridge's comic Yankee farmer in "Old Simon Dole" or Mary Mapes Dodge's working-class Irishwoman in "Kitty Maloney on the Chinese Question." Did Kellogg undergird restrictive middle-class female ideals in her overall demeanor or undermine them with her transformations on stage and her financial success as a performer? Did her insistence on dramatic reading rather than full actorly embodiment of those characters (such as within a play or in full costume) permit audiences to accept the radical alterations such women might undergo on stage? As Lampert notes, these women could not help but raise the subject of women's changing roles and positions in society, "even as their performances reinscribed a highly racialized and classed feminine ideal."[8] Such complex identifications and subversions of concrete gender performances not only replaced the conventional white male orator with a young single woman but also gave her the chance to transform several times before the eyes of her audience.

But as Kirt H. Wilson and Kaitlyn G. Patia remind us, such transformations and impersonations were not acceptable in all performers. Middle-class women might take on the persona of a comical Yankee farmer to great applause, and white men might perform the love and theft of blackface minstrelsy that constituted one of the most popular forms of musical comedy of midcentury, but black performers ran up against a wall comprising the many forms of racism that characterized African Americans as capable only of imitation. Neither the presence of actual black performers on stage nor the blackface performance by whites permitted the complex identifications embodied by Lampert's genteel young women. If white audiences were willing to place themselves in a position to think, even for only a moment, about the alternate possibilities for white women's public roles, they were manifestly unwilling to think about similar alternatives for African Americans. Indeed, as Wilson and Patia note, even formidable black leaders like Frederick Douglass could attest that imitation "could teach citizenship to freedmen and women through praxis," a path not to mere imitation of whites but instead to "cultural hybridity."[9] Were most Americans thinking when they attended such performances? Perhaps, but we must accept that in the nineteenth century, *thinking* could also mean the confirmation of assumptions, prejudices, and stereotypes that signaled stasis rather than social change.

Thinking *Together*

Performers' and audiences' insistence on extremely delimited roles for African Americans on stage reminds us to be cautious when we imagine lecture culture forging ties between everyone in a community. To imagine oratory as a magical, electric force that rivets an audience together takes on particular meanings when we realize that it could just as likely orient attendees *against* others in their towns. In 1956 the historian Carl Bode famously called the lyceum a "town meeting of the mind," but in the years since, our conceptions of these gatherings have undergone serious revision away from the romance inherent in that framing.[10] Most vividly, in 1988 the historian Lawrence W. Levine offered a very different characterization of American audiences: they were raucous, impossible crowds of hooligans with little interest in social niceties. Summing up the traveler Frances Trollope's accounts of attending performances in several cities during 1832, Levine draws attention to the informal dress, the "incessant spitting," the smell of "onions and whiskey," the thumping of feet instead of clapping, and the "general air of contempt for the decencies of life." In New York, Trollope saw "a lady performing the most maternal office possible." "Every man seemed to think his reputation as a citizen depended on the noise he made," she concluded sardonically.[11] Surely this amounts less to a "town meeting of the mind" than to a carnival.

In backing away from simply calling those audiences *American* and, instead, finding ways that they mirrored social divisions within the nation, these essays demonstrate a poignant tension between idealized views of audiences and the social divisions within them that had profound effects on nineteenth-century American culture as a whole. This stress on social tension is apt. Our scholarship needs to acknowledge both the idealized conceptions of these publics and the fraught divisions among different peoples. At its heart, the study of platform culture offers us many opportunities to analyze the broader debates over race, gender, class, and citizenship roles that took place in the long nineteenth century, for the dynamics that took place on stage and among the attendees both mirrored and commented directly on wider social divisions and exclusions.

That tense combination of calling forth unity while also demarcating divisions emerges powerfully in Ronald J. Zboray and Mary Saracino Zboray's essay on lecture culture during the Civil War when, as they suggest, it amounted to "a theater of war." Their focus on how men and women of many social backgrounds experienced popular lectures illustrates that sometimes lectures provided attendees with a sense of continuity back to antebellum peacetime, offering "knowledge, sociability, and a sense of belonging to a collective outside of home and family." Yet lecture culture had changed, too. Lyceums permitted speakers to address matters of politics and social reform, many of which fundamentally reflected on the war and its causes. Even when audience members sought diversion rather than political commentary or advocacy in their lecture attendance, they might well find on stage a white woman or an African American man or woman for the first time. Whereas such an appearance might have a profound effect, as when one white Wilmington woman professed herself to have "had no idea that [Frederick Douglass's] eloquence was of such a high order," for others it might amount to yet another reminder of the many disruptions that war wrought.[12]

For African Americans, as the Zborays demonstrate, these disruptions could be transformative—and they reflected a wider set of public events oriented toward creating not just an *American* public, or a *white* public, but what several scholars have called counterpublics: sites in which social subgroups define and express themselves as distinct from, and even in contrast to, a mainstream or dominant culture riddled with exclusions. The creation of the Galbreath Lyceum in Baltimore (as well as its associated publication, the *Lyceum Observer*), Philadelphia's Banneker Institute literary society, and other institutions created by and for African Americans illustrate yet another side of public speaking and performance during the long nineteenth century: the ways these performative sites might offer people the agency to create spaces for themselves in the social world.[13] The creation of such counterpublics reveals a parallel aspect of thinking together: a redefinition of *togetherness* that privileges the cohesion of one part of the public sphere in contradistinction to the rest.

Counterpublics could be expressly political in their self-creation and self-definition, as Tom F. Wright illustrates in his analysis of how Irish nationalism emerged in lecture culture. Lecture halls that featured discussions of Irish Americanness, Celtic heritage, and radical republicanism thus functioned to challenge dominant ideals of Anglo-Saxon superiority and conservative politics. Irish American republicans might raise funds for their cause, advocate radicalism, or contest mainstream scientific views of Anglo-Saxon racial dominance as ways to attract specific audiences of a like-minded counterpublic. Yet within the space of the lecture hall, something equally significant took place. Regardless of whether they donated funds or shared a vision for an independent Ireland, these attendees together helped to perform and articulate an Irish diaspora or a "Green Atlantic" of people proud of their ties to Ireland, invigorated by demonstrations of Irish eloquence, and happy to perceive that environment as offering an "oratory of resistance." "The lecture hall was not simply a place for the flattening out of social identities or conformity, but for the expression of complex ethnic affiliations," Wright concludes. The electric atmosphere of the public talk both directly and indirectly contributed to the Irish becoming white. "Engagement with institutions perceived as civic, such as the lecture, was a marker on the road to social respectability, legitimacy, and prestige," desires that paralleled the pleasure these Irish American audiences might take in the distinctively Irish nature of those events.[14]

Yet another form of togetherness and diaspora appeared in the Liberia Lyceum depicted by Bjørn F. Stillion Southard. The creation of this lyceum, which combined many aspects of a literary and debating society together with lecture series, drew heavily on American ideals for how such institutions helped to establish civic behaviors and consciousness. To set up such an institution in a hybrid colony made up of both native Africans and American migrants was to hold up highly specific models for nation building: it privileged American views of the importance of debate, mutual education, and specific forms of public assembly as crucial to the making of a public. Debating, explained lyceum leader Hilary Teage, "is a species of engagement in which the mind acquires dexterity of movement and elasticity of force," helping to make intellectually nimble and sophisticated citizens. In this regard, U.S. migrants played a major role in establishing the idealized forms of citizenship and civic engagement following American models, despite their earlier exclusion from those forms of citizenship due to their race. These migrants also incorporated a strong African American rhetorical tradition of "expressing views and creating identities."[15] Thus, as Stillion Southard notes, the translation of those views to the Liberian context forged a distinctive tie to the United States' black rhetorical forms of identification as well as to a broader set of values associated with America as a whole.

The final essay to examine the process by which lecture audiences "thought *together*" is Scott R. Stroud's analysis of Swami Vivekananda's late-century appearances at the 1893 World's Parliament of Religions—a moment of profoundly retrograde racial and xenophobic views in the United States. If there was any moment to expect deep public skepticism of a brown-skinned man lecturing about a religion that many Americans considered "heathen," this might be it. Yet as Stroud shows, the story is far more surprising. Vivekananda captivated his audiences; he demonstrated powerful ways of identifying with them as he spread a message of religious tolerance. His immediate message was to describe Hinduism to a crowd unlikely to understand its tenets and to emphasize in particular his own interpretation of the religion as exceptionally oriented toward universal acceptance of all world religions. But beyond that message, he appears to have won over his crowds through a uniquely appealing stage persona that exemplified the forms of acceptance of which he spoke. "He was an education, an illumination, a revelation!" effused one listener.[16] Thus, since his visit to the United States coincided with an enhanced American commitment to a sense of its own racial and cultural superiority, Vivekananda had an impressive effect, forging a powerful sense of religious and intellectual connection between nations and cultures.

Each of these essays indicates that we can provide no simple interpretation of audiences thinking *together* during the long nineteenth century. The "togetherness" produced among any given audience could shift profoundly by the next performance, the next group of attendees. But despite the actual social divisions that could fracture these public assemblies, one quality of lecture culture remains striking to the contemporary eye: Americans consistently idealized these gatherings at the same time that they continued to show up. Although they may have criticized a specific speaker or public address, men and women never questioned whether lecture culture was an edifying, important, and galvanizing aspect of culture at large. Public address and the spoken word became more important throughout the long nineteenth century, in part because to many, oratory appeared to be metaphorical of American ideals of community, mutual education, and a certain level of heterogeneity. The tension between social unity and social division provided an important electric friction to the public energies dedicated to lecture culture.

Looking Ahead

Participating in this effort to capture the dynamism of nineteenth-century practices of lecturing and learning has given me hope for an invigorated study of platform culture—one that maintains its interdisciplinary breadth while also finding more venues like this volume, and the conference from which it draws, that bring together diverse methods for the benefit of the field. In this respect, scholarship on print culture might serve as a model—a broad-ranging, interconnected set of works, conferences, and edited volumes that similarly brings together a variety of methods and theories while not erasing the disciplinary traditions that give our work meaning. Because our studies of cultures of orality often draw on printed sources—and because public speech overlaps and exists in tension with print during the nineteenth century, when these were the primary media for communication—it makes sense that scholars of the spoken word would draw inspiration from that field of study.

Even more in need of theorizing and interdisciplinary exchange is what performance theorist Diana Taylor calls the *repertoire,* or the ephemeral aspects of performance that can be so difficult to grasp from our current point in history.[17] No matter how many reviews, accounts, or transcripts of speeches we might retain, a complete analysis of any given performance remains beyond our grasp. But we can use our archival and printed evidence to begin to uncover the gestural repertoires, facial expressions, vocal techniques, and postures that would-be speakers learned as they prepared to convey emotion through their performances—a bodily repertoire that conveys important ideas about society, politics, identity, and memory. How did speakers conform to expectations for bodily comportment on stage while also conveying authenticity and true feeling? How did they break from the accepted range of physical postures to surprise or shock their auditors without appearing uncouth? Drawing on written accounts and a historically informed imagination, we might begin to comprehend what we cannot see or hear: the emotional punch of those gestures for the audiences who attended. "The world of unrecorded sounds is irreclaimable, so the disjunctions that separate our ears from what people heard in the past are doubly profound," writes the religious studies scholar Leigh Eric Schmidt as a preface to a work in which he makes the attempt anyway.[18] As difficult as it is to recapture the subtle effects and meanings of these performances, we need to try.

Consider this passage from Margaret Bayard Smith's 1824 novel *A Winter in Washington,* in which she describes sitting in the gallery of the House of Representatives to listen to "the favourite orator" of the day. "To-day, there was no walking about; no writing of letters, or reading of newspapers, in the hall; no whispering in the gallery," she begins, setting the stage for the experience of attending such a performance:

> He rose—and, in that easy and graceful manner, peculiarly his own; in that full and harmonious voice, whose very sound persuades; with that strength of argument, and warmth of eloquence, which convince and charm; he delivered those patriotic sentiments, presented those just views, and expressed those noble resolutions, which fixed the wavering, enlightened the ignorant, and kindled enthusiasm in all who listened. Attention hung upon his accents, conviction followed his reasoning, and unanimity of opinion crowned this most eloquent and powerful speech. For five long hours he spoke; sometimes pausing to rest, taking a glass of water to refresh himself; often changing his position; now gracefully leaning on the back of his chair; now standing erect,

with out-stretched arm; now eagerly bending forward, as if the better to reach the hearts of his listeners. His eye now thrown in a general glance round the whole assembly; now bent in inquiry, as if to catch coincidence of opinion from his friends, and now fixed with penetrating force on the face of an opponent, as if he could detect and destroy opposition with an eye-beam! His voice, his gestures, his looks, varied with his varying subjects; soft and persuasive, rapid and energetic, lofty and commanding, as the subject by turns required.[19]

Idealized, yes—not to mention fictional—yet this vignette gives us glimpses into the dynamics created between speaker and listeners in a culture that venerated these forms of public assembly, public deliberation, public performance. The forms of the spoken word about which we have written in this book always took place in embodied spaces with unpredictable levels of attention, unexpected outcomes, and unstable personal politics. Yet they also took place during an era that had long since come to see public speech as a democratizing force: public assemblies exemplified hope, social progress, the quest for knowledge. That they did not always reach those aims—often delivering instead racist stereotypes, cheap entertainment, demagoguery, or pandering flattery—should not allow us to lose sight of the grand ideals of electric, magical engagement made possible by nineteenth-century public speech. Only by maintaining a balance between fantasies of perfect eloquence, social and political realities, and the ephemerality of embodied performance can we begin to recover an American world where men and women wanted to think together.

NOTES

INTRODUCTION

1. William Deresiewicz, *Excellent Sheep: The Miseducation of the American Elite and the Way to a Meaningful Life* (New York: Free Press, 2014), 205.
2. Richard Susskind and Daniel Susskind, *The Future of the Professions: How Technology Will Transform the Work of Human Experts* (Oxford: Oxford University Press, 2015), 303.
3. Frederick Douglass, "The Trials and Triumphs of Self-Made Men: An Address Delivered in Halifax, England, on 4 January 1860," in *The Frederick Douglass Papers, Series One: Speeches, Debates, and Interviews*, vol. 3, *1855–63*, ed. John W. Blassingame (New Haven: Yale University Press, 1985), 294.
4. Carl Bode, *The American Lyceum: Town Meeting of the Mind* (New York: Oxford University Press, 1956), xii; Angela G. Ray, *The Lyceum and Public Culture in the Nineteenth-Century United States* (East Lansing: Michigan State University Press, 2005); Tom F. Wright, *Lecturing the Atlantic: Speech, Print, and an Anglo-American Commons, 1830–1870* (Oxford: Oxford University Press, 2017).
5. Cathy J. Cohen defines "a condition of marginality" as "deficiency in the economic, political, and social resources used to guarantee access to the rights and privileges assumed by dominant group members"; such a status is asserted and reinforced by systems of exclusion and exploitation, promulgated by those with greater power. Cohen, *The Boundaries of Blackness: AIDS and the Breakdown of Black Politics* (Chicago: University of Chicago Press, 1999), 37–38.
6. John Dewey, *Democracy and Education: The Middle Works*, vol. 9, *1899–1924*, ed. Jo Ann Boydston (Carbondale: Southern Illinois University Press, 1985), 9.
7. Robert Asen, *Democracy, Deliberation, and Education* (University Park: Pennsylvania State University Press, 2015), 10.
8. Joseph F. Kett, *The Pursuit of Knowledge Under Difficulties: From Self-Improvement to Adult Education in America, 1750–1990* (Stanford: Stanford University Press, 1994).
9. David M. Henkin, *The Postal Age: The Emergence of Modern Communications in Nineteenth-Century America* (Chicago: University of Chicago Press, 2006), 7.
10. Julie Winch, "Douglass, Sarah Mapps," in *African American Lives*, ed. Henry Louis Gates Jr. and Evelyn Brooks Higginbotham (Oxford: Oxford University Press, 2004), 241–42.
11. "Ladies' Department: Mental Feasts," *Liberator*, 21 July 1832. Scholars often quote from Douglass's address. For more detailed study of its content and context, see Marie Lindhorst, "Politics in a Box: Sarah Mapps Douglass and the Female Literary Association, 1831–1833," *Pennsylvania History* 65, no. 3 (1998): 263–78; Jacqueline Bacon and Glen McClish, "Reinventing the Master's Tools: Nineteenth-Century African-American Literary Societies of Philadelphia and Rhetorical Education," *Rhetoric Society Quarterly* 30, no. 4 (2000): 30–32; and Elizabeth McHenry, *Forgotten Readers: Recovering the Lost History of African American Literary Societies* (Durham: Duke University Press, 2002), 59–63.

12. "Ladies' Department: Mental Feasts"; "Ladies' Department: Address Read at a Mental Feast," *Liberator*, 8 December 1832. See Hilary J. Moss, "Jocelyn, Simeon Smith," in *Encyclopedia of Emancipation and Abolition in the Transatlantic World*, ed. Junius Rodriguez (London: Routledge, 2007), 315–16.

13. Ray, *Lyceum and Public Culture*, 106, 111, 297n86.

14. Thomas Augst, *A Clerk's Tale: Young Men and Moral Life in Nineteenth-Century America* (Chicago: University of Chicago Press, 2003); Angela G. Ray, "The Permeable Public: Rituals of Citizenship in Antebellum Men's Debating Clubs," *Argumentation and Advocacy* 41, no. 1 (2004): 1–16; Ray, *Lyceum and Public Culture*, 21–32; Dorothy B. Porter, "The Organized Educational Activities of Negro Literary Societies, 1828–1846," *Journal of Negro Education* 5, no. 4 (1936): 555–76; Emma Jones Lapsansky, "'Discipline to the Mind': Philadelphia's Banneker Institute, 1854–1872," in *A Question of Manhood: A Reader in U.S. Black Men's History and Masculinity*, vol. 1, ed. Darlene Clark Hine and Earnestine Jenkins (Bloomington: Indiana University Press, 1999), 399–414; Angela G. Ray, "Warriors and Statesmen: Debate Education Among Free African American Men in Antebellum Charleston," in *Speech and Debate as Civic Education*, ed. J. Michael Hogan, Jessica A. Kurr, Michael J. Bergmaier, and Jeremy D. Johnson (University Park: Pennsylvania State University Press, 2017), 25–35; Mary Kelley, *Learning to Stand and Speak: Women, Education, and Public Life in America's Republic* (Chapel Hill: University of North Carolina Press, 2006), 137; McHenry, *Forgotten Readers*, 57–79.

15. See Sydney E. Ahlstrom, *A Religious History of the American People*, 2nd ed. (New Haven: Yale University Press, 2004); Gary Dorrien, *The Making of American Liberal Theology: Imagining Progressive Religion, 1805–1900* (Louisville, Ky.: Westminster John Knox Press, 2001); and William R. Hutchinson, *The Modernist Impulse in American Protestantism* (Cambridge, Mass.: Harvard University Press, 1976).

16. Catherine R. Squires, "Rethinking the Black Public Sphere: An Alternative Vocabulary for Multiple Public Spheres," *Communication Theory* 12, no. 4 (2002): 459.

17. Julie Winch, "'You Have Talents—Only Cultivate Them': Philadelphia's Black Female Literary Societies and the Abolitionist Crusade," in *The Abolitionist Sisterhood: Women's Political Culture in Antebellum America*, ed. Jean Fagan Yellin and John C. Van Horne (Ithaca: Cornell University Press, 1994), 103, 117.

18. Shirley Wilson Logan, *Liberating Language: Sites of Rhetorical Education in Nineteenth-Century Black America* (Carbondale: Southern Illinois University Press, 2008), 65.

19. McHenry, *Forgotten Readers*, 17; Kelley, *Learning to Stand and Speak*, 143.

20. On threats in Philadelphia, see Lindhorst, "Politics in a Box," 266–68; on frontiersmen, see Angela G. Ray, "Learning Leadership: Lincoln at the Lyceum, 1838," *Rhetoric and Public Affairs* 13, no. 3 (2010): 349–87. Essays in this volume treat the other topics mentioned here.

21. Ray, *Lyceum and Public Culture*, 7–8, 176–78; Wright, *Lecturing the Atlantic*.

22. See Tom F. Wright, ed., *The Cosmopolitan Lyceum: Lecture Culture and the Globe in Nineteenth-Century America* (Amherst: University of Massachusetts Press, 2013).

23. "Ladies' Department: Extract from a Letter," *Liberator*, 14 July 1832; "Ladies' Department: Ella, a Sketch," *Liberator*, 4 August 1832; "Ladies' Department: Family Worship," *Liberator*, 8 September 1832. The author of each was designated "Sophanisba." See Margaret Malamud, "'A Kind of Moral Gladiatorship': Abolitionist Use of the Classics," *Arion* 23, no. 2 (2015): 61.

24. McHenry, *Forgotten Readers*, 63.

25. Jasmine Nichole Cobb, *Picture Freedom: Remaking Black Visuality in the Early Nineteenth Century* (New York: New York University Press, 2015), 17; on Douglass, see 67–69, 107–8.

26. Ray, "Learning Leadership," 357.

27. Ray, *Lyceum and Public Culture*, 21–23. On itinerancy, see Donald M. Scott, "Itinerant Lecturers and Lecturing in New England, 1800–1850," in *Itinerancy in New England and New York: The Dublin Seminar for New England Folklife, Annual Proceedings, 1984*, ed. Peter Benes and Jane Montague Benes (Boston: Boston University, 1986), 65–75.

28. Ray, *Lyceum and Public Culture*, 22. On the Alexandria Lyceum, see Benjamin Hallowell, *Autobiography of Benjamin Hallowell*, 2nd ed. (Philadelphia: Friends' Book Association, 1884), 128–29; Philip C. Brooks, "The Lyceum Company, 1838–1990," in *Historic Alexandria Antiques Show* (Alexandria, Va., 1990), 32–39; "History of The Lyceum," City of Alexandria, Virginia, updated 17 December 2015, http://alexandriava.gov/historic/lyceum/?id=38678.

29. Ray, *Lyceum and Public Culture*, 3–6, 15–20, 44, 263n3; Angela G. Ray, "How Cosmopolitan Was the Lyceum, Anyway?" in Wright, *Cosmopolitan Lyceum*, 26–28; Andrew C. Rieser, *The Chautauqua Moment: Protestants, Progressives, and the Culture of Modern Liberalism* (New York: Columbia University Press, 2003). On the Redpath Bureau, see John R. McKivigan, *Forgotten Firebrand: James Redpath and the Making of Nineteenth-Century America* (Ithaca: Cornell University Press, 2008), 113–52.

30. Bode, *American Lyceum*, xii.

31. Ronald J. Zboray and Mary Saracino Zboray, "The Portable Lyceum in the Civil War," herein.

32. Kirt H. Wilson and Kaitlyn G. Patia, "Authentic Imitation or Perverse Original? Learning about Race from America's Popular Platforms," herein.

33. See Simone Natale, *Supernatural Entertainments: Victorian Spiritualism and the Rise of Modern Media Culture* (University Park: Pennsylvania State University Press, 2016).

34. See Kett, *Pursuit of Knowledge Under Difficulties*, chap. 2.

35. See Donald M. Scott, "The Profession That Vanished: Public Lecturing in Mid-Nineteenth-Century America," in *Professions and Professional Ideologies in America*, ed. Gerald L. Geison (Chapel Hill: University of North Carolina Press, 1983), 15–18; and Ray, *Lyceum and Public Culture*, 37, 90.

36. Mid-twentieth-century communication theory characterizes this kind of noninstrumental, present-focused goal as "consummatory"; see, for example Leon Festinger, "Informal Social Communication," *Psychological Review* 57 (1950): 280–81; David K. Berlo, *The Process of Communication: An Introduction to Theory and Practice* (New York: Holt, Rinehart and Winston, 1960), 17–18; and Randall A. Lake, "Enacting Red Power: The Consummatory Function in Native American Protest Rhetoric," *Quarterly Journal of Speech* 69 (1983): 127–42.

37. Thomas Davidson, *The Education of the Wage-Earners*, ed. Charles M. Bakewell (Boston: Ginn and Company, 1904).

38. See Daniel Burnstein, *Next to Godliness: Confronting Dirt and Despair in Progressive Era New York City* (Urbana: University of Illinois Press, 2010); and John Louis Recchiuti, *Civic Engagement: Social Science and Progressive-Era Reform in New York City* (Philadelphia: University of Pennsylvania Press, 2007).

39. Autobiographical profiles of members of the Breadwinner's College exist in the form of lengthy survey responses written after Davidson's death in 1900. See the records of the Thomas Davidson Society, Thomas Davidson Papers, box 32, Sterling Memorial Library, Yale University (hereafter TDS-Yale).

40. Davidson, *Education of the Wage-Earners*, 104–5.

41. Morris R. Cohen, *A Dreamer's Journey: The Autobiography of Morris Raphael Cohen* (Boston: Free Press, 1949), 119.

42. Survey response of Mary Ryshpan, TDS-Yale.

43. Two of the many books published on these issues over the last few years include William J. Bennett and David Wilezol, *Is College Worth It?* (Nashville: Thomas Nelson, 2013); and Ryan Craig, *College Disrupted: The Great Unbundling of Higher Education* (New York: Palgrave Macmillan, 2015).

44. Carolyn Eastman, "Conclusion: Placing Platform Culture in Nineteenth-Century American Life," herein.

CHAPTER I

1. Ronald J. Zboray and Mary Saracino Zboray, *Literary Dollars and Social Sense: A People's History of the Mass Market Book* (New York: Routledge, 2005), 189–90. On the lyceum's cosmopolitanism, see Angela G. Ray, "How Cosmopolitan Was the Lyceum, Anyway?" in *The Cosmopolitan Lyceum: Lecture Culture and the Globe in Nineteenth-Century America*, ed. Tom F. Wright (Amherst: University of Massachusetts Press, 2013), 23–41; and Ronald J. Zboray and Mary Saracino Zboray, "Women Thinking: The International Popular Lecture and Its Audience in Antebellum New England," in ibid., 42–66.

2. For works that devote a few pages to the war, see David Mead, *Yankee Eloquence in the Middle West: The Ohio Lyceum, 1850–1870* (East Lansing: Michigan State College Press, 1951), 201–17; Carl Bode, *The American Lyceum: Town Meeting of the Mind* (New York: Oxford University Press, 1956), 247–49; Angela G. Ray, *The Lyceum and Public Culture in the Nineteenth-Century United States* (East Lansing: Michigan State University Press, 2005), 39, 43–44, 128, 136–37; Angela G. Ray, "What Hath She Wrought? Woman's Rights and the Nineteenth-Century Lyceum," *Rhetoric and Public Affairs* 9, no. 2 (2006): 188, 191, 193, 195; and Vern Wagner, "The Lecture Lyceum and the Problem of Controversy," *Journal of the History of Ideas* 15, no. 1 (January 1954): 131–33.

3. Bode, *American Lyceum*, 247.

4. Ray, *Lyceum and Public Culture*, 43, 114–37.

5. William Warren Rogers Jr., *Confederate Home Front: Montgomery During the Civil War* (Tuscaloosa: University of Alabama Press, 1999); Joan E. Cashin, ed., *The War Was You and Me: Civilians in the American Civil War* (Princeton: Princeton University Press, 2002); Paul Alan Cimbala and Randall M. Miller, eds., *Union Soldiers and the Northern Home Front: Wartime Experiences, Postwar Adjustments* (New York: Fordham University Press, 2002); Paul Alan Cimbala and Randall M. Miller, eds., *An Uncommon Time: The Civil War and the Northern Home Front* (New York: Fordham University Press, 2002); James Alan Marten, *Civil War America: Voices from the Home Front* (New York: Fordham University Press, 2007); Scott Reynolds Nelson and Carol Sheriff, *A People at War: Civilians and Soldiers in America's Civil War, 1854–1877* (New York: Oxford University Press, 2008); James Matthew Gallman, *Northerners at War: Reflections on the Civil War Home Front* (Kent: Kent State University Press, 2010); Ginette Aley and J. L. Anderson, eds., *Union Heartland: The Midwestern Home Front During the Civil War* (Carbondale: Southern Illinois University Press, 2013); Steven J. Ramold, *Across the Divide: Union Soldiers View the Northern Home Front* (New York: New York University Press, 2013).

6. The research was funded by a 2012 National Endowment for the Humanities Fellowship to Ronald J. Zboray (FA-56646-12) and, for Ronald J. Zboray and Mary Saracino Zboray, by a 2009 Joseph McKerns Research Grant Award from the American Journalism Historians Association, for research at the South Carolina Historical Society.

7. Ronald J. Zboray and Mary Saracino Zboray, "Research Essay: A Database of Civil War Readers," *AJHA Intelligencer* 31, no. 3 (2015): 2–3.

8. Our own work has been framed by third-wave audience studies that situate media's reception within contexts of everyday life. See Pertti Alasuutari, "Introduction:

Three Phases of Reception Studies," in *Rethinking the Media Audience: The New Agenda*, ed. Pertti Alasuutari (London: Sage, 1999), 1–21. For our audience analysis of the antebellum lyceum, see Zboray and Zboray, "Women Thinking."

9. Subtitle of Bode, *American Lyceum*.

10. See Ronald J. Zboray and Mary Saracino Zboray, *Everyday Ideas: Socioliterary Experience Among Antebellum New Englanders* (Knoxville: University of Tennessee Press, 2006), esp. chap. 10; and Zboray and Zboray, "Women Thinking."

11. In our discussion, we are mindful of the intersections of race with other axes of social difference, particularly class and gender. Kimberlé Crenshaw, "Demarginalizing the Intersections of Race and Sex: A Black Feminist Critique of Antidiscrimination Doctrine, Feminist Theory, and Antiracist Politics," *University of Chicago Legal Forum* 140 (1989): 139–67; Leslie McCall, "The Complexity of Intersectionality," *Signs: Journal of Women in Culture and Society* 30, no. 3 (2005): 1771–1800; Kim Vaz-Deville, "Intersectionality Theory in Historical Research: Telling Different American Stories," *Reviews in American History* 43, no. 2 (2015): 223–30.

12. Sarah Smith Cox Browne, Diary, 3 May 1862, Browne Family Papers, Schlesinger Library, Radcliffe Institute, Harvard University (hereafter BFP-SL).

13. See, for example, Mary Ann Hogg Brunot to Mary Ann Breading Hogg, 10 April 1863, Brunot Family Papers, series II, Senator John Heinz History Center (hereafter BFP-HHC); James W. Virtue, Diary, 5 February 1864, in "'May Live and Die a Miner': The 1864 Clarksville Diary of James W. Virtue," ed. Gary Dielman, *Oregon Historical Quarterly* 105, no. 1 (2004): 71; and Sarah Bartlett Bullock, Diary, 6 January 1864, Rhode Island Historical Society.

14. Emily Hawley Gillespie, Diary, 19 February and 18 September 1862, in *"A Secret to Be Burried": The Diary and Life of Emily Hawley Gillespie, 1858–1888*, ed. Judy Nolte Lensink (Iowa City: University of Iowa Press, 1989), 70, 82.

15. Sarah Ellen Browne to Albert Gallatin Browne, 20 January 1864, BFP-SL.

16. Caroline Barrett White, Diary, 16 November 1864, Caroline Barrett White Papers, 1844–1915, American Antiquarian Society (hereafter CBWP-AAS).

17. White, Diary, 9 January 1862, CBWP-AAS; Mary Henry, Diary, 24 and 26 January 1863, Joseph Henry Papers, Smithsonian Institution Archives.

18. Anna Farquhar to Eliza Brooke, 13 April 1865, Brooke Family Papers, Special Collections, University of Maryland Libraries (hereafter BFP-UM).

19. Ronald J. Zboray and Mary Saracino Zboray, "'My Unsocial Habit': Reading and Emergent Youth Subcultures in Civil War America," in *Lost Histories of Youth Culture*, ed. Christine Feldman-Barrett (New York: Peter Lang, 2015), 17–34.

20. Maria Lydig Daly, Diary, 27 April and 7 May 1862, in *Diary of a Union Lady, 1861–1865*, ed. Harold Earl Hammond (New York: Funk and Wagnalls, 1962), 123–25; Cousin Rose [Cass?] to Ann Wallace, 1 May 1861, Wallace-Dickey Family Papers, Abraham Lincoln Presidential Library; Hogg to Hogg, BFP-HHC; Sarah Smith Cox Browne, Diary, 8 January 1862, BFP-SL; Susan E. Parsons Forbes Brown, Diaries, 30 November 1863, American Antiquarian Society (hereafter AAS).

21. Susan R. Trautwine McManus, Diaries, 3 December 1861, Historical Society of Pennsylvania; Susan E. Parsons Forbes Brown, Diaries, 1 November 1864, AAS; Persis Sibley Andrews Black, Diary, 8 June 1862, Massachusetts Historical Society (hereafter MHS); J. Seymour Walton [writing about Mary in Utica, N.Y.], Diary, 4 November 1863, Newberry Library.

22. Delia Locke, Diary, 3 March, 27 September, and 30 November 1861, 6 July 1862, 14 March, 1 April, and 1 May 1863, 1 June 1864, Locke-Hammond Family Papers, Holt-Atherton Special Collections, University of the Pacific Library (hereafter LHP-UP).

23. Amherst College, *Obituary Record of the Graduates of Amherst College for the Academic Year Ending July 9, 1874* (Amherst, Mass.: Henry M. McCloud, 1874), 9–11.

24. Mary E. Willard, Diary, 29 October 1861, in *Nineteen Beautiful Years; or, Sketches of a Girl's Life*, ed. Frances E. Willard (New York: Harper and Brothers, 1864), 175.

25. Daly, Diary, 6 May 1863, 237.

26. Sarah Fulton to Edward A. Fulton, 4 April 1863, Edward A. Fulton Collection, Special Collections, University of Delaware Library.

27. Sarah Ellen Browne to Albert Gallatin Browne, 20 January 1864, BFP-SL.

28. See Emily Hawley Gillespie, Delaware County, Iowa, Diary, 26 March 1862, in Lensink, *Secret to Be Burried*, 72; Black, Diary, 31 March 1861, Paris Hill, Maine, MHS; Anna Farquhar, Olney, Maryland, 13 April 1865, BFP-UM; and Delia Locke, Diary, 2, 16, and 23 July 1864, Lockwood, California, LHP-UP.

29. Sara C. VanderHaagen and Angela G. Ray, "A Pilgrim Critic at Places of Public Memory: Anna Dickinson's Southern Tour of 1875," *Quarterly Journal of Speech* 100, no. 3 (2014): 353–54; Ray, *Lyceum and Public Culture*, 147–48.

30. Daly, Diary, 8 April 1865, 349.

31. Annie R. Stuart, Diary, 15 and 17 November 1861, Center for Archival Collections, Bowling Green State University (hereafter BGSU). On Dickinson, see, for example, Brown, Diary, 6 February 1865; Daniel F. Child [with sister Catherine], Diary, 11 February and 25 October 1864, and 6 February 1865, D. F. Child Papers, Massachusetts Historical Society (hereafter CP-MHS); and Cornelia Oatis Hancock to Rachel Nicholson Hancock, 20 January 1864, in *Letters of a Civil War Nurse: Cornelia Hancock, 1863–1865*, ed. Henrietta Stratton Jaquette (Lincoln: University of Nebraska Press, 1998), 39.

32. Stuart, Diary, 26 and 27 June 1862, BGSU. It is unlikely that the speaker was Abigail Bush since she was living in California during the war; Ann D. Gordon, ed., *The Selected Papers of Elizabeth Cady Stanton and Susan B. Anthony*, vol. 1, *In the School of Anti-Slavery, 1840–1866* (New Brunswick: Rutgers University Press, 1997), 125–26n5. A "Mrs. Bush" gave temperance lectures in Ohio in 1862 and spoke in the state on "the popular topics of the day" in 1864; see *Cadiz Democrat*, 5 March 1862; and *Western Reserve Chronicle*, 16 March 1864.

33. On Wendell Phillips, see Martha Osborne Barrett, South Danvers, to Moses Austin Cartland, 26 December 1861, Cartland Family Papers, Houghton Library, Harvard University; Child, Diary, 23 August 1861 and 1 March 1864, CP-MHS; and Browne, Diary, 3 December 1862, BFP-SL. On George Thompson, see Brown, Diary, 27 January 1865. On Theodore D. Weld, see Sarah Pugh to Mary Anne Estlin, 15 March 1863, in *Memorial of Sarah Pugh: A Tribute of Respect from Her Cousins* (Philadelphia: J. B. Lippincott, 1888), 103. See also Ray, *Lyceum and Public Culture*, 119.

34. Anne M. Ferris, Diary, December 1863, in *The Civil War Diaries of Anna M. Ferris*, ed. Harold B. Hancock (Wilmington: Historical Society of Delaware, 1961), 246–47.

35. Emilie Davis, Diary, 17 March 1863, in *Notes from a Colored Girl: The Civil War Pocket Diaries of Emilie Frances Davis*, ed. Karsonya Wise Whitehead (Columbia: University of South Carolina Press, 2014), 28.

36. *Philadelphia Inquirer*, 19 March 1863; Whitehead, *Notes*, 88–89, and annotation, 28.

37. Of the two diary editions—Whitehead, *Notes*; and Judith Giesberg, ed., *Emilie Davis's Civil War: The Diaries of a Free Black Woman in Philadelphia*, transcribed by the Memorable Days Project (University Park: Pennsylvania State University Press, 2014)—we mainly consult Whitehead.

38. Davis, Diary, 19 February 1863, 25.

39. Whitehead, *Notes*, 166; Davis, Diary, 22 March 1865, 183. See also Sara E. Lampert, "Black Swan / White Raven: The Racial Politics of Elizabeth Greenfield's American Concert Career, 1851–1855," *American Nineteenth Century History* 17, no. 1 (2016): 75–102.

40. Davis, Diary, 17 March, 25 April, and 4 December 1863, and 16 February 1865; and Whitehead, *Notes*, annotation, 28, 33, 57–58, 179.

41. Davis, Diary, 27 February 1865, 21 January 1864, 180, 108; and Whitehead, *Notes*, annotation, 180.

42. Davis, Diary, 28 and 25 January 1865, 7 December 1864, 8 March 1863, 177, 176, 142, 27; Whitehead, *Notes*, annotation, 177, 176, 142, 81, 91, 227.

43. Davis, Diary, 22 January, 5 and 19 February, and 5 March 1863, 22–23, 25, 27; Whitehead, *Notes*, annotation, 23. See also Emma Jones Lapsansky, "'Discipline to the Mind': Philadelphia's Banneker Institute, 1854–1872," in *A Question of Manhood: A Reader in U.S. Black Men's History and Masculinity*, vol. 1, ed. Darlene Clark Hine and Earnestine Jenkins (Bloomington: Indiana University Press, 1999), 399–414.

44. Davis, Diary, 21 March and 29 April 1865, 183, 188.

45. See Charlotte Forten, *The Journals of Charlotte Forten Grimké*, ed. Brenda Stevenson (New York: Oxford University Press, 1988), for example, 29 October, 5 and 19 November 1854, 30 and 31 January 1855, 14 December 1856, 18 October and 29 November 1857, 5 March 1858, 106, 109, 111, 125–26, 172–73, 262–63, 269, 290.

46. Ibid., 6 July 1862, 369.

47. Elizabeth McHenry, *Forgotten Readers: Recovering the Lost History of African American Literary Societies* (Durham: Duke University Press, 2002), 81–83. On a black literary society in Charleston, see Angela G. Ray, *"A Green Oasis in the History of My Life": Race and the Culture of Debating in Antebellum Charleston, South Carolina* (Salt Lake City: Department of Communication, University of Utah, 2014).

48. Christian A. Fleetwood to Isaac N. Rendall, 21 March 1911, Christian A. Fleetwood Papers, Library of Congress (hereafter CFP-LC). See also Zboray and Zboray, "'My Unsocial Habit,'" 29–30.

49. "Geemes" [James H. A. Johnson], "History of the Galbreath Lyceum," Domestic Department, *Lyceum Observer* 1, no. 2 (5 June 1863), CFP-LC.

50. Christian A. Fleetwood, Diary, 23 March 1863, CFP-LC.

51. Fleetwood, Diary, 19 May 1862, CFP-LC.

52. Ibid., 31 March 1862, CFP-LC.

53. Ibid., 13 January 1862, CFP-LC.

54. Christopher Phillips, *Freedom's Port: The African American Community of Baltimore* (Urbana: University of Illinois Press, 1997), 172.

55. Fleetwood, Diary, 22 September 1862, CFP-LC.

56. Ibid., 10 November 1862, CFP-LC.

57. *Baltimore Sun*, 20 March 1862; Fleetwood, Diary, 20 March 1862, CFP-LC.

58. Fleetwood, Diary, 22 April 1862, CFP-LC.

59. Ibid., 2 April 1862, CFP-LC.

60. Ibid., 22 March 1862, CFP-LC.

61. Christian A. Fleetwood, "Speech, 30 May 1877," CFP-LC.

62. Fleetwood, Diary, 4 and 18 March 1862, 15 January 1863, CFP-LC. On men and sewing societies, see Zboray and Zboray, *Everyday Ideas*, 132–33.

63. Fleetwood, Diary, 30 April 1863, CFP-LC.

64. *Lyceum Observer* 1, no. 2 (5 June 1863), CFP-LC. On the epigraph, see C. A. Goodrich and Noah Porter, *Webster's Complete Dictionary of the English Language, Thoroughly Revised* (Oxford: Oxford University Press, 1884), 1773.

65. "Speech of Mr. J. E. Green, of Detroit, Michigan, Delivered at the 1st Anniversary of the Emancipation of the District of Columbia, April 16th, in Washington," *Lyceum Observer* 1, no. 2 (5 June 1863): 3, 4, CFP-LC. See also "Gaand [sic] Emancipation Celebration," *Liberator*, 8 May 1863, 75.

66. Fleetwood, Diary, 3 July, 17 August, 29–30 September 1863, CFP-LC. See also "Fleetwood, Christian A.," *Compiled Military Service Records of Volunteer Union Soldiers Who Served with the United States Colored Troops, 2nd Through 7th Colored Infantry, 1861–65* (Washington, D.C.: National Archives and Records Administration, 1999), roll 0036.

67. Fleetwood, Diary, 31 December 1863, CFP-LC.

68. Amanda McDowell Burns, 22 July 1861, in *Fiddles in the Cumberlands*, ed. Lela McDowell Blankenship (New York: Richard R. Smith, 1943), 63.

69. Marcus Spiegel to Caroline Hamlin Spiegel, 17 December 1862, in *Your True Marcus: The Civil War Letters of a Jewish Colonel*, ed. Frank L. Byrne and Jean Powers Soman (Kent: Kent State University Press, 1985), 194.

70. John Harper to Albert Harper, 21 March 1862, Harper Family Papers, Senator John Heinz History Center.

71. Mary Emma Randolph to Walter G. Dunn, 20 February 1865, in *After Chancellorsville: Letters from the Heart: The Civil War Letters of Private Walter G. Dunn and Emma Randolph*, ed. Judith A. Bailey and Robert I. Cottom (Baltimore: Maryland Historical Society, 1998), 169.

72. Dunn to Randolph, 8 March 1865, 182; *Baltimore Sun*, 28 February 1865.

73. Fleetwood, Diary, 13 October 1863, CFP-LC. For one example of a young schoolteacher sending her lecture to her brother, see Thomas D. Christie to Sarah Christie, 16 July 1862, James C. Christie and Family Papers, Minnesota Historical Society (hereafter CFP-MIHS).

74. Shirley Wilson Logan, *Liberating Language: Sites of Rhetorical Education in Nineteenth-Century Black America* (Carbondale: Southern Illinois University Press, 2008), 18–24. African American periodicals such as the *Christian Recorder* fostered a similarly collective literary environment for soldiers by providing them with diverse reading matter to read aloud and otherwise share and by publishing their written expressions, such as letters. See Eric Gardner, *Black Print Unbound: The Christian Recorder, African American Literature, and Periodical Culture* (New York: Oxford University Press, 2015), chap. 5, esp. 151–57.

75. Fleetwood, Diary, 7 and 9 January, 21 and 19 May 1864, CFP-LC.

76. Ibid., 12 and 13 February 1864; on Butler as a lyceum member, see 23 March 1863, CFP-LC.

77. Ibid., 5 April 1864, CFP-LC. On Handy, see *Lyceum Observer* 1, no. 2 (5 June 1863), CFP-LC; and "Handy, Alfred Ward," *Compiled Military Service Records of Volunteer Union Soldiers*, roll 0037.

78. Fleetwood, Diary, 5 January and 2–3 December 1864, CFP-LC. On Hunter, see John David Smith, "Let Us All Be Grateful That We Have Colored Troops That Will Fight," in *Black Soldiers in Blue: African American Troops in the Civil War Era*, ed. John David Smith (Chapel Hill: University of North Carolina Press, 2005), 58; and "Rev. H. M. Turner," *Harper's Weekly* 7, no. 363 (12 December 1863): 796.

79. Fleetwood, Diary, 14 October 1863, CFP-LC.

80. Frank Morse to Ellen Morse, 12 October 1862, Frank C. Morse Papers, Massachusetts Historical Society. On reading letters aloud at home, see Ronald J. Zboray and Mary Saracino Zboray, "Cannonballs and Books: Reading and the Disruption of Social Ties on the New England Home Front," in Cashin, *War Was You and Me*, 250.

81. Susan Bradford Eppes, Diary, February 1864, in *Through Some Eventful Years: By Susan Bradford Eppes* (Macon, Ga.: J. W. Burke, 1926), 230–32.

82. Alonzo Miller to "Father and the Rest," 14 February 1864, in *Diaries and Letters, 1864–1865*, ed. Alonzo Miller (Prescott, Wis.: privately published, 1958), 8. See also Isaac Lyman Taylor, Diary, 3 December 1862, in Hazel C. Wolf, ed., "Campaigning with the First Minnesota: A Civil War Diary," pt. 3, *Minnesota History Magazine* 25, no. 3 (September 1944): 235.

83. Fleetwood, Diary, 5 January, 7 April, and 21 September 1864, CFP-LC.

84. Josiah Marshall Favill, Diary, 8 (on a camp newspaper) and 10 January 1864, in *The Diary of a Young Officer Serving with the Armies of the United States During the War of the Rebellion* (Chicago: R. R. Donnelley and Sons, 1909), 275–77.

85. Hasseltine Dunten to unknown recipient, 19 November 1863, in *Soldiers' Letters, from Camp, Battle-Field and Prison*, ed. Lydia Minturn Post (New York: Bunce and Huntington, 1865), 293.
86. Thomas D. Christie to Sarah J. Christie, 9 December 1863, CFP-MIHS. See also William M. McLain to unknown recipient, February 1865, in Post, *Soldiers' Letters*, 461.
87. Thomas D. Christie to Sarah J. Christie, 9 December 1863, CFP-MIHS.
88. James T. Currie, *Enclave: Vicksburg and Her Plantations, 1863–1870* (Jackson: University Press of Mississippi, 1980), 22–23; McLain, in Post, *Soldiers' Letters*, 461.
89. Quoted in Currie, *Enclave*, 23.
90. Thomas D. Christie to James C. Christie, 3 February 1864, CFP-MIHS.
91. William G. Christie to Alexander S. Christie, 20 December 1863, CFP-MIHS.
92. *Libby Chronicle*, 28 August 1863, in *The Libby Chronicle, Devoted to Facts and Fun: A True Copy of the Libby Chronicle as Written by the Prisoners of Libby in 1863* . . . , ed. Louis Napoléon Beaudry (Albany, N.Y.: Louis N. Beaudry, 1889), 5.
93. Peter Carlson, "'Meade's Army Annihilated!'" *Opinionator* (blog), *New York Times*, 12 July 2013, http://opinionator.blogs.nytimes.com/2013/07/12/meades-army-annihilated/.
94. *Libby Chronicle*, 21 August 1863, in Beaudry, *Libby Chronicle*, 1.
95. Frank E. Moran, "Libby's Bright Side: A Silver Lining in the Dark Cloud of Prison Life," in *Camp-Fire Sketches and Battle-Field Echoes of the Rebellion*, comp. W. C. King and W. P. Derby (Springfield, Mass.: W. C. King, 1887), 183–84.
96. *Libby Chronicle*, 28 August 1863, in Beaudry, *Libby Chronicle*, 5.
97. Ibid., 18 September 1863, 21.
98. Ibid.
99. Ibid., 26.
100. Ibid., 4 September 1863, 11.
101. Quote from the *Right Flanker* in Roy Alden Atwood, "The Right Flanker (NY, 1863–1864)," *The Handwritten Newspapers Project: An Annotated Bibliography and Historical Research Guide to Handwritten Newspapers from Around the World*, 22 July 2011, http://handwrittennews.com/category/united-states/new-york/.
102. *Rapidann*, 1 January 1864, B. H. Teague Family and Collected Papers, 1770–1899, South Carolina Historical Society.
103. John W. Hibbs, *Prison Times*, April 1865, New-York Historical Society, http://cdm16694.contentdm.oclc.org/cdm/ref/collection/p16694coll47/id/205.
104. Amanda Akin Stearns, Diary, 7 January 1864, in Amanda Akin Stearns, *The Lady Nurse of Ward E* (New York: Baker and Taylor, 1909), 141.
105. *Armory Square Hospital Gazette*, 20 January 1864, "Newspapers," *Civil War Washington*, http://civilwardc.org/texts/newspapers/cww.01131.html; on the demand for tickets to Dickinson's speech, see *Daily Constitutional Union*, 15 January 1864; on the speech, see Regular Correspondent of the *Evening Post*, "Miss Anna Dickinson's Lecture in Washington," *Liberator*, 29 January 1864.
106. Stearns, Diary, 18 December 1863, 12, 16, 19 January and 5 February 1864, 112, 148, 150–51, 155–56, 175–76.
107. Ibid., 16 January 1864, 150–51.
108. Ibid., 5 February 1864, 175–76.
109. Ibid., 16 January 1864, 151.
110. Ibid., 2 January 1864, 136–37; on being "too weary" to go to a lecture, see 21 December 1863, 115–16.
111. Ibid., 5 January 1864, 139.
112. Ibid., 9 and 11 January 1864, 142, 146 (Lord); 9 February 1864, 178 (Curtis).
113. Ibid., 17 February and 15 March 1864, 183–85, 205–6.
114. On the Soldiers' Rest, see Garrett Peck, *Walt Whitman in Washington, D.C.: The Civil War and America's Great Poet* (Charleston, S.C.: History Press, 2015), 41. On

Douglass's visit, see Julia Wilbur, Diary, 1 December 1864, Quaker and Special Collections, Haverford College, in *Diaries of Julia Wilbur, March 1860 to July 1866* (transcriptions by volunteers at Alexandria Archaeology), https://www.alexandriava.gov/uploadedFiles/historic/info/civilwar/JuliaWilburDiary1860to1866.pdf.

115. Wilbur, Diary, 1 December 1864. On Wilbur, see Lauren H. Roedner, "First Step Toward Freedom: Women in Contraband Camps in and Around the District of Columbia During the Civil War," *The Cupola: Scholarship at Gettysburg College* (2012), http://cupola.gettysburg.edu/student_scholarship/3/.

116. Wilbur, Diary, 1 December 1864.

117. Charles A. Mills and Andrew L. Mills, eds., *Alexandria, 1861–1865* (Charleston, S.C.: Arcadia, 2008), 26; "History of The Lyceum," City of Alexandria, Virginia, updated 17 December 2015, http://alexandriava.gov/historic/lyceum/?id=38678; Julia Susan Wheelock Freeman, Diary, 1 October 1862, in Julia S. Wheelock, *The Boys in White: The Experience of a Hospital Agent in and Around Washington* (New York: Lange and Hillman, 1870), 19, 21; Judith White Brockenbrough McGuire, 21 April 1862, in *Diary of a Southern Refugee During the War*, 3rd ed. (Richmond, Va.: J. W. Randolph and English, 1889), 167–68.

CHAPTER 2

1. William Northrop Morse, "Lectures on Electricity in Colonial Times," *New England Quarterly* 7, no. 2 (1934): 364–74; Ebenezer Kinnersley and William Johnson, *A Course of Experiments, in That Curious and Entertaining Branch of Natural Philosophy, Call'd* [sic] *Electricity Accompanied with Lectures on the Nature and Properties of the Electric Fire, by William Johnson* ... (New York: Printed by H. Gaine, at the Bible and Crown, in Hanover-Square, 1765).

2. See especially Larry Stewart, *The Rise of Public Science: Rhetoric, Technology, and Natural Philosophy in Newtonian Britain, 1660–1750* (New York: Cambridge University Press, 1993); and James Delbourgo, *A Most Amazing Scene of Wonders: Electricity and Enlightenment in Early America* (Cambridge, Mass.: Harvard University Press, 2006). See also William Clark, Jan Golinski, and Simon Schaffer, eds., *The Sciences in Enlightened Europe* (Chicago: University of Chicago Press, 1999); Jan Golinski, "A Noble Spectacle: Phosphorus and the Public Cultures of Science in the Early Royal Society," *Isis* 80 (1989): 11–39; Simon Schaffer, "Natural Philosophy and Public Spectacle in the Eighteenth Century," *History of Science* 21, no. 1 (1983): 1–43; and Ian Inkster, "The Public Lecture as an Instrument of Science Education for Adults: The Case of Great Britain, c. 1750–1850," *Paedagogica Historica* 20 (1980): 80–107.

3. Ronald J. Zboray and Mary Saracino Zboray, "Women Thinking: The International Popular Lecture and Its Audience in Antebellum New England," in *The Cosmopolitan Lyceum: Lecture Culture and the Globe in Nineteenth-Century America*, ed. Tom F. Wright (Amherst: University of Massachusetts Press, 2013), 42–66; Ronald J. Zboray and Mary Saracino Zboray, *Everyday Ideas: Socioliterary Experience Among Antebellum New Englanders* (Knoxville: University of Tennessee Press, 2006), esp. chaps. 7 and 10.

4. Linda K. Kerber, *Women of the Republic: Intellect and Ideology in Revolutionary America* (Chapel Hill: University of North Carolina Press, 1980); Lindal Buchanan, *Regendering Delivery: The Fifth Canon and Antebellum Women Orators* (Carbondale: Southern Illinois University Press, 2005); Mary Kelley, *Learning to Stand and Speak: Women, Education, and Public Life in America's Republic* (Chapel Hill: University of North Carolina Press, 2006); Carolyn Eastman, *A Nation of Speechifiers: Making an American Public After the Revolution* (Chicago: University of Chicago Press, 2009), esp. chap. 2.

5. Alfred F. Young, *Masquerade: The Life and Times of Deborah Sampson, Continental Soldier* (New York: Vintage, 2005). See also Sandra Gustafson, *Eloquence Is Power: Oratory and Performance in Early America* (Chapel Hill: University of North Carolina Press, 2000), 246–57; and Karlyn Kohrs Campbell, "Gender and Genre: Loci of Invention and Contradiction in the Earliest Speeches by U.S. Women," *Quarterly Journal of Speech* 81, no. 4 (1995): esp. 485–90.

6. Excluding advertisements for college "lectures" for matriculated students, of the approximately 250 commercial lecturers advertised in American newspapers from 1740 to 1820, at least 60 identified themselves as schoolteachers, active college professors, or vocational schoolmasters in music, business, and other fields. Because of the era's wide use of handbills and postings, newspaper advertisements alone are an unreliable measure of lecture activity, but empirical data show that school-affiliated lecturers were among the most prominent and active lecturers of the era.

7. Vyacheslav Khrapak, "Reflections on the American Lyceum: The Legacy of Josiah Holbrook and the Transcendental Sessions," *Journal of Philosophy and History of Education* 64, no. 1 (2014): 61–62; Anya Kamenetz, *DIY U: Edupunks, Edupreneurs, and the Coming Transformation of Higher Education* (Chelsea, Vt.: Chelsea Green, 2010).

8. Eva B. Armstrong and Claude K. Deischer, "Dr. Henry Moyes, Scotch Chemist: His Visit to America, 1785–1786," *Journal of Chemical Education* 24 (1947): 169–74; Henry Moyes, *Heads of a Course of Lectures on the Philosophy of Chemistry and Natural History* (Boston, 1785); Jennifer E. Monaghan, *A Common Heritage: Noah Webster's Blue-Backed Speller* (New York: Archon, 1983), 93.

9. All newspapers quoted in this chapter were accessed via the digital database *America's Historical Newspapers*.

10. William Jones, *Poems Consisting Chiefly of Translations from the Asiatick Languages . . .* (London: W. Bowyer and J. Nichols, 1777). Jones admits that most of his Arabic "translations" were imitations inspired by his broad reading (vii–viii).

11. "Portugal Matrimônios, 1670–1910," Benjamin Barons and Margarett [sic] Hardy, 27 January 1748; "Portugal, Select Baptisms, 1570–1910," Elizabeth Harriot Barons, 1749; "British Postal Service Appointment Books, 1737–1969," Benjamin Barons; "England and Wales, Prerogative Court of Canterbury Wills, 1384–1858," Benjamin Barons, probate date, 14 April 1783, all accessed at Ancestry.com. Benjamin's work as customs collector is described in Maurice Henry Smith, *The Writs of Assistance Case* (Berkeley: University of California Press, 1978), esp. 184–201. See also "Westminster Marriages," John O'Connor and Elizabeth Harriet [sic] Barons, 6 June 1776, at FindMyPast.com.

12. *Pennsylvania Evening Herald*, 6 October 1787; Jean Pierre Baptist Nougaret, *Anecdotes of the Reign of Lewis the XVIth, Present King of France*, trans. John O'Connor with the assistance of John Mary (New York: F. Childs, 1787).

13. *Pennsylvania Mercury*, 7 June, 13 July 1787; *Philadelphia Independent Gazetteer*, 16 June 1787.

14. Eliza Harriot O'Connor to Sarah Franklin Bache, 17 June 1787, American Philosophical Society.

15. *Pennsylvania Evening Herald*, 6 October 1787; *Philadelphia Independent Gazetteer*, 17 May 1788.

16. *Maryland Gazette*, 9 December 1787; *Maryland Journal and Baltimore Advertiser*, 21 December 1787.

17. Donald Dean Jackson and Dorothy Twohig, eds., *The Diaries of George Washington*, vol. 5 (Charlottesville: University Press of Virginia, 1976–79), 158–59; "To George Washington from George Lux, 9 January 1788," "To George Washington from Eliza Harriot O'Connor, 17 June 1788," and "From George Washington to Eliza Harriot O'Connor, 20 June 1788," all in *The Papers of George Washington*, Confederation Series, vol. 6, *1 January*

1788–23 September 1788, ed. W. W. Abbot (Charlottesville: University of Virginia Press, 1997), 24–25, 334–35, 343–44; "To George Washington from Eliza Harriot O'Connor, 7 October 1788," in *The Papers of George Washington*, Presidential Series, vol. 1, *24 September 1788–31 March 1789*, ed. Dorothy Twohig (Charlottesville: University of Virginia Press, 1987), 40–41.

18. *Norfolk and Portsmouth Journal*, 16 July 1788; *Philadelphia Federal Gazette*, 28 February 1790.

19. *Charleston City Gazette*, 18, 24 November 1790; *Supplement to Daily Advertiser*, 21 April 1791; *City Gazette*, 25 November 1791.

20. *State Gazette of South Carolina*, 16 June 1791; *Columbian Herald or Independent Courier of North-America*, 21 June 1791; *Supplement to City Gazette*, 10 October 1791. Nixon's brush with the O'Connors may have been instructive: he later began to use public lectures at his lyceum, the Attic Society for the Advancement of Science, in conjunction with commercial advertising for his academy. See *Charleston City Gazette*, 10 April 1795.

21. *Charleston City Gazette*, 1, 13, 30 March, 1 May 1792; *South Carolina Gazette*, 13 August 1793; *South Carolina State Gazette*, 29 November 1799; "Eliza Harriot O'Connor," 18 June 1811, Richland County Probate Court, South Carolina, in *South Carolina Wills and Probate Records, 1670–1980*, Ancestry.com.

22. Adderley: *New York Commercial Advertiser*, 13 November 1800; Lathrop: *Boston Daily Advertiser*, 27 October 1813; Ramsay: *New York Commercial Advertiser*, 30 July 1807; Senter: *Newport Mercury*, 2 April 1814; Darby: *New York Columbian*, 25 August 1819; *Poulson's*, 2 March 1822; Slack: *New Bedford Mercury*, 12 May, 28 June 1822.

23. See *Albany Gazette*, 15 September 1818; Joseph Lancaster, *Epitome of Some of the Chief Events and Transactions of Joseph Lancaster* (New Haven, Conn.: Baldwin and Peck, 1833); Joseph McCadden, "Joseph Lancaster and the Philadelphia Schools," *Pennsylvania History* 3, no. 4 (1936): 225–39; Joseph McCadden, "Joseph Lancaster and Philadelphia," *Pennsylvania History* 4, no. 1 (1937): 6–20; and Patricia Crain, "Children of Media, Children as Media: Optical Telegraphs, Indian Pupils, and Joseph Lancaster's System for Cultural Replication," in *New Media, 1740–1915*, ed. Lisa Gitelman and Geoffrey B. Pingree (Cambridge, Mass.: MIT Press, 2003), 61–89.

24. A satire of lecture culture and women's patronage, "Hints to Lecturers," reprinted from London, appears in the *Northern Whig*, 28 July 1818. See Jane Marcet, *Conversations on Chemistry, in Which the Elements of That Science Are Familiarly Explained and Illustrated by Experiments* (London: Longman, Hurst, Rees, and Orme, 1806); Saba Bahar, "Jane Marcet and the Limits to Public Science," *British Journal for the History of Science* 34, no. 1 (2001): 29–49; and John H. Griscom, comp., *Memoir of John Griscom, Late Professor of Chemistry and Natural Philosophy* . . . (New York: Robert Carter and Bros., 1859), 50–56, 98.

25. Fitz-Greene Halleck, *Fanny: With Other Poems* (New York: Harper and Bros., 1839), 49. "Fanny" first appeared in 1819 and was revised several times over the following years.

26. *Boston Gazetteer*, 2 November 1803. See also Eastman, *Nation of Speechifiers*, chap. 2.

27. *Baltimore Patriot*, 23 November 1815; Zboray and Zboray, "Women Thinking," 49.

28. Zboray and Zboray, "Women Thinking," 45; Zboray and Zboray, *Everyday Ideas*, chap. 10; Elizabeth Palmer Peabody to Maria Chase, 8 March 1826, Peabody Family Papers, Sophia Smith Collection, Smith College.

29. Dorothy W. Porter, *Early Negro Writing, 1760–1837* (1971; repr., Baltimore: Black Classic Press, 1995), 123–40; Elizabeth McHenry, *Forgotten Readers: Recovering the Lost History of African American Literary Societies* (Durham: Duke University Press, 2002).

30. Marilyn Richardson, ed., *Maria W. Stewart, America's First Black Woman Political Writer, Essays and Speeches* (Bloomington: Indiana University Press, 1987); Carla L. Peterson, *Doers of the Word: African-American Women Speakers and Writers in the North, 1830–1880* (New York: Oxford University Press, 1995); Shirley Wilson Logan, *"We Are Coming": The Persuasive Discourse of Nineteenth-Century Black Women* (Carbondale: Southern Illinois University Press, 1999), esp. chap. 2.

31. *Providence Patriot*, 7 April 1821.

32. Granville Ganter, "Mistress of Her Affairs: Anne Laura Clarke, Traveling Lecturer of the 1820s," *New England Quarterly* 87, no. 4 (2014): 709–46. Clarke's lectures on North and South American history are held at the Historic Northampton museum in Massachusetts.

33. Anne Laura Clarke (hereafter ALC) to Amos Eaton, from Rutland, Vermont, 1833, Simon Grantz Collection, Philadelphia Library Company. In this remarkable letter, Clarke reviews her lecture tours of the previous seven years and thanks Eaton for his warm support of her when they first met in 1826. On Eaton as a lecturer addressing women, see Emanuel D. Rudolph, "History of the Botanical Teaching Laboratory in the United States," *American Journal of Botany* 83, no. 5 (1996): 661–67.

34. Daniel Rosenberg and Anthony Grafton, *Cartographies of Time* (New York: Princeton Architectural Press, 2010). See also Susan Schulten, *Mapping the Nation: History and Cartography in Nineteenth-Century America* (Chicago: University of Chicago Press, 2012).

35. ALC to Elizabeth Clarke, 26 October 1826, folder 5, ALC Collection, Historic Northampton; ALC to Elizabeth Clarke, early November 1826, Shaw-Hudson House. See reviews of ALC lectures in *Troy Sentinel*, 3 October 1826; *Albany Argus*, 8 November and 27 December 1826, 8 January 1827. Thanksgiving was a state holiday.

36. Donald M. Scott, "The Profession That Vanished: Public Lecturing in Mid-Nineteenth-Century America," in *Professions and Professional Ideologies in America*, ed. Gerald L. Geison (Chapel Hill: University of North Carolina Press, 1983), 15.

37. For critiques of the declensionist paradigm, see Gregory Clark and S. Michael Halloran, eds., *Oratorical Culture in Nineteenth-Century America: Transformations in the Theory and Practice of Rhetoric* (Carbondale: Southern Illinois University Press, 1993); Thomas Augst, "Humanist Enterprise in the Marketplace of Culture," in Wright, *Cosmopolitan Lyceum*, 223–40; and Angela G. Ray, "How Cosmopolitan Was the Lyceum, Anyway?" in Wright, *Cosmopolitan Lyceum*, esp. 23–24. On the multidimensional aspects of the lyceum, see also Angela G. Ray, *The Lyceum and Public Culture in the Nineteenth-Century United States* (East Lansing: Michigan State University Press, 2005), chaps. 1–2.

38. Nancy Hoffman, introduction to *Woman's "True" Profession: Voices from the History of Teaching*, ed. Nancy Hoffman (Old Westbury, N.Y.: Feminist Press, 1981), xv. See also Joel Perlmann and Robert A. Margo, *Women's Work? American School Teachers, 1650–1920* (Chicago: University of Chicago Press, 2001); and Geraldine J. Clifford, *Those Good Gertrudes: A Social History of Women Teachers in America* (Baltimore: Johns Hopkins University Press, 2014).

CHAPTER 3

1. James Joyce, *Ulysses* (Oxford: Oxford University Press, 2008), 316.

2. David Brundage, *Irish Nationalists in America: The Politics of Exile, 1798–1998* (Oxford: Oxford University Press, 2016).

3. Tom F. Wright, *Lecturing the Atlantic: Speech, Print, and an Anglo-American Commons, 1830–1870* (Oxford: Oxford University Press, 2017).

4. Thomas Wentworth Higginson, "The American Lecture-System," *Macmillan's Magazine* 18 (May 1868): 49.

5. Andrew Chamberlin Rieser, "Lyceums, Chautauquas, and Institutes for Useful Knowledge," in *Encyclopedia of American Cultural and Intellectual History*, vol. 3, ed. Mary Kupiec Cayton and Peter W. Williams (New York: Charles Scribner's Sons, 2001), 354.

6. See Elizabeth M. Dillon, *New World Drama: The Performative Commons in the Atlantic World, 1649–1849* (Durham: Duke University Press, 2014), v–vii; and Lewis Hyde, *Commons as Air: Revolution, Art, and Ownership* (New York: Farrar, Straus and Giroux, 2010), xx.

7. The most important recent work on nationalism is Brundage's *Irish Nationalists in America*, which develops and challenges some of the contentions in Kerby A. Miller, *Emigrants and Exiles: Ireland and the Irish Exodus to North America* (Oxford: Oxford University Press, 1989). See also Diarmid A. Finnegan, "Race, Space and Politics in Mid-Victorian Ireland: The Ethnologies of Abraham Hume and John McElheran," *Historical Geography* 42 (2014): 152–70.

8. Peter D. O'Neill and David Lloyd, *The Black and Green Atlantic: Cross-Currents of the African and Irish Diasporas* (Basingstoke: Palgrave Macmillan, 2009); Angela F. Murphy, *American Slavery, Irish Freedom: Abolition, Immigrant Citizenship, and the Transatlantic Movement for Irish Repeal* (Baton Rouge: Louisiana State University Press, 2010).

9. Henry Ward Beecher in the *Independent*, quoted in "Meagher Demonstration," *New York Daily Tribune*, 9 June 1852.

10. "Robert [sic] Francis Meagher," *Farmer's Cabinet*, 17 June 1852; Thomas Francis Meagher, *Speeches on the Legislative Independence of Ireland* (New York: J. S. Redfield, 1853), 89.

11. *New York Tribune*, quoted in "From Our New York Correspondent," *Freeman's Journal*, 14 December 1852; "Thomas Francis Meagher," *Freeman's Journal*, 14 December 1852.

12. "Lecture by Thomas F. Meagher: Australia," *New York Times*, 26 November 1852.

13. Michael Cavanagh, *Memoirs of General Thomas Francis Meagher* (Worcester, Mass.: Messenger Press, 1892), 424.

14. Bryan McGovern, *John Mitchel: Irish Nationalist, Southern Secessionist* (Knoxville: University of Tennessee Press, 2009), 150. See also James Quinn, *John Mitchel* (Dublin: Historical Association of Ireland by University College Dublin Press, 2008), 64.

15. Franklin Pierce, Inaugural Address, 4 March 1853, in *A Compilation of the Messages and Papers of the Presidents*, comp. James D. Richardson, vol. 6 (New York: Bureau of National Literature, 1897), 2731.

16. Yonatan Eyal, *The Young America Movement and the Transformation of the Democratic Party, 1828–1861* (Cambridge: Cambridge University Press, 2007), 107.

17. John Mitchel, *Jail Journal; or, Five Years in British Prisons* (New York: The Citizen, 1854), 289.

18. "Arrival of John Mitchel," *New York Herald*, 30 November 1853. See also Paul R. Wylie, *The Irish General: Thomas Francis Meagher* (Norman: University of Oklahoma Press, 2007); and Timothy Egan, *The Immortal Irishman: The Irish Revolutionary Who Became an American Hero* (New York: Houghton Mifflin Harcourt, 2016), 145.

19. "Mr. Meagher in Philadelphia: Enthusiastic Reception," *New York Herald*, 22 February 1853; "From Our New York Correspondent."

20. "Ripening of the Revolution in Ireland: Lecture by John Mitchel," *New York Times*, 17 January 1856.

21. "Movements of Thomas Francis Meagher," *New York Herald*, 19 January 1853.

22. "Meagher Demonstration."

23. "Arrival of Thomas Francis Meagher," *New York Herald*, 29 May 1852.

24. "Young Ireland and 1848, by Thomas Francis Meagher," *New York Daily Tribune*, 26 May 1853.
25. *St. Louis Leader*, quoted in "Political Sayings and Doings," *New York Herald*, 24 November 1856.
26. "From Our Brooklyn Correspondent," *Frederick Douglass' Paper*, 4 January 1855.
27. Ibid.
28. "Mr. Meagher in Philadelphia."
29. "Ripening of the Revolution in Ireland."
30. "From Our Brooklyn Correspondent."
31. Ibid.
32. "John Mitchel's Lecture," *Cincinnati Daily Press*, 19 June 1860.
33. See Cavanagh, *Memoirs of General Thomas Francis Meagher*, 337.
34. "Lecture of John Mitchel in Boston," *New York Herald*, 29 December 1853; "Daniel O'Connell: A Lecture by Thomas Francis Meagher," *New York Times*, 15 December 1854.
35. Miller, *Emigrants and Exiles*, 311.
36. John Mitchel, *Memoir of Thomas Devin Reilly: A Lecture Delivered by John Mitchel, in the Tabernacle, New-York, on Dec. 29th, 1856* (New York: P. M. Haverty, 1857), 3.
37. "John Mitchel in Boston," *New York Herald*, 1 January 1854.
38. "Ripening of the Revolution in Ireland."
39. "Lectures on Irish Orators," San Francisco Musical Hall, 24 January 1854, quoted in Gary R. Forney, *Thomas Francis Meagher: Irish Rebel, American Yankee, Montana Pioneer* ([Ennis, Mont.?]: G. R. Forney, 2003), 71.
40. "Young Ireland and 1848."
41. "Mr. T. F. Meagher's Lecture on Australia," *Freeman's Journal*, 17 December 1852.
42. "Lecture of Mr. Thomas Francis Meagher on Australia," *New York Herald*, 26 November 1852.
43. "Ripening of the Revolution in Ireland."
44. "John Mitchel on European Politics," *St. Louis Republican*, 29 November 1856.
45. Ibid.; "Mr. Mitchel's Lecture at the Music Hall," *Boston Herald*, 29 December 1853.
46. "From Our Dublin Correspondent," *National Anti-Slavery Standard*, 11 December 1851.
47. "Popular Lectures: The French Exiles at the Tabernacle," *New York Herald*, 22 February 1853.
48. "John Mitchel: His Speech and His Position," *New York Herald*, 24 December 1853.
49. Ibid.; "Lectures: Meagher," *Sacramento Daily Union*, 1 February 1854.
50. Ralph Waldo Emerson, "The Anglo-American" (1853), in *The Selected Lectures of Ralph Waldo Emerson*, ed. Ronald A. Bosco and Joel Myerson (Athens: University of Georgia Press, 2005), 191.
51. *Boston Pilot*, quoted in "Mr. Meagher's Lecture: Opposition of the Catholic Press," *Brooklyn Eagle*, 18 January 1853. See also Richard J. Purcell and John F. Poole, "Political Nativism in Brooklyn," *Journal of American Irish Historical Society* 32 (1941): 10–56.
52. "Mr. Meagher's Lecture," *Brooklyn Daily Eagle*, 26 May 1853.
53. "Lectures: Meagher."
54. "John Mitchel."
55. These pieces were collected in Henry Giles, *Lectures and Essays on Irish and Other Subjects* (New York: D. and J. Sadier, 1869). For accounts of his lecturing, see David Mead, *Yankee Eloquence in the Middle West: The Ohio Lyceum, 1850–1870* (East Lansing: Michigan State College Press, 1951), 62–69.
56. Henry Giles, "The Spirit of Irish History," in *Lectures and Essays*, 9.
57. Henry Giles, "Irish-Born Citizens," in *Lectures and Essays*, 156.

58. "Mr. Henry Giles's Lecture," *New York Times*, 26 March 1863.

59. "Lecture: The Celtic and Anglo-Saxon Races," *New York Daily Tribune*, 24 March 1852.

60. See Robert Knox, *The Races of Man: A Fragment* (Philadelphia: Lea and Blanchard, 1850); and Robert Knox, "New Theory of Race: Celt v. Saxon," *The Lancet* 70, no. 1774 (1857): 218–20.

61. Peter Adams, *The Bowery Boys: Street Corner Radicals and the Politics of Rebellion* (Westport, Conn.: Praeger, 2005), 30; Charles Levin, *A Lecture on Irish Repeal: In Elucidation of the Fallacy of Its Principles, and in Proof of Its Pernicious Tendency, in Its Moral, Religious, and Political Aspects* (Philadelphia, 1844); "People's Lectures: Theodore Parker on Anglo-Saxons," *New York Herald*, 25 February 1853; Emerson, "Anglo-American," 191.

62. See Cian T. McMahon, *The Global Dimensions of Irish Identity: Race, Nation, and the Popular Press* (Chapel Hill: University of North Carolina Press, 2015), 22–23.

63. Thomas D'Arcy McGee, "National Creed," in the first issue of *Nation*, 1848.

64. "Characteristics of the Irish Celt: Moral, Social and Religious," *Brooklyn Eagle*, 30 January 1854.

65. See Finnegan, "Race, Space and Politics," 164–65.

66. "Lectures," *New York Herald*, 3 January 1855.

67. "The Celt and the Saxon," *New York Daily Tribune*, 29 March 1855.

68. "English Policy in America," *New York Daily Tribune*, 5 January 1855.

69. "Celt and the Saxon."

70. Quoted in McMahon, *Global Dimensions of Irish Identity*, 96.

71. Noel Ignatiev, *How the Irish Became White* (New York: Routledge, 1995).

72. "Mr. Mitchel's Reply," *Boston Herald*, 29 December 1853.

73. "John Mitchel in Boston," *New York Herald*, 1 January 1854.

74. "Mr. Mitchel's Lecture at the Music Hall."

75. "New Orleans Delivery of 'Ireland in '48,'" quoted in Cavanagh, *Memoirs of General Thomas Francis Meagher*, 339.

76. Brundage, *Irish Nationalists in America*, 81.

77. "An Old Subscriber in Indiana, in Renewing His Subscription," *Daily National Era*, 30 January 1854.

78. Henry Ward Beecher in the *Independent*, quoted in "John Mitchel and Slavery," *National Anti-Slavery Standard*, 28 January 1854.

79. See Fionnghuala Sweeney, *Frederick Douglass and the Atlantic World* (Liverpool: Liverpool University Press, 2007).

CHAPTER 4

1. Tom F. Wright, introduction to *The Cosmopolitan Lyceum: Lecture Culture and the Globe in Nineteenth-Century America*, ed. Tom F. Wright (Amherst: University of Massachusetts Press, 2013), 1–19.

2. Heather A. Haveman, "Antebellum Literary Culture and the Evolution of American Magazines," *Poetics* 32 (2004): 5–28.

3. Angela G. Ray, *The Lyceum and Public Culture in the Nineteenth-Century United States* (East Lansing: Michigan State University Press, 2005); Andrew C. Rieser, *The Chautauqua Moment: Protestants, Progressives, and the Culture of Modern Liberalism* (New York: Columbia University Press, 2003).

4. Paul Stob, "William James's 'True American Theory': *The Varieties of Religious Experience* and Transatlantic Intellectual Culture," in Wright, *Cosmopolitan Lyceum*, 130–48; Robert Arbour, "Mr. Emerson's Playful Lyceum: Polyvocal Promotion on the Lecture

Circuit," in Wright, *Cosmopolitan Lyceum*, 93–112; Robert A. Gross, "Talk of the Town," *American Scholar* 84 (2015): 31–43.

5. See, for example, Louis Agassiz, "The Diversity of Origin of the Human Species," *Christian Examiner* 49 (1850): 141–42.

6. David N. Livingstone, *Nathaniel Southgate Shaler and the Culture of American Science* (Tuscaloosa: University of Alabama Press, 1987), 138.

7. Nathaniel S. Shaler, "The Nature of the Negro," *Arena* 3 (1890): 24–25.

8. For a brief description of Agassiz's lyceum activity, see John Evelev, *Tolerable Entertainment: Herman Melville and Professionalism in Antebellum New York* (Amherst: University of Massachusetts Press, 2006), 137. See also A. Augustus Wright, ed., *Who's Who in the Lyceum* (Philadelphia: Pearson Brothers, 1906), 23.

9. For one example of this debate, see Kirt H. Wilson, *The Reconstruction Desegregation Debate: The Politics of Equality and the Rhetoric of Place, 1870–1875* (East Lansing: Michigan State University Press, 2002).

10. Nathaniel Shaler, "The Negro Problem," *Atlantic Monthly*, November 1884, 700.

11. Shaler, "Nature of the Negro," 28.

12. Nathaniel Shaler, *The Neighbor: The Natural History of Human Contacts* (Boston: Houghton, Mifflin and Co., 1904), 134.

13. Ray, *Lyceum and Public Culture*, 41; Sara E. Lampert, "Bringing Music to the Lyceumites: The Bureaus and the Transformation of Lyceum Entertainment," in Wright, *Cosmopolitan Lyceum*, 67–89.

14. See Kirt H. Wilson, "The Racial Politics of Imitation in the Nineteenth Century," *Quarterly Journal of Speech* 89 (2003): 89–108.

15. Among some black writers and speakers, imitation was viewed as a general human quality. Alexander Crummell, for example, argued that imitation was a trait common to people of all races who were striving toward the highest stages of civilization. See Alexander Crummell, "The Destined Superiority of the Negro," in *Destiny and Race: Selected Writings, 1840–1898*, ed. Wilson Jeremiah Moses (Amherst: University of Massachusetts Press, 1992), 194–205.

16. W. T. Lhamon Jr., *Jump Jim Crow: Lost Plays, Lyrics, and Street Prose of the First Atlantic Popular Culture* (Cambridge, Mass.: Harvard University Press, 2003), 2.

17. Ibid., 4.

18. David R. Roediger, *The Wages of Whiteness: Race and the Making of the American Working Class* (New York: Verso, 2007), 115–16.

19. Ray, *Lyceum and Public Culture*, 17.

20. Ibid., 41.

21. Dale Cockrell, *Demons of Disorder: Early Blackface Minstrels and Their World* (Cambridge: Cambridge University Press, 1997), chap. 4.

22. Saidiya V. Hartman, *Scenes of Subjection: Terror, Slavery, and Self-Making in Nineteenth-Century America* (New York: Oxford University Press, 1997), 29–32.

23. See Noel Ignatiev, *How the Irish Became White* (New York: Routledge, 1995).

24. Augusta Browne, "Negro Minstrelsy," *Christian Advocate and Journal* 29, no. 4 (January 1854): 13.

25. Plato, *Republic*, trans. Paul Shorey, in *The Collected Dialogues of Plato*, ed. Edith Hamilton and Huntington Cairns (New York: Pantheon Books, 1961), 3.398a–b.

26. "Southern Trio and Mart King," 1900/1909, Redpath Chautauqua Collection, Special Collections Department, University of Iowa Libraries, reproduced in digital facsimile in *Traveling Culture: Circuit Chautauqua in the Twentieth Century*, http://digital.lib.uiowa.edu/cdm/compoundobject/collection/tc/id/63132/rec/2. Occasionally the sisters added a third member, either Ethel Mae Raymond or a Miss Estes; see "The Southern Trio," *Deseret Evening News*, 27 December 1902, 10.

27. "Once Famous Singer Is Now Jobless Cook," *Washington Times*, 9 July 1922, 6.
28. "Southern Trio and Mart King."
29. "Once Famous Singer Is Now Jobless Cook."
30. "At the White House," *New York Tribune*, 15 April 1902, 6.
31. "Once Famous Singer Is Now Jobless Cook."
32. "The Woman's Club Has Men's Night," *Music News* 6 (May 1914): 28.
33. "Once Famous Singer Is Now Jobless Cook."
34. *Folk-Songs of [the] American Negro*, collected and harmonized by Harriet Turner (Boston: Boston Music Co., 1925).
35. *Chattanooga News*, quoted in "Mrs. William Calvin Chilton: Monodramist," 1904/1932, Redpath Chautauqua Collection, reproduced in *Traveling Culture*, http://digital.lib.uiowa.edu/cdm/compoundobject/collection/tc/id/46678/rec/3. See also "Monodramist Is Real Artist in Southern Negro Impersonations," *Fairmont West Virginian*, 1 July 1916, 5.
36. "Mrs. William Calvin Chilton: Monodramist," 1908, Redpath Chautauqua Collection, reproduced in *Traveling Culture*, http://digital.lib.uiowa.edu/cdm/compoundobject/collection/tc/id/41380/rec/1.
37. Quoted in "Mrs. William Calvin Chilton," 1904/1932.
38. S. W. Paris, "Committeeman Reviews Alkahest," *Lyceum Magazine*, 26 August 1916, 24.
39. "The Day's Gossip," *New York Tribune*, 23 July 1897, 5.
40. "Chautauqua Features," *New York Observer and Chronicle*, 12 September 1895, 339.
41. Jacques Bert Martin Vest, "Making Authenticity: Polk Miller and the Evolution of American Popular Culture" (master's thesis, Virginia Commonwealth University, 2010), 4.
42. Quoted in ibid., 9.
43. Ibid., 11, 16.
44. Quoted in ibid., 74.
45. Quoted in ibid., 79.
46. These songs have since been rereleased. See Polk Miller, *Polk Miller and His Old South Quartette*, Tompkins Square Records, 2008, compact disc.
47. Richard Mook, "Sound Review: 'Polk Miller and His Old South Quartette,'" *Journal of American Folklore* 126 (2013): 335.
48. Quoted in Barbara L. Webb, "'The Real Character of the Negro on the Stage': African American Theatre as Risk and Possibility, 1890–1908" (PhD diss., Northwestern University, 2003), 112.
49. Quoted in Henry T. Sampson, *The Ghost Walks: A Chronological History of Blacks in Show Business, 1865–1910* (Metuchen, N.J.: Scarecrow, 1988), 6.
50. Quoted in Eileen Southern, introduction to *Out of Bondage*, in *African American Theater*, vol. 9, ed. Eileen Southern (New York: Garland, 1994), xv.
51. See Plato, *Republic*, 3.398a–b; Elizabeth Belfiore, "A Theory of Imitation in Plato's *Republic*," *Transactions of the American Philological Association* 114 (1984): 126–27.
52. Jocelyn Buckner, "'Spectacular Opacities': The Hyers Sisters' Performances of Respectability and Resistance," *African American Review* 45, no. 3 (2012): 309–23.
53. Ibid., 311.
54. "Amusements," *Cleveland Morning Daily Herald*, 19 December 1871, 4.
55. *Mechanics' Hall—Worcester Benefit Post 10, G.A.R., . . . March 7, 1877: Out of Bondage . . .* (Worcester, Mass., 1877), American Antiquarian Society.
56. Eileen Southern states that the Hyers Sisters Combination remained in existence until about 1893, while Errol Hill identifies 1891 as the year of the group's final

performance. See Southern, introduction to *Out of Bondage*, xiv; Errol Hill, "The Hyers Sisters: Pioneers in Black Musical Comedy," in *The American Stage: Social and Economic Issues from the Colonial Period to the Present*, ed. Ron Engle and Tice L. Miller (Cambridge: Cambridge University Press, 1993), 115–30.

57. Wilson, *Reconstruction Desegregation Debate*.

58. John Ernest, introduction to *The Escape; or, A Leap for Freedom: A Drama in Five Acts*, by William Wells Brown (Knoxville: University of Tennessee Press, 2001), x.

59. H. C. Wright, "William Wells Brown—His Dramas—Their Power for Good," *Liberator*, 8 October 1858, 163.

60. John Ernest, "The Reconstruction of Whiteness: William Wells Brown's *The Escape; or, A Leap for Freedom*," *PMLA* 113 (1998): 1109.

61. William Wells Brown, *The Escape; or, A Leap for Freedom* (Boston: R. F. Wallcut, 1858), 8.

62. Ernest, introduction to *The Escape*, xxxi.

63. Brown, *Escape*, 25.

64. Ibid., 44.

65. Ibid., 24.

66. Daphne Brooks, *Bodies in Dissent: Spectacular Performances of Race and Freedom, 1850–1910* (Durham: Duke University Press, 2006), 2.

67. Wilson, "Racial Politics of Imitation," 103.

68. Crummell, "Destined Superiority of the Negro," 198, 201.

CHAPTER 5

1. Eric Burin notes that a small percentage of settler-colonists were African by birth, but even these individuals were traveling to Liberia after having spent time in servitude in the United States. See Burin, *Slavery and the Peculiar Solution: A History of the American Colonization Society* (Gainesville: University Press of Florida, 2005), table 2.

2. Tom W. Shick, *Behold the Promised Land: A History of Afro-American Settler Society in Nineteenth-Century Liberia* (Baltimore: Johns Hopkins University Press, 1980), 19–41.

3. Peter Gibian, "The Lyceum as Contact Zone: Bayard Taylor's Lectures on Foreign Travel," in *The Cosmopolitan Lyceum: Lecture Culture and the Globe in Nineteenth-Century America*, ed. Tom F. Wright (Amherst: University of Massachusetts Press, 2013), 168–202.

4. See Angela G. Ray, "What Hath She Wrought? Woman's Rights and the Nineteenth-Century Lyceum," *Rhetoric and Public Affairs* 9, no. 2 (2006): 183–213; Angela G. Ray, "Frederick Douglass on the Lyceum Circuit: Social Assimilation, Social Transformation?" *Rhetoric and Public Affairs* 5, no. 4 (2002): 625–47; Gibian, "Lyceum as Contact Zone"; and Evan Roberts, "The Peripatetic Career of Wherahiko Rawei: Māori Culture on the Global Chautauqua Circuit, 1893–1927," in Wright, *Cosmopolitan Lyceum*, 203–20.

5. Tom F. Wright, *Lecturing the Atlantic: Speech, Print, and an Anglo-American Commons, 1830–1870* (Oxford: Oxford University Press, 2017), 3, 5.

6. Thomas Jefferson, *Notes on the State of Virginia* (Philadelphia: Prichard and Hall, 1788), query 14; Thomas Jefferson to Edward Coles, 25 August 1814, Thomas Jefferson Papers, Library of Congress.

7. See P. J. Staudenraus, *The African Colonization Movement, 1816–1865* (New York: Columbia University Press, 1961), 26–28; and Douglas R. Egerton, "'Its Origin Is Not a Little Curious': A New Look at the American Colonization Society," *Journal of the Early Republic* 5, no. 4 (1985): 463–80.

8. Henry Clay used these phrases in his opening speech at the germinal meeting of the ACS on 21 December 1816. The motivations of the group were discussed by Clay as well as the featured speaker of the evening, Elias B. Caldwell. See *National Intelligencer*, 24 December 1816, 2.

9. Burin, *Slavery and the Peculiar Solution*, table 2. Although the ACS was the dominant colonization group, serving as the umbrella organization for state societies and auxiliaries, the Maryland State Colonization Society (MSCS) established a separate colony in Liberia in 1834. Located south of Monrovia in Cape Palmas, the Maryland-in-Liberia colony also contributed to the influx of African Americans to West Africa (approximately 1,025 settler-colonists between 1834 and 1851). See Papers of the Maryland State Colonization Society, 1817–1902, Manumission Lists, 1832–1834, Film No. M 13248-1, Records of Manumissions Reported to the Board of State Colonization Managers, http://mdhistory.net/msa_sc5977/scm013248/html/msa_sc5977_scm13248-0124.html.
For a brief time, the Mississippi Colonization Society established a separate colony because its white supporters believed that the ACS was not giving Mississippi settler-colonists the same level of attention as other states' emigrants. Some also posit that the Mississippi colonization supporters perceived the ACS as an abolitionist group. From 1831 to 1840 the colony, which first resided on the St. Paul River near Monrovia before moving to the mouth of the Sinoe River, functioned as a third American colony in Liberia. In 1840 it was absorbed into the ACS-led colony in Monrovia. See Alan Huffman, *Mississippi in Africa: The Saga of the Slaves of Prospect Hill and Their Legacy in Liberia Today* (Jackson: University Press of Mississippi, 2010), 153–55.

10. For example, see Bell I. Wiley, ed., *Slaves No More: Letters from Liberia, 1833–1869* (Lexington: University Press of Kentucky, 1980), 36, 57, 105, 138, 163, 193.

11. The Maryland-in-Africa colony was governed by the MSCS until 1854, when it became a part of the independent Republic of Liberia.

12. Angela G. Ray, "How Cosmopolitan Was the Lyceum, Anyway?" in Wright, *Cosmopolitan Lyceum*, 26–28.

13. Angela G. Ray, *The Lyceum and Public Culture in the Nineteenth-Century United States* (East Lansing: Michigan State University Press, 2005), 20, 41.

14. [Josiah Holbrook], "Associations of Adults for Mutual Education," *American Journal of Education* 1, no. 10 (October 1826): 594.

15. Josiah Holbrook, "American Lyceum," *American Journal of Education* 4, no. 1 (January/February 1829): 50.

16. Ray, *Lyceum and Public Culture*, 27.

17. Ray, "What Hath She Wrought?" 197.

18. Waldo W. Braden, "The Beginnings of the Lyceum, 1826–1840," *Southern Speech Journal* 20, no. 2 (1954): 133.

19. Ray, *Lyceum and Public Culture*, 19.

20. "Republicanism of Lyceums," *Family Lyceum* 1, no. 22 (12 January 1833): 86.

21. Ray, *Lyceum and Public Culture*, 13–47.

22. Ibid., 113.

23. Dorothy B. Porter, "The Organized Educational Activities of Negro Literary Societies, 1828–1846," *Journal of Negro Education* 5, no. 4 (1936): 557–58.

24. See Robert L. Harris Jr., "Charleston's Free Afro-American Elite: The Brown Fellowship Society and the Humane Brotherhood," *South Carolina Historical Magazine* 82, no. 4 (1981): 289–310; Michael P. Johnson and James L. Roark, "'A Middle Ground': Free Mulattoes and the Friendly Moralist Society in Antebellum Charleston," *Southern Studies* 21 (1982): 246–65; and Angela G. Ray, *"A Green Oasis in the History of My Life": Race and the Culture of Debating in Antebellum Charleston, South Carolina* (Salt Lake City: Department of Communication, University of Utah, 2014).

25. Donald M. Scott, "Print and the Public Lecture System, 1840–60," in *Printing and Society in Early America*, ed. William L. Joyce, David D. Hall, Richard D. Brown, and John B. Hench (Worcester, Mass.: American Antiquarian Society, 1983), 284–85. See also Ray, *Lyceum and Public Culture*, 102.

26. Carl Patrick Burrowes, *Power and Press Freedom in Liberia, 1830–1970: The Impact of Globalization and Civil Society on Media-Government Relations* (Trenton, N.J.: Africa World Press, 2004), 66. The MSCS Cape Palmas colony had the Cape Palmas Lyceum, the Hall Palmas Reading Club, the Cape Palmas Reading Room and Library Association, the Female Benevolent Society, and the Russwurm Literary Association. See Winston James, *The Struggles of John Brown Russwurm: The Life and Writings of a Pan-Africanist Pioneer, 1799–1851* (New York: New York University Press, 2010), 95; and Charles A. Earp, "The Role of Education in the Maryland Colonization Movement," *Journal of Negro History* 26, no. 3 (1941): 386.

27. Richard L. Hall, *On Afric's Shore: A History of Maryland in Liberia, 1834–1857* (Baltimore: Maryland Historical Society, 2003), 348.

28. Quoted in *Liberia Herald*, 31 May 1845, 1.

29. See, for example, *Charter, Constitution and By-Laws of the Troy Lyceum of Natural History* (Troy, N.Y.: John F. Prescott, 1850), 3; and Daniel Appleton White, *An Address Delivered at Ipswich, Before the Essex County Lyceum, at Their First Annual Meeting* (Salem, Mass.: Foote and Brown, 1830), 52.

30. Hall, *On Afric's Shore*, 348.

31. Shirley Wilson Logan, *Liberating Language: Sites of Rhetorical Education in Nineteenth-Century Black America* (Carbondale: Southern Illinois University Press, 2008), chaps. 3–4.

32. Other Liberian mutual education and rhetorical societies are listed above. Another newspaper—*Africa's Luminary*—was based out of Bossa Cove and was run by white missionaries.

33. See Burrowes, *Power and Press Freedom in Liberia*, 27–86.

34. Alan Neely, "Teague, Colin," in *Biographical Dictionary of Christian Missions*, ed. Gerald H. Anderson (New York: Macmillan Reference USA, 1998), 660; Tom W. Shick, *Emigrants to Liberia, 1820 to 1843: An Alphabetical Listing* (Newark, Del.: Liberian Studies Association in America, 1971), 96.

35. *Maryland Colonization Journal* 4, no. 10 (April 1848): 167.

36. This group is also called the Richmond Baptist Missionary Society or the Richmond African Baptist Missionary Society.

37. *Maryland Colonization Journal* 4, no. 10 (April 1848): 167. Some reports erroneously date Teage's arrival in West Africa to 1819. See, for example, *African Repository* 29, no. 10 (October 1853): 302.

38. Burrowes, *Power and Press Freedom in Liberia*, 39.

39. D. Elwood Dunn and Svend E. Holsoe, *Historical Dictionary of Liberia* (Metuchen, N.J.: Scarecrow, 1985), 166.

40. James, *Struggles of John Brown Russwurm*, 76.

41. *National Intelligencer*, 24 December 1816, 2.

42. *Liberia Herald*, 31 May 1845, 1; Plato, *Gorgias*, trans. W. D. Woodhead, in *The Collected Dialogues of Plato*, ed. Edith Hamilton and Huntington Cairns (New York: Pantheon Books, 1961), 462d–465e.

43. Brian Vickers, *In Defence of Rhetoric* (Oxford: Oxford University Press, 1988), 88–90.

44. *Liberia Herald*, 31 May 1845, 1. See also Russell's "Liberia No. 1," *Liberia Herald*, 6 November 1846, 6, subsequently reprinted in the *African Repository and Colonial Journal* 23, no. 2 (February 1847): 48–53.

45. *Liberia Herald*, 31 May 1845, 1.

46. Bjørn F. Stillion Southard, "The Rhetorical Origins of the African Colonization Movement in the United States" (PhD diss., University of Maryland, 2009), 28–76.

47. Bruce Dorsey, "A Gendered History of African Colonization in the Antebellum United States," *Journal of Social History* 34, no. 1 (2000): 78, 84.

48. *National Intelligencer*, 24 December 1816, 2.

49. Burrowes, *Power and Press Freedom in Liberia*, 139.

50. Linda K. Kerber, *Women of the Republic: Intellect and Ideology in Revolutionary America* (Chapel Hill: University of North Carolina Press, 1980). An example of the rhetoric of republican motherhood in Liberian discourse can be found in another speech delivered at the Liberia Lyceum and reprinted in the *Liberia Herald*. In an address on 9 February 1848, E. J. Roye stated, "You Ladies of this new Republic cannot know too well the great influence you exert either for weal or wo[e] upon every citizen. . . . It is your province, ladies, to put your signal veto and condemnation on any immodest thing, to discountenance independently of a sacrifice of any temperal [sic] good, all counterfeit characters either among your own or our sex"; *Liberia Herald*, 30 June 1848, 35.

51. See, for example, William Lloyd Garrison, *Thoughts on African Colonization . . .* (Boston: Garrison and Knapp, 1832); and David Walker, *Walker's Appeal, in Four Articles . . .* (Boston: David Walker, 1830).

52. James, *Struggles of John Brown Russwurm*, 72–74.

53. *Liberia Herald*, 31 May 1845, 1.

54. Henry Louis Gates Jr., *The Signifying Monkey: A Theory of African-American Literary Criticism* (New York: Oxford University Press, 1988), 130–31.

55. Elizabeth McHenry, *Forgotten Readers: Recovering the Lost History of African American Literary Societies* (Durham: Duke University Press, 2002), 85.

56. [Holbrook], "Associations," 594.

57. *Liberia Herald*, 31 May 1845, 1.

58. Holbrook, "American Lyceum," 47.

59. *Liberia Herald*, 31 May 1845, 1.

60. Ibid.

61. Ibid., 10.

62. Ibid.

63. David Kazanjian, *The Brink of Freedom: Improvising Life in the Nineteenth-Century Atlantic World* (Durham: Duke University Press, 2016), 232–33, 229.

CHAPTER 6

1. Ralph Waldo Emerson, *Nature* (New York: Renaissance Classics, 2012), 51.

2. Thomas Augst, "Humanist Enterprise in the Marketplace of Culture," in *The Cosmopolitan Lyceum: Lecture Culture and the Globe in Nineteenth-Century America*, ed. Tom F. Wright (Amherst: University of Massachusetts Press, 2013), 224.

3. See Joseph F. Kett, *The Pursuit of Knowledge Under Difficulties: From Self-Improvement to Adult Education in America, 1750–1990* (Stanford: Stanford University Press, 1994); Mary Kelley, *Learning to Stand and Speak: Women, Education, and Public Life in America's Republic* (Chapel Hill: University of North Carolina Press, 2006); and Shirley Wilson Logan, *Liberating Language: Sites of Rhetorical Education in Nineteenth-Century Black America* (Carbondale: Southern Illinois University Press, 2008).

4. Naturally, Plato and Dewey were opposed on educational philosophy, and Dewey would object to any educational program that began, as religion does, with fixed Truths or conclusions. My point here is simply that maintaining the group—its *paideia*, continuity, purity—is a central focus of educational philosophy that is at the heart of arguments

ranging from Plato's *Republic* to Dewey's *Democracy and Education*. See D. C. Phillips and Harvey Siegel, "Philosophy of Education," in *Stanford Encyclopedia of Philosophy*, ed. Edward N. Zalta (Stanford University, Winter 2015), article published 2 June 2008; last modified 15 August 2013, https://plato.stanford.edu/archives/win2015/entries/education-philosophy/.

5. The term *Mormonism* encompasses movements that separated from the LDS Church as well as the broader culture that has emerged from Joseph Smith's revelations. Here I favor the term *Mormon* because I am discussing the spectrum of experience that grew out of Smith's original movement. I occasionally use the term *LDS* to point to beliefs or statements published by that church.

6. The Mormon (mainly LDS) belief that humans can become like God derives from Smith's early revelations. It continues to be taught as a basic principle in LDS theology. See, for example, chapter 47 of the Church's official manual, *Gospel Principles* (Salt Lake City: Church of Jesus Christ of Latter-day Saints, 2012). On Smith's life, see Richard Bushman, *Rough Stone Rolling: A Cultural Biography of Mormonism's Founder* (New York: Vintage, 2005); and Fawn Brodie, *No Man Knows My History: The Life of Joseph Smith*, 2nd ed. (New York: Vintage, 1995).

7. "LDS Church Now Ranks 4th Largest in U.S.," *Deseret News*, 10 March 2007.

8. See Nathan O. Hatch, *The Democratization of American Christianity* (New Haven: Yale University Press, 1989); and Whitney R. Cross, *The Burned-Over District: The Social and Intellectual History of Enthusiastic Religion in Western New York, 1800–1850* (Ithaca: Cornell University Press, 1950).

9. See M. David Litwa, *Becoming Divine: An Introduction to Deification in Western Literature* (Eugene, Ore.: Cascade Books, 2013), 197.

10. Harold Bloom, *The American Religion: The Emergence of the Post-Christian Nation* (New York: Simon and Schuster, 1992), 127.

11. T. A. Frall, "The 100 Most Significant Americans of All Time," *Smithsonian Magazine*, 17 November 2014.

12. Bloom, *American Religion*, 127.

13. Peter Manseau, *One Nation, Under Gods: A New American History* (New York: Little Brown, 2015), 302.

14. Bloom, *American Religion*, 99.

15. Joseph Smith, *History*, 1:10–14, in *Pearl of Great Price* (Salt Lake City: Church of Jesus Christ of Latter-day Saints, 1989).

16. Ibid.

17. Ibid., 1:10–14, 16–19.

18. *Populism* here refers not to a particular political movement but to an orientation that can be adapted for different purposes, a mode of addressing different individuals that calls together an agitational public around a particular issue. See Michael Kazin, *The Populist Persuasion: An American History* (New York: Basic Books, 1995).

19. See Cross, *Burned-Over District*.

20. Hatch, *Democratization*, 13.

21. Ibid., 9–10.

22. Although these factors are widely known to correlate with religiosity, a recent Gallup study confirms that poverty and the lack of a strong social safety net that supports upward mobility are evident in highly religious cultures. See Steve Crabtree, "Religiosity Highest in World's Poorest Nations," *Gallup*, 31 August 2010, http://www.gallup.com/poll/142727/religiosity-highest-world-poorest-nations.aspx. See also Hatch, *Democratization*, 4–5; and John L. Brooke, *The Refiner's Fire: The Making of Mormon Cosmology, 1644–1844* (New York: Cambridge University Press, 1996), 237–38.

23. Hatch, *Democratization*, 125.

24. Bushman, *Rough Stone Rolling*, 113.

25. For a more complete discussion of the Nauvoo years, see chapter 19 of the LDS Church's own publication *Church History in the Fullness of Times: Student Manual* (Salt Lake City: Church of Jesus Christ of Latter-day Saints, 2002), available online at https://www.lds.org/manual/church-history-in-the-fulness-of-times-student-manual/chapter-nineteen-life-in-nauvoo-the-beautiful?lang=eng. See also Brodie, *No Man Knows My History*, 256–74.

26. Here I am referencing Hatch's *Democratization of American Christianity*. In the introduction he comments at length on the breaking down of distinctions between the learned and the unlearned, the elite and the common. But of course there remained extremely problematic inequities between men and women, as well as people of color or foreign birth and white Americans, even, and in some cases especially, among new religious communities.

27. Bushman, *Rough Stone Rolling*, 385. On the high rituals of Mormon temple worship and administration, see Hugh Nibley, *Temple and Cosmos: Beyond This Ignorant Present* (Salt Lake City: Deseret Books, 1992); David John Buerger, *The Mysteries of Godliness: A History of Mormon Temple Worship* (Salt Lake City: Signature Books, 1994); and Brooke, *Refiner's Fire*. On the logistics of Mormon temple worship, including staffing, see "Mormon Temples: How They Work," *By Common Consent*, 18 November 2010, https://bycommonconsent.com/2010/11/18/mormon-temples-how-they-work-part-3/. On the low/high bifurcation in Mormon religious practice, see "Low Church / High Church," *Wheat and Tares*, 27 May 2014. For an official statement by the current LDS Church, see "Joseph Smith's Teachings About Priesthood, Temple, and Women," *Church of Jesus Christ of Latter-day Saints*, https://www.lds.org/topics/joseph-smiths-teachings-about-priesthood-temple-and-women?lang=eng.

28. Herbert Leventhal, *In the Shadow of the Enlightenment: Occultism and Renaissance Science in Eighteenth-Century New England* (New York: New York University Press, 1976), 129–31; Robert Freke Gould, *A Concise History of Freemasonry* (London: Gale and Polden, 1951), 340–42; D. Michael Quinn, *Early Mormonism and the Magic World View* (Salt Lake City: Signature Books, 1998), 10.

29. Quoted in Lance S. Owens, "Joseph Smith: America's Hermetic Prophet," http://gnosis.org/ahp.htm, originally published in *Gnosis: A Journal of Western Inner Traditions* (Spring 1995).

30. Quinn, *Early Mormonism*, 16.

31. B. H. Roberts, *A Comprehensive History of the Church*, 6 vols. (Salt Lake City: Church of Jesus Christ of Latter-day Saints, 1930), 1:26–27. See also Quinn, *Early Mormonism*, 31.

32. "Dowsing," in *American Folklore: An Encyclopedia*, ed. Jan Harold Brunvand (New York: Garland, 1996), 432.

33. Clyde R. Forsberg Jr., *Equal Rites: The Book of Mormon, Masonry, Gender, and American Culture* (New York: Columbia University Press, 2004), 32–40.

34. Reed C. Durham, "Is There No Help for the Widow's Son?" presidential address to the Mormon History Association, Nauvoo, Illinois, 20 April 1974, available online in an unauthorized transcription by Melvin B. Hogan, http://www.mormonismi.net/tempeli/durhamin_puhe1974.shtml. See also Albert Gallatin Mackey, "Enoch," in *An Encyclopedia of Freemasonry and Its Kindred Sciences* (New York: Masonic History Company, 1913), 1:244–46.

35. Owens, "Joseph Smith."

36. Durham, "Is There No Help?"

37. See Kenneth W. Godfrey, "Freemasonry and the Temple," in *Encyclopedia of Mormonism*, last modified 24 March 2008, http://eom.byu.edu/index.php/Freemasonry_and_the_Temple.

38. Durham, "Is There No Help?"

39. Owens, "Joseph Smith."

40. Wright, introduction to *Cosmopolitan Lyceum*, 3; Augst, "Humanist Enterprise," 224.

41. Joshua G. Gunn argues that learned discourses act as an occultic form of communication, creating barriers against the uninitiated and exalting opportunities for the initiated; Gunn, *Modern Occult Rhetoric: Mass Media and Drama of Secrecy in the Twentieth Century* (Tuscaloosa: University of Alabama Press, 2005).

42. On Smith's communication with God, see Bushman, *Rough Stone Rolling*, 129; and Richard Bushman, "Little Narrow Prison of Language: The Rhetoric of Revelation," *Religious Educator* 1, no. 1 (2000): 90–104.

43. Brooke, *Refiner's Fire*, 245.

44. See Joseph Smith, "The King Follett Sermon," reprinted in *Ensign*, April 1971. All quotations of the discourse in this chapter come from this version.

45. Patricia Bizzell and Bruce Herzberg, introduction to *The Rhetorical Tradition: Readings from Classical Times to the Present*, ed. Bizzell and Herzberg (Boston: Bedford / St. Martin's, 2001), 35.

46. Brooke, *Refiner's Fire*, 281.

47. The LDS Church supports these doctrinal claims by pointing to scriptures such as Genesis 1:26–27, 2:17, and 3:22 and Psalm 82:6. But the notion of human deification was also acknowledged and taught by the early Christian fathers. See, for example, Norman Russell, *The Doctrine of Deification in the Greek Patristic Tradition* (New York: Oxford University Press, 2006). On similar teachings in the Hermetic and Kabbalistic traditions, see Bloom, *American Religion*, 99–101.

48. Brooke, *Refiner's Fire*, 4; Bloom, *American Religion*, 101.

49. Brooke, *Refiner's Fire*, 254.

50. This phrasing is used both in Isaiah 28:10 of the King James Version of the Bible and in 2 Nephi 28:30 of the Book of Mormon.

51. Brooke, *Refiner's Fire*, 254.

52. Mormons believe in the Christian theology of grace but tend to view grace as a foundation rather than a culmination. For them, grace opens the door to the more radical doctrine of exaltation, which Smith elucidates here.

53. Joseph Smith, *History of the Church* (Salt Lake City: Church of Jesus Christ of Latter-day Saints, 1902), 4:588.

54. Doctrine and Covenants 93:36.

55. Ibid., 130:18–19.

56. Lorenzo Snow, *Teachings of the Presidents of the Church* (Salt Lake City: Church of Jesus Christ of Latter-day Saints, 2011), chap. 5.

57. See Paul Stob, "William James's 'True American Theory': The Varieties of Religious Experience and Transatlantic Intellectual Culture," in Wright, *Cosmopolitan Lyceum*, 130–48.

58. Terryl Givens, *People of Paradox: A History of Mormon Culture* (New York: Oxford University Press, 2007).

59. Harold Bloom, "Will This Election Be the Mormon Breakthrough?" *New York Times*, 13 November 2011.

CHAPTER 7

Sara E. Lampert would like to thank Angela G. Ray and Paul Stob as well as the participants in the Popular Knowledge, Public Stage conference at the Alexandria Lyceum in 2015; the American Antiquarian Society for funding some of this research with a Kate B. and Hall J. Peterson Fellowship; and her writing partner, Lisa Ann Robertson.

1. Sallie Joy White, "Matters in Boston," *Milwaukee Sentinel*, 19 February 1878.
2. Gertrude Kellogg Diaries, 2 February 1878, Kellogg Family Papers, New-York Historical Society (hereafter KFP-NYHS).
3. White, "Matters in Boston."
4. Marjorie Eubank, "The Redpath Lyceum Bureau from 1868 to 1901" (PhD diss., University of Michigan, 1968); Sara E. Lampert, "Bringing Music to the Lyceumites: The Bureaus and the Transformation of Lyceum Entertainment," in *The Cosmopolitan Lyceum: Lecture Culture and the Globe in Nineteenth-Century America*, ed. Tom F. Wright (Amherst: University of Massachusetts Press, 2013), 67–89.
5. *Redpath Lyceum* [circular], 1878–79, 1–6.
6. These numbers are based on analysis of circulars of the Redpath Lyceum Bureau (briefly, Boston Lyceum Bureau) for 1869, 1871–72, 1872–73, 1875, and 1878–79. Apart from 1878–79, which is found in KFP-NYHS, the American Antiquarian Society holds the circulars. See also Angela G. Ray, "What Hath She Wrought? Woman's Rights and the Nineteenth-Century Lyceum," *Rhetoric and Public Affairs* 9, no. 2 (2006): 191.
7. Eubank, "Redpath Lyceum Bureau," 311.
8. Nan Johnson, *Gender and Rhetorical Space in American Life: 1866–1910* (Carbondale: Southern Illinois University Press, 2002).
9. Excerpted in Eubank, "Redpath Lyceum Bureau," 202–3.
10. Eubank compares the appeal and pursuit of dramatic reading in this period with the popularity of tap dancing in the 1930s, each imagined in its own time as a "sure, short road to fame"; ibid., 202.
11. Jane Hunter, *How Young Ladies Became Girls: The Victorian Origins of American Girlhood* (New Haven: Yale University Press, 2003), 3–5.
12. Frances Cogan, *All-American Girl: The Ideal of Real Womanhood in Mid-Nineteenth-Century America* (Athens: University of Georgia Press, 1989), 4.
13. Barbara Welter, "The Cult of True Womanhood, 1820–1860," *American Quarterly* 18 (1966): 151–74.
14. Cogan, *All-American Girl*, 4.
15. For treatment of key patterns in the careers of women lecturers on the post–Civil War platform, see Lisa Tetrault, "The Incorporation of American Feminism: Suffragists on the Postbellum Lyceum," *Journal of American History* 96, no. 4 (March 2010): 1027–56; and Ray, "What Hath She Wrought?"
16. Gertrude Kellogg Diaries, 18 May 1864, KFP-NYHS.
17. Bruce McConachie, *Melodramatic Formations: American Theatre and Society, 1820–1870* (Iowa City: University of Iowa Press, 1992); Faye Dudden, *Women in the American Theatre: Actresses and Audiences, 1790–1870* (New Haven: Yale University Press, 1994); Richard Butsch, *The Making of American Audiences: From Stage to Television, 1750–1990* (New York: Cambridge University Press, 2000).
18. Dudden, *Women in the American Theatre*.
19. Melanie Dawson, *Laboring to Play: Home Entertainment and the Spectacle of Middle-Class Cultural Life, 1850–1920* (Tuscaloosa: University of Alabama Press, 2005); Hunter, *How Young Ladies Became Girls*.
20. Fanny also studied elocution for a time, but she pursued a career as a concert pianist.
21. Gertrude Kellogg Diaries, 24 March and 25 June 1864, KFP-NYHS.
22. Ibid., 14 May 1869.
23. Ibid., 31 December 1864.
24. Ibid., 26 December 1867.
25. Anna Cora Mowatt, *Autobiography of an Actress; or, Eight Years on the Stage* (Boston: Ticknor, Reed, and Fields, 1854).

26. David Grimsted, *Melodrama Unveiled: American Theater and Culture, 1800–1850* (1968; repr., Berkeley: University of California Press, 1987); Claudia Durst Johnson, *Church and Stage: The Theater as Target of Religious Condemnation in Nineteenth Century America* (Jefferson, N.C.: McFarland, 2008).

27. Peter Buckley, "Paratheatricals and Popular Stage Entertainment," in *The Cambridge History of American Theatre, Beginnings to 1870*, vol. 1, ed. Don B. Wilmeth and Christopher Bigsby (New York: Cambridge University Press, 1998), 424–81.

28. John R. McKivigan, *Forgotten Firebrand: James Redpath and the Making of Nineteenth-Century America* (Ithaca: Cornell University Press, 2008), esp. 119–21, 132–33.

29. Lampert, "Bringing Music to the Lyceumites."

30. Donald M. Scott, "The Popular Lecture and the Creation of a Public in Mid-Nineteenth-Century America," *Journal of American History* 66, no. 4 (March 1980): 795.

31. *Redpath Lyceum*, 1878–79, 21.

32. *Redpath's Lyceum*, 1875, special circular on W. S. Andrews; *Lyceum Magazine*, June 1873, 5.

33. *Lyceum Magazine*, June 1873, 5.

34. At midcentury, the most established white-collar occupation open to women was education, which would be joined by nursing and medicine after the Civil War. Women also entered new forms of office labor as typists, clerical workers, and telegraph operators. Platform performance drew on skills developed in a normal school education but offered earning potential on an unprecedented scale. See Elyce J. Rotella, *From Home to Office: U.S. Women at Work, 1870–1930* (Ann Arbor: UMI Research Press, 1981).

35. Kellogg Diaries, 17 October and 20 November 1868; Hathaway and Pond to Charles White Kellogg, 4 October 1878, KFP-NYHS.

36. Kellogg Diaries, 1 November 1865.

37. Ibid., 2 May 1869.

38. Ibid., 1 February 1870.

39. "The Drama," *New York Tribune*, 1 February 1870. Kellogg identifies Winter as the author of the column in her diary entry for 3 February 1870.

40. Ibid.

41. Kellogg Diaries, 1 February 1870.

42. "The Reading of Miss Gertrude Kellogg," *Buffalo Courier*, 9 March 1870.

43. Ibid.

44. "The Drama."

45. "Reading of Miss Gertrude Kellogg."

46. Merritt Caldwell, *A Practical Manual of Elocution: Embracing Voice and Gesture* (Philadelphia: Sorin and Ball, 1845), 17–18.

47. Charles Walter Brown, *The American Star Speaker and Model Elocutionist* (Chicago: M. A. Donohue, 1902), 22.

48. *Recitations by Miss Gertrude Kellogg, Tuesday and Wednesday Evenings, March 26th and 27th, 1878 . . . First Presbyterian Church, Plattsburgh*, program, KFP-NYHS.

49. This piece had been part of Kellogg's repertoire from the beginning of her career. She performed Oliver Wendell Holmes and then Browning's "Good News" at one of her first public performances in 1869. *Franklin Literary Society. Complimentary Musical and Literary Entertainment. Polytechnic Institute. Monday, Evening, February 15, 1869*, program, KFP-NYHS.

50. The popularity of pieces in regional vernacular is illustrated by a handwritten poster used to promote a Kellogg engagement that lists an entire program. Both "Old Simon Dole" and "Miss Maloney" are highlighted by large block letters, the former underlined. *Miss Gertrude Kellogg Will Give Readings at the Armory of the G. Mil. Academy*, hand-painted poster, KFP-NYHS.

51. *Redpath Lyceum,* 1878–79, 35.
52. Ibid. In the circular, White's review is marked *Lowell Courier,* 15 February 1878.
53. *Redpath Lyceum,* 1878–79, 35.
54. *Laura Dainty: Humorous and Dramatic Recitations* (Boston: Redpath Lyceum Bureau, 1879–80), 15, 11, 8, 10.
55. Ibid., 15.
56. *Redpath Lyceum,* 1878–79, 35.
57. *Laura Dainty,* 14–15.
58. Ibid., 3.
59. Richard H. Brodhead, *Cultures of Letters: Scenes of Reading and Writing in Nineteenth-Century America* (Chicago: University of Chicago Press, 1993), 119–21.
60. J. T. Trowbridge, *The Emigrant's Story, and Other Poems* (Boston: Houghton, Mifflin and Co., 1874), 38–48.
61. Robert Allen, *Horrible Prettiness: Burlesque and American Culture* (Chapel Hill: University of North Carolina Press, 1991), esp. 163–78; Gillian Rodger, *Champagne Charlie and Pretty Jemima: Variety Theater in the Nineteenth Century* (Urbana: University of Illinois Press, 2010).
62. *Redpath Lyceum,* 1878–79, 35.
63. *Plattsburgh Republican,* 20 March 1878; also in *Redpath Lyceum,* 1878–79, 35.
64. Elizabeth Cady Stanton, "Our Girls," in *The Selected Papers of Elizabeth Cady Stanton and Susan B. Anthony,* vol. 3, *National Protection for National Citizens, 1873 to 1880,* ed. Ann D. Gordon (New Brunswick: Rutgers University Press, 2003), 487–89, 485.
65. Ibid., 488.
66. Lisa Strange, "Dress Reform and the Feminine Ideal: Elizabeth Cady Stanton and the 'Coming Girl,'" *Southern Communication Journal* 68, no. 1 (2002): 1–13.

CHAPTER 8

1. See Leon Botstein, "Language and Music: The Mendelssohnian Aesthetic," in *Mendelssohn and His World,* ed. R. Larry Todd (Princeton: Princeton University Press, 1991), 26–32.
2. Among the essential reference sources created during this era of music scholarship are Alexandre Choron and François Joseph Marie Fayolle, *Dictionnaire historique des musiciens, artistes et amateurs* (Paris, 1810–11); Ernst Ludwig Gerber, *Neues historisch-biographisches Lexikon der Tonkünstler* (Leipzig, 1812–14); François-Joseph Fétis, *Biographie universelle des musiciens et bibliographie générale de la musique* (Paris, 1835–44); John Weeks Moore, *Complete Encyclopaedia of Music* (Boston, 1854); Hugo Riemann, *Musik-Lexikon* (Leipzig, 1882); and George Grove, *A Dictionary of Music and Musicians* (London, 1879–90).
3. See Judith Tick, "Passed Away Is the Piano Girl: Changes in American Musical Life, 1870–1900," in *Women Making Music: The Western Art Tradition, 1150–1950,* ed. Jane Bowers and Judith Tick (Urbana: University of Illinois Press, 1985), 325–48.
4. See Norma P. Atkinson, "An Examination of the Life and Thought of Zina Fay Peirce, an American Reformer and Feminist" (PhD diss., Ball State University, 1983).
5. E. Douglas Bomberger, "The German Musical Training of American Students, 1850–1900" (PhD diss., University of Maryland, College Park, 1991).
6. See Margaret William McCarthy, "Amy Fay's Reunions with Franz Liszt: 1875, 1876, 1885," *Journal of the American Liszt Society* 24 (1988): 23–32.
7. Amy Fay to her family, Weimar, 8 October 1873, reprinted in Amy Fay, *Music-Study in Germany* (Chicago: Jansen, McClurg and Co., 1880), 269–70.

8. Amy Fay to her family, Berlin, 29 September 1870, reprinted in *Music-Study in Germany*, 95–96.

9. A.F., "In Weimar with Liszt: From a Young Lady's Letters Home," *Atlantic Monthly* 33, no. 198 (April 1874): 417–29; A.F., "Some Great Contemporary Musicians: From a Young Lady's Letters Home," *Atlantic Monthly* 34, no. 204 (October 1874): 453–65. These letters are discussed in Robert Dumm and Karen A. Shaffer, "Amy Fay, American Pianist: Something to Write Home About," *Maud Powell Signature: Women in Music* 1, no. 2 (Fall 1995): 4–8, 29.

10. A.F., "Some Great Contemporary Musicians," 453.

11. Margaret William McCarthy, *Amy Fay: America's Notable Woman of Music* (Warren, Mich.: Harmonie Park Press, 1995), 51.

12. Ethelbert Nevin, cited in McCarthy, *Amy Fay*, 83.

13. See, for instance, her articles "Deppe System Vindicated," *The Etude* 3, no. 4 (April 1885): 79; "Deppe Method Again," *The Etude* 6, no. 6 (June 1888): 96; and "Miss Amy Fay on the Deppe Method," *The Etude* 11, no. 7 (July 1893): 144. See also Amy Fay, *The Deppe Finger Exercises for Rapidly Developing an Artistic Touch in Piano Forte Playing, Carefully Arranged, Classified and Explained* (Chicago: S. W. Straub and Co., 1890).

14. Rivé-King's trailblazing efforts were recognized in John C. Fillmore, "Piano Teachers and Concert Pianists," *Dwight's Journal of Music* 37, no. 11 (1 September 1877): 84–85. Her career is discussed in Leslie Petteys, "Julie Rivé-King, American Pianist" (DMA diss., University of Missouri–Kansas City, 1987).

15. "Concert in Aid of St. Luke's Home," *Boston Daily Globe*, 17 February 1876, 4.

16. Thomas would become personally important to the Fay family years later when he married Amy's sister Rose after the death of his first wife. See Rose Fay Thomas, *Memoirs of Theodore Thomas* (New York: Moffat, Yard, 1911).

17. "Concerts," *Dwight's Journal of Music* 34, no. 24 (3 March 1877): 399.

18. Letter to her family, quoted in Margaret William McCarthy, "Fay, Amy Muller," in *American National Biography*, ed. John A. Garraty and Mark C. Carnes, 24 vols. (New York: Oxford University Press, 1999), 7:772.

19. Diane Price Herndl, *Invalid Women: Figuring Feminine Illness in American Fiction and Culture, 1840–1940* (Chapel Hill: University of North Carolina Press, 1993), 116–22.

20. George P. Upton, "The Piano Recitals of the Week," *Chicago Tribune*, 18 May 1879, 11. This assessment is confirmed by "The Amy Fay Concert," *Chicago Inter Ocean*, 13 May 1879, 2.

21. "Gossip of the World," *Brainard's Musical World* 20, no. 3 (March 1883): 42.

22. "Musical," *Chicago Inter Ocean*, 3 March 1883, 13.

23. This description had appeared as part of the reporting on the inaugural concert at the auditorium in 1877: "The Hershey Hall Concert," *Chicago Tribune*, 21 January 1877, 2.

24. "Musical Notes at Home," *Chicago Tribune*, 1 April 1883, 24.

25. "Miss Fay's Piano Conversations," *Chicago Inter Ocean*, 7 April 1883, 13.

26. Quoted from a "Chicago Paper" in *St. Albans (Vt.) Daily Messenger*, 5 April 1883.

27. "Miss Fay's Piano Conversations," *Chicago Weekly Magazine*, 7 April 1883, 10. This article was the longest and most detailed of the reviews.

28. George P. Upton, "Chicago: Miss Amy Fay," *Brainard's Musical World* 20, no. 4 (April 1883): 60.

29. George P. Upton, "Miss Amy Fay," *Brainard's Musical World* 20, no. 5 (May 1883): 76.

30. "Miss Amy Fay's Recitals," *Chicago Daily Tribune*, 15 April 1883, 15.

31. "Her appearance and manner as she talks are fascinating, the only criticism seeming to be that she 'does not talk enough!'"; "Miss Fay's Piano Conversations," *Chicago Weekly Magazine*, 10.

32. "Chicago Notes," *Musical Visitor* 12, no. 11 (1 November 1883): 293.

33. A copy of this brochure is housed in carton 1, folder 1, of the Fay Family Collection, Schlesinger Library, Radcliffe College (hereafter FFC-SL).

34. "Miss Fay's Matinee," *New York Times*, 4 June 1891, 4.

35. Mark N. Grant, *Maestros of the Pen: A History of Classical Music Criticism in America* (Boston: Northeastern University Press, 1998), 88.

36. Ibid., 81.

37. "Musical Comment: Miss Fay's Entertainment," *New York Tribune*, 4 June 1891, 6.

38. See John Louis Recchiuti, *Civic Engagement: Social Science and Progressive-Era Reform in New York City* (Philadelphia: University of Pennsylvania Press, 2007).

39. Amy Fay to Zie [Melusina Fay Peirce], dated 13 November 1901, although the portion quoted below was written on 15 November, carton 1, folder 12, FFC-SL.

40. George P. Upton, "Chicago, May 20th," *Brainard's Musical World* 20, no. 6 (June 1883): 92.

41. Upton's observation that most musicians know nothing outside their art goes back to the tension between music and language. Since music begins where words leave off, marrying the two in an intelligible yet also artistic way is the fundamental challenge of the genre.

42. R. Allen Lott, "Perry, Edward Baxter," in *Grove Dictionary of American Music*, 2nd ed., ed. Charles Hiroshi Garrett, 8 vols. (New York: Oxford University Press, 2013), 6:443.

43. [W. S. B. Mathews], "Editorial Bric-a-Brac," *Music* 7, no. 2 (December 1894): 183–88.

44. See Sondra Wieland Howe, "The NBC Music Appreciation Hour: Radio Broadcasts of Walter Damrosch, 1928–1942," *Journal of Research in Music Education* 51, no. 1 (2003): 64–77; and George Martin, *The Damrosch Dynasty: America's First Family of Music* (Boston: Houghton Mifflin, 1983), 358–74.

45. See Theodor W. Adorno, *Essays on Music*, selected, with introduction, commentary, and notes by Richard Leppert, trans. Susan H. Gillespie (Berkeley: University of California Press, 2002).

46. Bernstein's Young People's Concerts with the New York Philharmonic are described on the website of the Leonard Bernstein Office, https://leonardbernstein.com/.

47. "Amy Fay at Work," *Musical Courier* 75, no. 19 (8 November 1917): 7, quoted in McCarthy, *Amy Fay*, 132.

48. A blog post by a professor at the University of Virginia summarizes the tension inherent in this form of performance: Michael J. Puri, "On the Lecture-Recital," *Musicology Now: Lively Facts and Opinions, Brought to You by the American Musicological Society* (blog), 24 February 2014, http://musicologynow.ams-net.org/2014/02/on-lecture-recital.html.

CHAPTER 9

1. *The Life of Swami Vivekananda*, 6th ed., vol. 1 (Kolkata, India: Advaita Ashrama, 1989), 342–44.

2. Ibid., 345.

3. Ibid., 385.

4. Sister Nivedita, introduction to *The Complete Works of Swami Vivekananda*, 17th ed., vol. 1 (Kolkata, India: Advaita Ashrama, 1986), x.

5. Stephen Prothero, "Mother India's Scandalous Swamis," in *Religions of the United States in Practice*, ed. Colleen McDannell, 2 vols. (Princeton: Princeton University Press, 2001), 2:418–19.

6. Ibid., 418.

7. Amiya P. Sen, *Swami Vivekananda* (New Delhi: Oxford University Press, 2000), 19–29.

8. Ibid., 21.

9. J. N. Pankratz, "The Response of the Brahmo Samaj," in *Modern Indian Responses to Religious Pluralism*, ed. Harold G. Coward (Albany: State University of New York Press, 1987), 19–38.

10. Ibid., 16. See also Romain Rolland, *The Life of Ramakrishna* (Kolkata, India: Advaita Ashrama, 2008).

11. Swami Sunirmalananda, *Alasinga Perumal: An Illustrious Disciple of Swami Vivekananda* (Chennai, India: Sri Ramakrishna Math, 2012), 109.

12. *Life of Swami Vivekananda*, 403.

13. Asim Chaudhuri, *Swami Vivekananda in Chicago: New Findings* (Kolkata, India: Advaita Ashrama, 2012), 67.

14. *Life of Swami Vivekananda*, 405–6.

15. Richard Hughes Seager, *The World's Parliament of Religions: The East/West Encounter, Chicago, 1893* (Bloomington: Indiana University Press, 1995), 10–11.

16. Ibid., 25–27.

17. Walter R. Houghton, *Neely's History of the Parliament of Religions and Religious Congresses of the World's Columbian Exposition* (Chicago: F. Tennyson Neely, 1894), 15–16.

18. John Henry Barrows, ed., *The World's Parliament of Religions: An Illustrated and Popular Story of the World's First Parliament of Religions, Held in Chicago in Connection with the Columbian Exposition of 1893*, 2 vols. (Chicago: Parliament Publishing Company, 1893), 1:68.

19. Ibid.

20. Quoted in Seager, *World's Parliament of Religions*, 78.

21. Barrows, *World's Parliament of Religions*, 2:1581.

22. Marie Louise Burke, *Swami Vivekananda in the West: New Discoveries*, 4th ed., vol. 1 (Kolkata, India: Advaita Ashrama, 1992), 73–76.

23. Seager, *World's Parliament of Religions*, 50.

24. Burke, *Swami Vivekananda in the West*, 80.

25. Barrows, *World's Parliament of Religions*, 1:166, 168.

26. Chaudhuri, *Swami Vivekananda in Chicago*, 87–89.

27. Ibid., 89.

28. Romain Rolland, *The Life of Vivekananda and the Universal Gospel* (Kolkata, India: Advaita Ashrama, 2012), 29–30.

29. Chaudhuri, *Swami Vivekananda in Chicago*, 106.

30. Quoted in Burke, *Swami Vivekananda in the West*, 105.

31. *Reminiscences of Swami Vivekananda*, 4th ed. (Kolkata, India: Advaita Ashram, 2004), 426.

32. Ibid., 218.

33. Ibid., 140.

34. Ibid., 414–15.

35. Vivekananda, *Complete Works*, 3.

36. Ibid.

37. Ibid.

38. Ibid.

39. Ibid., 4.

40. Burke, *Swami Vivekananda in the West*, 102. Other reports also confirm this, for example, *Boston Evening Transcript*, 5 April 1894; see *Life of Swami Vivekananda*, 426–27.

41. Burke, *Swami Vivekananda in the West*, 103.

42. *Life of Swami Vivekananda*, 418.

43. J. T. Sunderland, "The World's Parliament of Religions," *The Unitarian* 8, no. 10 (1893): 446–47.
44. Vivekananda, *Complete Works*, 5.
45. Ibid.
46. Sunderland, "World's Parliament of Religions," 447.
47. Chaudhuri, *Swami Vivekananda in Chicago*, 93.
48. Burke, *Swami Vivekananda in the West*, 108.
49. Ibid., 112.
50. Ibid.
51. Vivekananda, *Complete Works*, 6.
52. See Carl T. Jackson, *The Oriental Religions and American Thought: Nineteenth-Century Explorations* (Westport, Conn.: Greenwood Press, 1981), 89–93.
53. Vivekananda, *Complete Works*, 6.
54. Ibid., 1:7. See also Abhik Roy and Michele L. Hammers, "Swami Vivekananda's Rhetoric of Spiritual Masculinity: Transforming Effeminate Bengalis into Virile Men," *Western Journal of Communication* 78 (2014): 545–62; Anupama Arora, "'A Black Pagan in Orange Clothes': Swami Vivekananda's American Travels," *LIT: Literature Interpretation Theory* 27 (2016): 71–89.
55. Seager, *World's Parliament of Religions*, 164.
56. Vivekananda, *Complete Works*, 7.
57. Ibid., 8.
58. Ibid., 14.
59. Ibid., 14–15.
60. Quoted in Gopal Stavig, *Western Admirers of Ramakrishna and His Disciples* (Kolkata, India: Advaita Ashrama, 2010), 616.
61. Vivekananda, *Complete Works*, 17.
62. Ibid., 18.
63. See Carl T. Jackson, *Vedanta for the West: The Ramakrishna Movement in the United States* (Bloomington: Indiana University Press, 1994).
64. Vivekananda, *Complete Works*, 19.
65. Ibid., 20.
66. Burke, *Swami Vivekananda in the West*, 131–32.
67. Vivekananda, *Complete Works*, 21.
68. Ibid., 23.
69. Ibid.
70. Barrows, *World's Parliament of Religions*, 2:1338–46.
71. Vivekananda, *Complete Works*, 24.
72. Ibid.
73. Ibid.
74. Burke, *Swami Vivekananda in the West*, 180.
75. *Life of Swami Vivekananda*, 458.
76. Jackson, *Vedanta for the West*, 48–66.
77. Swami Vivekananda, *Lectures from Colombo to Almora*, 3rd ed. (Kolkata, India: Advaita Ashrama, 1933).

CONCLUSION

1. Increase Cooke, *The American Orator: or, Elegant Extracts in Prose and Poetry; Comprehending a Diversity of Oratorical Specimens, Principally Intended for the Use of Schools and Academies* (New Haven, Conn.: Sidney's Press, 1811), 85. See also Peter Gibian, "Walt

Whitman, Edward Everett, and the Culture of Oratory," *Intellectual History Newsletter* 16 (1994): 20. This metaphor of electricity tied oratory to the concept of sensibility, that acute sensitivity to complex emotional or aesthetic influences so prized by refined men and women in the eighteenth and nineteenth centuries. See Sarah Knott, *Sensibility and the American Revolution* (Chapel Hill: University of North Carolina Press, 2009), 4–15.

2. Carolyn Eastman, *A Nation of Speechifiers: Making an American Public After the Revolution* (Chicago: University of Chicago Press, 2009); Sandra M. Gustafson, *Eloquence Is Power: Oratory and Public Performance in Early America* (Chapel Hill: University of North Carolina Press, 2000); Sandra M. Gustafson, "Orality and Literacy in Transatlantic Perspective," *19: Interdisciplinary Studies in the Long Nineteenth Century* 18 (2014), http://19.bbk.ac.uk; Christopher Looby, *Voicing America: Language, Literary Form, and the Origins of the United States* (Chicago: University of Chicago Press, 1998); Tom F. Wright, *Lecturing the Atlantic: Speech, Print, and an Anglo-American Commons, 1830–1870* (Oxford: Oxford University Press, 2017). See also Adam Fox, *Oral and Literate Culture in England, 1500–1700* (New York: Oxford University Press, 2000); Jack Goody, *The Domestication of the Savage Mind* (Cambridge: Cambridge University Press, 1977); Joseph S. Meisel, *Public Speech and the Culture of Public Life in the Age of Gladstone* (New York: Columbia University Press, 2001); and Alessandro Portelli, *The Text and the Voice: Writing, Speaking, and Democracy in American Literature* (New York: Columbia University Press, 1994).

3. Granville Ganter, "Women's Entrepreneurial Lecturing in the Early National Period," herein.

4. Joseph F. Kett, *The Pursuit of Knowledge Under Difficulties: From Self-Improvement to Adult Education in America, 1750–1990* (Stanford: Stanford University Press, 1994).

5. An 1883 review in the *Chicago Inter Ocean*, quoted in E. Douglas Bomberger, "Talking Music: Amy Fay and the Origins of the Lecture Recital," herein.

6. Angela G. Ray, *The Lyceum and Public Culture in Nineteenth-Century United States* (East Lansing: Michigan State University Press, 2005); Paul Stob, *William James and the Art of Popular Statement* (East Lansing: Michigan State University Press, 2013). See also Robert Arbour, "Mr. Emerson's Playful Lyceum: Polyvocal Promotion on the Lecture Circuit," in *The Cosmopolitan Lyceum: Lecture Culture and the Globe in Nineteenth-Century America*, ed. Tom F. Wright (Amherst: University of Massachusetts Press, 2013), 93–112.

7. Richard Benjamin Crosby, "Secret Knowledge, Public Stage: Joseph Smith's King Follett Discourse," herein.

8. Sara E. Lampert, "The 'Perfect Delight' of Dramatic Reading: Gertrude Kellogg and the Post–Civil War Lyceum," herein.

9. Kirt H. Wilson and Kaitlyn G. Patia, "Authentic Imitation or Perverse Original? Learning About Race from America's Popular Platforms," herein. See also Eric Lott, *Love and Theft: Blackface Minstrelsy and the American Working Class* (New York: Oxford University Press, 1993).

10. Carl Bode, *The American Lyceum: Town Meeting of the Mind* (New York: Oxford University Press, 1956). For similarly influential accounts of the nation-building capacity of the lyceum, see Donald M. Scott, "The Popular Lecture and the Creation of a Public in Mid-Nineteenth-Century America," *Journal of American History* 66, no. 4 (March 1980): 791–809; and Mary Kupiec Cayton, "The Making of an American Prophet: Emerson, His Audiences, and the Rise of the Culture Industry in Nineteenth-Century America," *American Historical Review* 92 (1987): 597–620.

11. Lawrence W. Levine, *Highbrow/Lowbrow: The Emergence of Cultural Hierarchy in America* (Cambridge, Mass.: Harvard University Press, 1988), 25–26.

12. Ronald J. Zboray and Mary Saracino Zboray, "The Portable Lyceum in the Civil War," herein.

13. Ibid. For more on counterpublics, see Robert Asen and Daniel C. Brouwer, eds., *Counterpublics and the State* (Albany: State University of New York Press, 2001); Michael Warner, *Publics and Counterpublics* (New York: Zone Books, 2002); Catherine R. Squires, "Rethinking the Black Public Sphere: An Alternative Vocabulary for Multiple Public Spheres," *Communication Theory* 12, no. 4 (2002): 446–68; and Joanna Brooks, "The Early American Public Sphere and the Emergence of the Black Print Counterpublic," *William and Mary Quarterly*, 3rd ser., 62, no. 1 (January 2005): 67–93.

14. Tom F. Wright, "Mobilizing Irish America in the Antebellum Lecture Hall," herein.

15. Bjørn F. Stillion Southard, "A Lyceum Diaspora: Hilary Teage and a Liberian Civic Identity," herein.

16. Reminiscence quoted in Scott R. Stroud, "Hinduism for the West: Swami Vivekananda's Pluralism at the World's Parliament of Religions," herein.

17. Diana Taylor, *The Archive and the Repertoire: Performing Cultural Memory in the Americas* (Durham: Duke University Press, 2003).

18. Leigh Eric Schmidt, *Hearing Things: Religion, Illusion, and the American Enlightenment* (Cambridge, Mass.: Harvard University Press, 2000), 15.

19. Margaret Bayard Smith, *A Winter in Washington; or, Memoirs of the Seymour Family*, vol. 1 (New York: E. Bliss and E. White, 1824), 147–48.

CONTRIBUTORS

E. Douglas Bomberger is Professor of Music at Elizabethtown College. His research examines such topics as the cosmopolitan style in nineteenth-century American music; the influential American Composers' Concert movement of the 1880s; and America's preeminent nineteenth-century composer, Edward MacDowell. His book on changes in American musical culture during 1917 is forthcoming from Oxford University Press.

Richard Benjamin Crosby is Associate Professor of Speech in the English Department at Iowa State University. His research focuses on civil-religious rhetoric in the United States. He is also interested in the way minority religious groups find and maintain footholds in an unaccommodating culture. He is working on a monograph that examines the rhetorical history and significance of the Washington National Cathedral.

Carolyn Eastman is Associate Professor of History at Virginia Commonwealth University. Her research explores the ways that men and women in the past interacted with politics and cultural notions of belonging and exclusion via the media of writing, oratory, and visual images. Her prizewinning book A Nation of Speechifiers: Making an American Public After the Revolution was published in 2009 by the University of Chicago Press.

Granville Ganter is Associate Professor of English at St. John's University. His research centers on oratory, rhetoric, and performance from the colonial period through the Civil War, and he has published on such figures as Ralph Waldo Emerson, Frederick Douglass, and Anne Laura Clarke. He is the editor of The Collected Speeches of Sagoyewatha, or Red Jacket, published by Syracuse University Press in 2006.

Sara E. Lampert is Assistant Professor of History at the University of South Dakota. Her work explores women's and gender history in the early United States, with particular attention to popular entertainment and women's changing relationship with public life in the nineteenth century. She is working on a monograph about female celebrity and the transformations of American theater and culture between 1790 and 1850.

Kaitlyn G. Patia is Visiting Assistant Professor of Rhetoric Studies at Whitman College. Her research examines the rhetoric of social change, focusing primarily on historical efforts by politically marginalized groups to create a more just world. She is working on a monograph about the rhetoric and activism of W. E. B. Du Bois and Jane Addams.

Angela G. Ray is Associate Professor of Communication Studies at Northwestern University. Her research focuses on rhetorical criticism and history, emphasizing popular media, education, and social reform in the nineteenth-century United States. Her award-winning book The Lyceum and Public Culture in the Nineteenth-Century United States was published in 2005 by Michigan State University Press.

Bjørn F. Stillion Southard is Assistant Professor of Communication Studies at the University of Georgia. His work investigates early U.S. public address, particularly discourses of race and law. His current work focuses on the "peculiar rhetoric" of white and black supporters of the African colonization movement.

Paul Stob is Associate Professor of Communication Studies at Vanderbilt University. His research investigates the intersection of rhetoric and intellectual culture, paying particular attention to public lecturing in the Gilded Age and Progressive Era. He is the author of William James and the Art of Popular Statement, published in 2013 by Michigan State University Press.

Scott R. Stroud is Associate Professor of Communication Studies at the University of Texas at Austin. His research explores the ways that diverse cultures and thinkers have integrated rhetorical means into schemes of moral improvement. He is the author of John Dewey and the Artful Life, published by Pennsylvania State University Press in 2011, and Kant and the Promise of Rhetoric, published by Pennsylvania State University Press in 2014.

Kirt H. Wilson is Associate Professor of Communication Arts and Sciences at the Pennsylvania State University. He has published widely in the areas of African American public discourse, nineteenth-century political communication, the civil rights movement, memory, and public deliberation. He is the author of The Reconstruction Desegregation Debate: The Politics of Equality and the Rhetoric of Place, 1870–1875, published by Michigan State University Press in 2002.

Tom F. Wright is Senior Lecturer in American Literature at the University of Sussex, England, specializing in nineteenth-century writing and cultural history. He is the editor of The Cosmopolitan Lyceum: Lecture Culture and the Globe in Nineteenth-Century America, published by the University of Massachusetts Press in 2013, and the author of Lecturing the Atlantic: Speech, Print, and an Anglo-American Commons, 1830–1870, published by Oxford University Press in 2017.

Mary Saracino Zboray is Visiting Scholar in the Department of Communication at the University of Pittsburgh. Her research focuses on antebellum cultural history and nineteenth-century literary culture. She has authored four books with Ronald J. Zboray: A Handbook for the Study of Book History in the United States, published in 2000 by the Center for the Book, Library of Congress; Literary Dollars and Social Sense: A People's History of the Mass Market Book, published in 2005 by Routledge; Everyday Ideas: Socioliterary Experience Among Antebellum New Englanders, published in 2006 by the University of Tennessee Press; and Voices Without Votes: Women and Politics in Antebellum New England, published in 2010 by the University of New Hampshire Press.

Ronald J. Zboray is Professor of Communication and Director of Cultural Studies at the University of Pittsburgh. His research investigates the intersections of print media production, distribution, and reception. In addition to the books authored with Mary Saracino Zboray, he is author of A Fictive People: Antebellum Economic Development and the American Reading Public, published in 1993 by Oxford University Press. The Zborays are working on a monograph titled The Bullet in the Book: Volumes That Saved Civil War Soldiers' Lives and are coediting U.S. Popular Print Culture to 1860, volume 5 of The Oxford History of Popular Print Culture.

INDEX

Page numbers in *italics* refer to illustrations.

abolitionist lectures, 5–7, 29–31, 32, 39
   See also Civil War *entries*
Adams, Gerry, 56
Adderley, Thomas, 48
Adorno, Theodor, 167
advertising function, entrepreneurial lecturing. *See* women's entrepreneurial lecturing, late 1700s
African Americans
   in Civil War lyceum culture, 25–26, 29–32, 34, 35, 197, 210n74
   in early 1800s lyceum culture, 5–7, 8–9, 51, 100, 101
   in Irish American oratory, 69–70
   Shaler's arguments, 72–74, 83–84
   Talking Book trope, 109–11
   See also Liberia *entries*; racial mimesis
African Society, Boston, 51
Agassiz, Louis, 28, 34, 39, 72–73, 74
alchemy comparison, human deification doctrine, 125–26
Alexandria Lyceum, 9, *10*, 40
American Colonization Society, 97, 99, 104–5, 108, 111, 222nn8–9
American Lyceum (Bode), 23
American Revolution, in Irish oratory, 59, 63
Anagarika Dharmapala, 184
Andrews, William, 138
Anglo-American commons, 57–59, 98
Anglo-Saxon racial ideas, 66–67
Art Institute of Chicago, 172, 174
Asen, Robert, 3
Ashmun, Jehudi, 104
Atlantic Monthly, 72, 155
atman concept, Vivekananda's explanation, 181–82
audience power, impact on rhetoric, 189–90
Augst, Thomas, 54, 113, 122
Autobiography of an Actress (Mowatt), 136

Bache, Sarah Franklin, 46

Baltimore Lyceum, 32
Banneker Institute, 30
"Barbara Freitchie" (Whittier), 140, 141, 142, 229n49
Barons, Benjamin, 45–46
Barons, Eliza Harriot (later O'Connor), 43–48, 192
Barons, Mary Margaret (earlier Hardy), 45
Barrows, John Henry, 173, 174, 175
battlefield participants, Civil War lyceum culture, 25–26, 33–39, 210n74
Beach, Amy, 156
Beecher, Henry Ward, 26, 28, 59
Belfiore, Elizabeth, 84
Bernstein, Leonard, 167–68
Binns, John, 61
blackface minstrelsy, 76–79, 86
   See also racial mimesis
Bloom, Harold, 115–16
Bloomfield-Zeisler, Fannie, 156
Boardman, George Dana, 185
Bode, Carl, 10, 23, 25, 196
Bodies in Dissent (Brooks), 92
Bomberger, E. Douglas
   biographical highlights, 237
   chapter by, 150–68
   comments on, 18, 192
Bonney, Charles Carroll, 173, 174
Boston Globe, 157
Boston Lyceum Bureau, 228n6
Boston Pilot, 63, 65, 68
Brahmo Samaj, 171
Brainard's Musical World, 159, 166
Breadwinner's College, 13–14
Brooke, John L., 120, 123, 126, 127
Brooklyn speech, Meagher's, 61
Brooks, Daphne, 92
Brown, Moses T., 138
Brown, Solomon G., 32
Brown, William Wells, 88–93
Browne, Augusta, 78
Browne, Nellie, 26–27, 28

Browne, Sarah, 26
Browning, Robert, 140, 141, 142, 144, 229n49
Brownlow, William Gannaway, 34
Brune, John C., 31
Buchanan, Lindal, 42
Buckner, Jocelyn, 85
Buffalo Courier, 141
Buffalo Express, 145
Buntline, Ned, 67
Burgess, Ebenezer, 104
Burin, Eric, 221n1
Burr, Hetty, 7
Burrowes, Carl, 109
Bush, Mrs., 29, 208n32
Bushman, Richard, 118
Butler, John, 34

Caldwell, Elias B., 108
Capers, Henry D., 35
Carey, Lott, 104
Carpenter, Edward, 52
Carpenter, John Alden, 168
Carreño, Teresa, 156
Cary, Alice, 142
Cato character, in *The Escape*, 88–91
Cavada, Lt. Col., 36
Celtic identity themes, Irish American lecture circuit, 57, 66–70
Chase, Maria, 50
Chattanooga News, 81
chautauqua presentations, 10, 81–82
Chicago Amusement Bureau, 162
Chicago Evening Journal, 176
Chicago Inter Ocean, 159, 160–61
Chicago Tribune, 160, 162
Chicago Weekly Magazine, 161
Chickering Hall performance, Fay's, 163–64
Chilton, Josephine, 81
Chopin concerto, Fay's performance, 157–58
Christian Advocate and Journal, 78
Christian leaders, at World's Parliament of Religions, 173–74, 178, 180
Christian Recorder, 210n74
Christie, Thomas, 35–36
Christie, William, 36
Christine, Sister, 176
churches, lyceum activity in, 9, 29, 30, 32, 34, 35
Cicero, 123
citizenship duties, in Mitchel's oratory, 69
civic identity development, Teage's role in Liberia, 103–11

Civil War, Irish American orators, 59, 60, 69–70
Civil War era, lyceum culture
  battlefield participation, 33–39, 210n74
  home front activities, 26–33
  scholarship framework, 23–26
  summarized, 12–13, 15–16, 40, 196–97
Clark, Cotton, 136
Clarke, Anne Laura, 43, 52–54, 192, 215n33
classical architecture, implications, 9, 172, 174
Clay, Henry, 105, 222n8
Cobb, Jasmine Nichole, 9
Cogan, Frances, 133, 149
Cohen, Cathy J., 203n5
Cohen, Morris, 13–14
collective inquiry. *See* thinking together practices, overview
college education, contemporary criticisms, 1, 14
Columbian Centinel, 51
Columbian Exposition, 172–73
Complete Encyclopedia (Moore), 150
Comstock, A., 100
consummatory communication, defined, 205n36
Conversations on Chemistry (Marcet), 49
Cook, Joseph, 180
correspondence, Civil War, 24, 33–34
Craig, John D., 50
creation as organization, in King Follett Discourse, 126
Crittenden, Alonzo, 54
Crosby, Richard Benjamin
  biographical highlights, 237
  chapter by, 113–29
  comments on, 17, 193–94
Crummell, Alexander, 32, 92–93, 219n15
Curtis, George William, 28, 39

Dainty, Laura, 144–46
Daly, Maria, 28–29
Damrosch, Walter, 167
Darby, William, 48, 52
"Darius Green and His Flying Machine" (Trowbridge), 142, 144
Davidson, Thomas, 13, 14
Davis, Emilie Frances, 25, 29–30
Davitt, Michael, 70
debates
  Civil War era, 31–32, 35, 36
  in Teage's lyceum support speech, 106–9, 198

deception detection purpose, Teage's lyceum support speech, 109
Deming, Henry C., 34
democratic impulses and Mormonism origins, 117–19, 127–28
democratic religious culture, appeal, 114
Democratization of American Christianity (Hatch), 226n26
democratization of knowledge, 189–90
Deppe, Ludwig, 153, 156
Deresiewicz, William, 1
Dewey, John, 2–3, 113, 224n4
Dharmapala, Anagarika, 184
dialect imitations, European American performances, 81–82
diary accounts, Civil War lyceum activity
African American writers, 29–33
sourcing process, 24
white women writers, 26–29
Dickinson, Anna, 28–29, 30, 34, 37, 39
A Dictionary of Music and Musicians (Grove), 150
divining rods, 120–21
Doctor Quash character, 76
Dodge, Mary Mapes, 142, 147, 194–95
Dorsey, Bruce, 108
Douglass, Frederick, 2, 23, 29, 30, 39, 70, 92
Douglass, Grace Bustill, 5
Douglass, Robert, Sr., 5
Douglass, Sarah Mapps, 5–7, 8–9
Dr. Gaines character, in *The Escape,* 89–92
dramatic reading genre
audience expectations, 141
expansion of, 130–31, 136–38
and the feminine ideal, 144–48
as gendered opportunity, 131–33, 136, 138–40, 149, 228n10
regional culture appeal, 146–47
role of socioeconomic class, 132–33, 139
variety within, 138–39
See also Kellogg, Gertrude
Dresel, Otto, 151
Dunn, Walter, 34
Durham, Reed C., 121
Dutta, Narendranath. *See* Vivekananda, Swami *entries*
Dwight's Journal of Music, 157–58, 159
Dyer, A. D., 32

Eastman, Carolyn
biographical highlights, 237
chapter by, 187–201
comments on, 18–19, 42

Eaton, Amos, 52, 215n33
educational affiliations, commercial lectures. *See* women's entrepreneurial lecturing, late 1700s
education and knowledge
for democratization, 189–90
in Holbrook's lyceum claims, 100–101
national community variations, 113–15
and religion, 189
in Teage's lyceum arguments, 107, 110–11
See also specific topics, e.g., Fay, Amy Muller; Mormonism
electricity metaphor, public speech, 187, 234n1
Emerson, Ralph Waldo, 65, 67, 113, 128–29
"endowment" rituals, 121–22
Enoch legend, 121, 126
entertainment/education boundaries, overview, 10–11, 191–95
See also specific topics, e.g., Fay, Amy Muller; racial mimesis
Eppes, Susan, 34–35
Equiano, Olaudah, 70
Ernest, John, 90
The Escape (Brown), 88–93
Essipoff, Annette, 156
Estes, Miss, 80, 219n26
Eubank, Marjorie, 228n10
European American performers, racial mimesis, 75–83
exaltation doctrine. *See* human deification doctrines

"Fanny" (Halleck), 49
Faraday, Michael, 49
Fay, Amy Muller
early concert performances, 156–59
legacy, 166–68
music training, 151, 153
photo of, 152
piano conversations innovation, 18, 159–66, 192, 231n31
writings of, 153–56, 164–65
Fay, Melusina "Zina" (later Peirce), 151, 155, 164
Fazio, Kellogg's reading, 134
Ferris, Anne, 29
Field, Kate, 140
Fincke, Martha Brown, 176
Fisk Jubilee Singers, 83
Fleetwood, Christian E., 25, 31–32, 34, 35
folk magic subculture, 114, 120–22, 125–27, 227n41
See also Mormonism

244 INDEX

Follett, King, 122–23
Forgotten Readers (McHenry), 31
Forsberg, Clyde R., Jr., 121
Forten, Charlotte, 30–31, 101
Fowler, Lorenzo Niles, 28
Fowler, Orson Squire, 28
Frederick Douglass' Paper, 61–62
Freemasonry, 117, 120, 121–22
frog parable, Vivekananda's, 178–79
Fulton, Sarah, 28

Gage, Matilda Joslyn, 29
Gaines characters, in *The Escape*, 89–92
Galbreath Lyceum, 31, 32, 34
Gandhi, Virchand, 178
Gannett, Deborah Sampson, 42
Ganter, Granville
   biographical highlights, 237
   chapter by, 41–55
   comments on, 16, 192
Garrison, William Lloyd, 5
Gates, Henry Louis, Jr., 110
Gazetteer, 45
Germany, musical conservatories, 153, 156
Gibbons, Cardinal, 174
Gibbs, Jonathan Clarkson, 30
Gilbert Lyceum, 30
Giles, Henry, 66
Givens, Terryl, 129
gladiatorial engagement, in Teage's lyceum support speech, 108–9
global republicanism, oratory, 60, 63–65
God as human, doctrine, 115, 124–28, 225n6
golden plates, in Mormonism, 117
"Good News" (Browning), 229n49
Gordon, John B., 81
Gough, John B., 28, 39, 190
grace principle, Mormonism, 128, 227n52
Grafton, Anthony, 53
Grant, Mark N., 163, 164
Greeley, Horace, 30
Green, J. E., 32
Greenfield, Elizabeth Taylor, 30
Greenwood, Grace, 138
Grimké, Angelina, 52
Grimké, Sarah, 52
Griscom, John, 49–50
Grove, George, 150
Gunn, Joshua G., 227n41

Hall, Richard L., 102
Halleck, Fitz-Greene, 49–50
Handy, Alfred Ward, 34
Hardy, Mary Margaret (later Barons), 45

Hardy the Younger, Sir Charles, 45
Harper, Albert, 34
Harper, Frances Ellen Watkins, 23, 30
Harper, John, 34
Harper's magazine, 35–36
Hatch, Nathan O., 117–18, 226n26
Hathaway, George, 132, 140
Haven, Joseph, 27
Hawley, Emily, 26
Hearst, William Randolph, 79
Henderson, W. J., 163
Henkin, David M., 5
Henry, Major, 36–37
Hermeticism comparison, human deification doctrine, 125–26
Herndl, Diane Price, 158
Hershey Hall, Chicago, 160
Higginson, Thomas Wentworth, 57
higher education, contemporary criticisms, 1, 14
Hill, Errol, 220n56
Hill, James H., 31
Holbrook, Josiah, 9, 57, 76, 77, 100–101, 110–11
Holmes, Oliver Wendell, 142, 229n49
Holy Ghost, in Mormonism, 119–20, 129
home front activities, Civil War lyceum culture
   African American category, 29–32
   characterized, 24–25, 33
   white women category, 25–29
Hopkins, Jerome, 159
Hospital Gazette, 37
hospitals, Civil War era, 37, 39, 40
Howe, Julia Ward, 138
"How They Brought the News from Ghent to Aix" (Browning), 140, 141, 144
human deification doctrines, 114, 125–28, 193–94, 225n6, 227n47
Hunchback, Kellogg's reading, 134
Hungarian Revolution, 60
Hunter, William H., 34
Hyers, Anna Madah, 11, 84–88
Hyers, Emma Louise, 11, 84–88
Hyers Sisters Concert Company, 84–88, 220n56

imitation, as human trait, 219n15
   See also racial mimesis
intelligence principle, in Mormonism, 126–28
Invalid Women (Herndl), 158
Irish American mobilization, lecture circuit overview, 15, 56–57, 70–71, 197–98

as Anglo-American commons challenge,
    57–59
  with Celtic identity themes, 57, 66–70
  with nationalism-oriented rhetoric,
    56–57, 59–66
  slavery issue, 69–70

Jail Journal (Mitchell), 59
James, William, 193
Jefferson, Thomas, 98–99
Jim Crow character, 76
Joachim, Joseph, 154
Jocelyn, Simeon Smith, 6
Johnson, Nan, 131
Jones, Sir William, 45
Joyce, James, 56

Kabbalah teachings, 121, 126
Kazanjian, David, 112
Kellar, Mr., 35
Kelley, Mary, 7, 42
Kelley, William Darrah, 30
Kellogg, Charles, 134
Kellogg, Demis, 134
Kellogg, Fanny, 134
Kellogg, Gertrude
  advertising flyer, 143
  career preparation and beginnings,
    133–36
  as cultural change example, 17, 148–49,
    194–95
  dialect and interpretation mastery,
    146–47
  family support significance, 139–40, 149
  Mowatt's career compared, 136–37
  portrait of, 137
  program variety, 142, 144, 229n49, n50
  responses to her readings, 130, 140–41,
    144, 145, 147–48
Kellogg, Peter, 134
Kemble, Fanny, 134
Kerber, Linda, 42, 109
Kett, Joseph F., 4, 192
King Follett Discourse, 115, 122–28, 129,
    193–94
Kinnersley, Ebenezer, 41
"Kitty Maloney on the Chinese Question"
    (Dodge), 142, 147, 195
knowledge and religion, 189
  See also Mormonism
Knox, Robert, 66–67
Kossuth, Lajos, 60, 64, 65
Krehbiel, Henry E., 163–64
Kullak, Theodor, 153, 166

Lamar, A. W., 81
Lampert, Sara E.
  biographical highlights, 237
  chapter by, 130–49
  comments on, 17, 74–75, 194–95
Lancaster, Joseph, 48–49
Lathrop, John, Jr., 48
learning and religion. *See* Mormonism
lecture approach, King Follett Discourse,
    123–24
lecture recitals, 166–68
  See also Fay, Amy Muller
Lecturing the Atlantic (Wright), 57
Levin, Charles, 67
Levine, Lawrence W., 196
Lhamon, W. T., Jr., 76
Libby Chronicle, 36–37
Libby Lyceum Association, 36
Libby Prison, 36–37
Liberating Language (Logan), 34
Liberator newspaper, 5, 6, 7, 8, 88
Liberia, American colonization, 98–99,
    104–5, 221n1, 222nn8–9
Liberia Herald, 102, 103, 104–5
Liberia Lyceum
  overview, 17, 97–98, 111–12, 198
  comparisons with Anglo-American
    lyceum culture, 102–3
  Roye's republican motherhood speech,
    224n50
  significance of Teage's speech about,
    105–11
Life of Ulysses S. Grant (Deming), 34
Liszt, Franz, 153, 154, 156, 166
literary societies
  African American, 101
  Civil War era, 31, 32, 35
  Philadelphia, 7, 46
Livermore, Mary, 23
Logan, Shirley Wilson, 7, 34, 102
logic declaration, in King Follett Discourse,
    126
London Times, 67–68
Longfellow, Henry Wadsworth, 151, 155
Lord, John, 39
Lux, George, 47
Lyceum and Public Culture (Ray), 23
lyceum bureaus, impact, 9–10, 131, 136, 138
lyceum culture, overview, 9–11, 97–98,
    99–102
  See also specific topics, e.g., Civil War era;
    Liberia Lyceum
lyceum diaspora. *See* Liberia Lyceum
Lyceum Magazine, 81, 132

Lyceum Observer, 32, 34

Macaulay, T. B., 142
magic lantern, in Clarke's lectures, 43
Manseau, Peter, 116
Marcet, Jane, 49
marginalized groups, overview
  defined, 203n5
  knowledge pursuit approaches, 2–4, 194–95
  scholarship consequence, 23–24, 203n5
Markievicz, Constance, 56
Marshall, Josiah, 35
Martin, John Sella, 30
Maryland Colonization Journal, 104
Maryland State Colonization Society, 222n9
Masonic traditions, 117, 120, 121–22
  See also Mormonism
Mathews, W. S. B., 166
McCarthy, Margaret, 155
McDowell, Amanda, 33
McElheran, John, 57, 67–70
McGee, Thomas D'Arcy, 67
McHenry, Elizabeth, 7, 8, 31, 51, 110
McLaughlin, Peter, 67
Mead, David, 23
Meagher, Thomas Francis, 56–57, 59–66
Mendelssohn, Felix, 150
mental feast metaphor, 5–6
Menter, Sophie, 156
Metropolitan Hall lecture, Meagher's, 59
Midway Plaisance, Columbian Exposition, 172–73
Miller, Kerby, 63
Miller, Polk, 81–83, 93–94
Mills, Samuel J., 104
minstrelsy, 76–79, 86
  See also racial mimesis
Mississippi State Colonization Society, 222n9
Miss Tapioca character, in *The Escape*, 90
Mitchel, John, 56–57, 59–66, 69–70
Monrovia. *See* Liberia *entries*
Mook, Richard, 82–83
Moore, John Weeks, 150
Mormonism
  as American quintessence, 17, 114–15, 128–29
  and folk magic beliefs, 120–22, 125–26
  and Freemasonry traditions, 121–22
  God as human, doctrine, 126, 227n47
  grace principle, 227n52
  human deification doctrine, 114, 125–27, 193–94, 225n6, 227n47

  King Follett Discourse, 115, 122–28
  origin story and national context, 116–19
  populism thread, 117–19, 127–28, 226n26
  system structure, 119–20
  term clarification, 225n5
Mowatt, Anna, 136–37
Moyes, Henry, 43–44
Mrs. Gaines character, in *The Escape*, 91–92
musical blackness, European American performances, 79–83, 93–94
Musical Courier, 168
Musical Visitor, 162
Music Hall, Boston, 26, 69, 136
Music journal, 166
Music News, 79
Music-Study in Germany (Fay), 155, 168

Narendranath Dutta. *See* Vivekananda, Swami *entries*
National Anti-Slavery Standard, 70
nationalism-oriented rhetoric, exiled Irish orators, 56–57, 59–66
"Nature" (Emerson), 113
Nauvoo, establishment of, 118, *119*
NBC Music Appreciation Hour, 167
"Negro Minstrelsy" (Browne), 78
"The Negro Problem" (Shaler), 72–74
The Neighbor (Shaler), 73–74
nervousness barriers, Fay's, 158–59
Nevin, Ethelbert, 156
newspapers
  Civil War era, 32, 34, 36–37, *38*
  and lyceum culture success, 101–2
  See also specific periodicals, e.g., *Chicago Inter Ocean*; *Liberia Herald*
New York Herald, 63, 65–66
New York Philharmonic, 167–68
New York Times, 63, 163
New York Tribune, 61, 140–41, 163–64
Nivedita, Sister, 170
Nixon, William, 48, 214n20
Northrup, Filmer S. C., 182

occult. *See* folk magic subculture
O'Connell, Daniel, 63, 70
O'Connor, Eliza Harriot (born Barons), 43–48, 192
O'Connor, John, 46–48
O'Gorman, Mr., 28
"Old Simon Dole" (Trowbridge), 142, 146–47, 229n50
"The One Hoss Shay" (Holmes), 142
One Nation, Under Gods (Manseau), 116

"Our Girls" (Stanton), 148–49
Out of Bondage drama, 86–88
Owens, Lance S., 121

Paine, John Knowles, 151
Parker, Theodore, 67
Parnell, Charles, 56, 70
Patia, Kaitlyn
  biographical highlights, 238
  chapter by, 72–94
  comments on, 11, 16–17, 195
Peabody, Elizabeth Palmer, 50
Peculiar Sam drama, 86, 88
Peirce, Charles Sanders, 151
Peirce, Melusina "Zina" Fay, 151, 155, 164
Perry, Edward Baxter, 166
persuasion, changing importance, 189–90
Philadelphia Female Anti-Slavery Society, 5–7
Philadelphia Inquirer, 29
Phillips, Wendell, 28, 30, 34
physiognomic arguments, Irish American lecture circuit, 66–67, 68
piano conversations format
  adoption by other performers, 166–68
  Fay's introduction of, 18, 159–66, 192, 231n31
"The Pied Piper" (Browning), 142
Pierce, Franklin, 59
platform culture, oratory's changing role, 100–101, 188–91, 193
  See also thinking together practices, overview
Plato, 78, 84, 106, 113, 224n4
Pleyel, Marie, 156
pluralism advocacy, Vivekananda's, 18, 177–79, 182–83, 184–85
poetry, 32, 37, 45, 47, 49
political oratory, changes, 190–91
Polk Miller and His Old South Quartette, 82–83, 93–94
polygenism, 72–73
popular vs. institutional learning, overview, 3–4
populism, term clarification, 225n18
populism and Mormonism, 117–19, 127–28, 226n26
Porter, Dorothy, 51, 101
poverty and religiosity, 118, 225n18
priesthoods, in Mormonism, 119–20
print culture, 187–88, 189
prisoner participation, Civil War lyceum culture, 36–37
Prison Times, 37, 38

Prothero, Stephen, 170
Pung Kwang Yu, 175

Quinn, D. Michael, 120

racial mimesis
  African American performances, 83–93, 195
  assumptions for analysis, 74–75
  culture threat arguments, 73–74, 93–94
  European American performances, 75–83
  learning argument summarized, 11, 16–17, 72–74
radio lecture recitals, 167
Ramakrishna, 171
Ramakrishnananda, Swami, 169
Ramsey, Alexander, 48
Randolph, Mary Emma, 34
Rapidann newspaper, 37
Ray, Angela G.
  biographical highlights, 238
  chapter by, 1–19
  comments on, 23, 54, 74–75, 100, 101, 193
Read, T. B., 140, 141
real womanhood concept, Cogan's, 133, 149
Redmond, John, 56
Redpath, James, 84
Redpath Lyceum Bureau, 10, 84–88, 131, 132, 136, 144, 228n6
Remond, Charles, 70
republican motherhood concept, Kerber's, 42, 109, 224n50
Republic (Plato), 78
revivalist movements and Mormonism origins, 117–19
rhetoric, changing role, 100–101, 188–91, 193
  See also specific topics, e.g., Irish American mobilization; Teage, Hilary
Rhodehamel, Frank, 176
Rice, Thomas Dartmouth, 76, 77
Richmond African Missionary Society, 104
Rieser, Andrew Chamberlin, 57
Right Flanker newspaper, 37
Rivé-King, Julie, 156
Robinson, William E., 66
Roediger, David, 76
Rolland, Romain, 175–76
Rollins, Stephen, 36
Roosevelt, Edith, 79
Rosenberg, Daniel, 53
Rowson, Susanna, 50
Roye, E. J., 224n50

Russwurm, John Brown, 104–5
Ryshpan, Mary, 14

Salem Lyceum building, 9
Samaroff, Olga, 156
Sambo character, 76
Sanborn, Kate, 172, 176–77
San Francisco Chronicle, 84
Schumann, Clara, 156
Schumann, Robert, 151, 156, 163
science
  as lecture subject, 43–44, 48, 50, 52–53
  in Vivekananda's Hinduism lecture, 181–82
  in women's education, 46, 49–50, 52–53
Scott, Donald M., 54, 101–2
Seager, Richard, 172
self/soul, Vivekananda's explanation, 181–82, 186
Sen, Amiya, 171
Senter, Nathaniel G., 48
settler-colonists, African American. *See* Liberia *entries*
Shaler, Nathaniel, 72–74, 83–84, 88
Sheehy-Skeffington, Hanna, 56
"Sheridan's Ride" (Read), 140, 141
Sherwood, William, 166
Slack, David B., 48
slavery depiction, in *The Escape*, 88–91
Slayton Lyceum Bureau, 10, 186
Smith, John H., 30
Smith, Joseph. *See* Mormonism
Smith, Margaret Bayard, 200–201
Smithsonian Magazine, 115
soldier participation, Civil War lyceum culture, 25–26, 33–39, 210n74
soul/self, Vivekananda's explanation, 181–82, 186
Southern, Eileen, 220n56
Southern Trio, 80, 219n26
Spencer, Herbert, 171
Spiegel, Caroline, 33
Spiegel, Marcus, 33
Squires, Catherine R., 7
Stanford, Anthony L., 30
Stansbury, Anna, 146
Stanton, Elizabeth Cady, 148–49
Stearns, Amanda Aikin, 39
Stewart, John W., 51
Stewart, Maria Miller, 51
Stillion Southard, Bjørn F.
  biographical highlights, 238
  chapter by, 97–112
  comments on, 17, 198

Stob, Paul
  biographical highlights, 238
  chapter by, 1–19
  comments on, 193
Stone, Billy, 33
Streight, Abel Delos, 39
Stroud, Scott R.
  biographical highlights, 238
  chapter by, 169–86
  comments on, 18, 198–99
Stuart, Annie R., 29
Stuart, Ruth McEnery, 81
Sunderland, J. T., 178, 179
Susskind, Daniel, 1
Susskind, Richard, 1

Talking Book trope, 109–10
Tausig, Carl, 153
Taylor, Bayard, 28, 34
Taylor, Diana, 200
Teage, Colinett, 104
Teage, Collin, 104
Teage, Frances, 104
Teage, Hilary
  civic activity in Liberia, 104–5
  on lyceum's role, 105–9, 110–12, 198
  and Talking Book trope, 109–11
televised concerts, 167–68
theater, cultural status change, 134, 137–38
  See also Kellogg, Gertrude
Theodore Thomas Orchestra, 157–58
thinking together practices, overview
  complexity of purposes, 11–14
  contemporary challenges, 1–2, 14
  entertainment/education boundaries, 191–93
  experimentation history, 2–3
  by marginalized groups, 2–4, 194–95, 197
  physical space implications, 8–11
  religious truth seeking, 189, 193–94
  role of audience, 18–19, 189–90, 193
  scholarship future, 199–201
  social bonding issues, 5–8, 12–14, 195–99, 205n36
  See also specific topics, e.g., Irish American mobilization; Mormonism
Thomas, Theodore, 157
Trollope, Frances, 196
Trowbridge, J. T., 142, 144, 229n50
true womanhood concept, Welter's, 133
truth-seeking purpose, in Teage's lyceum support speech, 109
Turner, Estelle, 79–80

Turner, Harriet, 79–80

Union Literary Society of Vicksburg, 35–36
United States Christian Commission, 35
Upton, George P., 158–59, 161–62, 232n41

Vandenhoff, George, 138
Vedanta philosophy, 180–81
Vedanta Society, 186
versatile mimesis, Hyers Sisters performances, 84–88
Vest, Jacques, 82
Vestvali, Felicita, 135
Virgil, Almon Kincaid, 168
"Virginia" (Macaulay), 142
Vivekananda, Swami
  post-Parliament lecture tour, 185–86
  travel path to World's Parliament, 169–72
Vivekananda, Swami (speaking at World's Parliament of Religions)
  audience reception, 175–76, 198–99
  Buddhism-Hinduism comparison, 184
  criticisms of Christian missionaries, 183–84
  delivery style, 176–77
  Hinduism lecture, 179–83
  opening statement, 175–76
  pluralism advocacy, 18, 177–79, 182–83, 184–85

Wagner, Richard, 150, 167
Walker, David, 51
Ward, Artemus, 28
war-time lectures. *See* Civil War era, lyceum culture
Washington, George, 43, 45, 47
Washington Times, 79
Watkins, William J., 32
Watkins Harper, Frances Ellen, 23, 30
Webb, Barbara L., 83
Webster, Noah, 44
Welter, Barbara, 133
Wheatley, Phillis, 110
Wheaton, Miss, 51
White, Jacob C., Sr., 30
White, Sallie Joy, 130, 144
White, W. S., 37
White City site, Columbian Exposition, 172–73
whiteness and racial mimesis, 76–83
Whittier, John Greenleaf, 140, 141, 142, 229n49
Wilbur, Julia, 39
Wilde, Oscar, 70

Willard, Emma, 53–54
Williams, James H., 31
Wilson, Kirt H.
  biographical highlights, 238
  chapter by, 72–94
  comments on, 11, 16–17, 92, 195
Winch, Julie, 7
Winter, William, 140–41
A Winter in Washington (Smith), 200–201
women
  Civil War lecture-going, 25–29
  in dramatic reading genre, 131–32
  as Liberian settler-colonists, 108–9
  occupation opportunities, 229n34
  in Smith's Mormonism, 122, 126
  in Vivekananda's Hinduism lecture, 181
  See also specific individuals, e.g., Douglass, Sarah Mapps; Fay, Amy Muller; Kellogg, Gertrude
women's entrepreneurial lecturing, late 1700s
  Clarke's activity, 43, 52–54, 215n33
  cultural context, 16, 41–44, 49–51, 54–55, 213n6
  O'Connor's activity, 43–48
working class entertainment, minstrelsy, 76–77
World's Parliament of Religions, 9, 173–75
  See also Vivekananda, Swami *entries*
Wright, Frances, 52
Wright, Henry C., 88
Wright, John Henry, 172
Wright, Tom F.
  biographical highlights, 238–39
  chapter by, 56–71
  comments on, 16, 98, 122, 197

Yankee Eloquence (Mead), 23
Yeats, W. B., 70
"the yips," Fay's, 158–59
Young, Edward, 45
Young People's Concerts, 167–68
"The Young Soldier" (Cary), 142

Zboray, Mary Saracino
  biographical highlights, 239
  chapter by, 23–40
  comments on, 10–11, 12, 15–16, 41–42, 50–51, 196–97
Zboray, Ronald J.
  biographical highlights, 239
  chapter by, 23–40
  comments on, 10–11, 12, 15–16, 41–42, 50–51, 196–97

Other books in the series:

Karen Tracy, *Challenges of Ordinary Democracy: A Case Study in Deliberation and Dissent* / VOLUME 1

Samuel McCormick, *Letters to Power: Public Advocacy Without Public Intellectuals* / VOLUME 2

Christian Kock and Lisa S. Villadsen, eds., *Rhetorical Citizenship and Public Deliberation* / VOLUME 3

Jay P. Childers, *The Evolving Citizen: American Youth and the Changing Norms of Democratic Engagement* / VOLUME 4

Dave Tell, *Confessional Crises and Cultural Politics in Twentieth-Century America* / VOLUME 5

David Boromisza-Habashi, *Speaking Hatefully: Culture, Public Communication, and Political Action in Hungary* / VOLUME 6

Arabella Lyon, *Deliberative Acts: Democracy, Rhetoric, and Rights* / VOLUME 7

Lyn Carson, John Gastil, Janette Hartz-Karp, and Ron Lubensky, eds., *The Australian Citizens' Parliament and the Future of Deliberative Democracy* / VOLUME 8

Christa J. Olson, *Constitutive Visions: Indigeneity and Commonplaces of National Identity in Republican Ecuador* / VOLUME 9

Damien Smith Pfister, *Networked Media, Networked Rhetorics: Attention and Deliberation in the Early Blogosphere* / VOLUME 10

Katherine Elizabeth Mack, *From Apartheid to Democracy: Deliberating Truth and Reconciliation in South Africa* / VOLUME 11

Mary E. Stuckey, *Voting Deliberatively: FDR and the 1936 Presidential Campaign* / VOLUME 12

Robert Asen, *Democracy, Deliberation, and Education* / VOLUME 13

Shawn J. Parry-Giles and David S. Kaufer, *Memories of Lincoln and the Splintering of American Political Thought* / VOLUME 14

J. Michael Hogan, Jessica A. Kurr, Michael J. Bergmaier, and Jeremy D. Johnson, eds., *Speech and Debate as Civic Education* / VOLUME 15

Typeset by
BOOKCOMP, INC.

Printed and bound by
SHERIDAN BOOKS

Composed in
SCALA

Printed on
NATURES NATURAL